Triumphal forms

Triumphal forms

Structural patterns in Elizabethan poetry

By ALASTAIR FOWLER

Fellow of Brasenose College, Oxford

CAMBRIDGE

AT THE UNIVERSITY PRESS 1970

Published by the Syndics of the Cambridge University Press
Bentley House, 200 Euston Road, London N.W.1
American Branch: 32 East 57th Street, New York, N.Y.10022

© Cambridge University Press 1970

Library of Congress Catalogue Card Number 75 105498

Standard Book Number: 521 07747 8

Printed in Great Britain
at the University Printing House, Cambridge
(Brooke Crutchley, University Printer)

Contents

Illustrations

Preface

This book is about numerical organization in works of literature, especially English poetry of the Elizabethan period. It studies the composition of substantive and formal elements into spatial patterns, in an age when all art was thought of spatially. Some now regard numerology as an occasional device, comparable with acrostics. Yet it was widely used by ancient Latin authors, common to the best medieval and renaissance poets and almost universal in the period 1580–1680, when it reached its greatest height of sophistication. The best poems of that time are generally interesting from a numerological point of view; though of course the converse need not obtain. My subject, then, is the largely unstudied level of organization of poetic form, intermediate between prosody and structure; merging with the former in complex stanza forms (sestina, canzone), with the latter in patterns of substantive elements (episodes, catalogues, processions). Numerology has as great interest, potentially, as either of its neighbours; yet it is practically a virgin province of the critical continent.

For its neglect there are good historical reasons. Most obviously and fundamentally, we have come to despise the notion that literature is spatial in character. No longer *ut pictura poesis*. And with its structural and symbolic functions, stanzaic organization lost most of its interest in the eighteenth century, until at last it was relegated to a humble place under the heading of prosody. When Wordsworth (as

De Vere reports) said he was puzzled by 'a subtle metrical sweetness' in *Epithalamion* 'the secret of which he could never wholly discover', he was in all probability quite oblivious of the secret pattern Professor Hieatt has recently demonstrated in the poem's large-scale metrical organization. Nineteenth-century attempts to find an expressive *raison d'être* for the stanza failed, and made way for *vers libre*. For when the link with internal structure broke, all metrical organization beyond the phrase seemed external decoration. To this we must add that the whole system of symbolism that numerology depends on is a dead language. Who now has enough knowledge of Scripture to remember how many generations intervened between Abraham and Christ? Or enough interest in Pythagoreanism to be moved by recognition of the *tetractys*?—let alone enough faith in the significance of numbers to manipulate them into their symbolic parts. Less obviously, interest in numerology may have declined because fewer practised the poetic art than in Elizabethan times, when readers of court poetry had first-hand knowledge of composition and structural methods. Some numerology has perhaps always been hidden, however. Singleton may be right to compare Dante's numerical patterns to inaccessible carvings in medieval cathedrals, visible to God and the angels but not to men. The mathematical harmonies governing renaissance architecture, and rediscovered for our own age by Professor Wittkower, are equally independent of subjective perception.

For some the current attempt to recover appreciation of literary numerology displays all the follies of which autonomous speculative criticism is capable: for others, it vindicates descriptive analysis as a heuristic instrument. As may be imagined, I take the second view. But I have to admit the prematurity, at least, of this study. What makes it premature is not merely the paucity of individual numerological analyses of high quality. A still more rudimentary difficulty exists: the absence of reliable information about the external facts of poetic form. Contrary to what one might suppose, for example, the development of the stanza has never been fully charted. For that matter, there has been no comprehensive history of prosody at all since Saintsbury's impressionistic sketch (1906–10). Even simple statistics are lacking, such as would enable a numerologist to determine, say, what percentage of elegies were composed in seven-line stanzas, or with line totals of 120, during particular historical periods. Being *ante tempus*, the present book undefinitively aims simply to arouse interest and to suggest future lines of exploration.

The interest of numerological criticism is twofold. First, it makes possible a more fully intelligible descriptive analysis. By bridging the gap between form and content it not only shows what internal considerations led to the external proportions but can even sometimes stimulate fresh appreciation of the meaning. Self-referring passages relating to the work's own structural patterns must remain obscure without it. Nor can we adequately account for the Elizabethan poet's characteristic sureness of direction, without referring to the numerological maps by which he could always tell where he was going and what came next. Secondly, numerological criticism holds out the hope of a better understanding of poetry's relations with the sister arts music and architecture. For, if the doctrines *ut pictura poesis* and *ut architectura poesis* ever had validity, this should be plainest where poetry is most visual: in structural patterns of lines and stanzas. These doctrines, in reality far from vague, implied a completely spatial conception of literature, of which figure poems were only one manifestation, noticeable because bizarre. Literary and architectural theorists shared many ideas, especially that of creation by number and proportion: when he spoke in his *Poetice* (1561) of the poet as an *alter deus*, Scaliger was repeating Alberti's claim (1435) that the painter 'will feel himself another God'. We should never, of course, allow ourselves to forget that comparisons between the arts are only more or less remote analogies. Elizabethan poets were no more trying to write architecture than Palladian architects with their octave proportions were composing music in stone. Nevertheless, if we are to have such analogies at all, numerological criticism may help to make them less impressionistic.

A subject as large as numerical organization, necessarily involving much detail, could hardly be treated in a single volume. Consequently I have selected two sorts of pattern from among many: other books could be written about other sorts. The chosen two, however, triumphal patterns and temporal patterns, are the commonest, and often occur in conjunction. They are also among the most significant; for the triumph embodied some of the profoundest aspirations of the renaissance, while meditations on time and the structure of history many of the finest poems of the sixteenth and seventeenth centuries.

Chapter 1, on evidence for the existence of numerical composition, may be passed over by those to whom such evidence seems superfluous or irrelevant. Chapters 2–5 deal with triumphal patterns involving symmetry or significant central points. Similar iconology is traced in extra-literary forms (2), in the substantive structure of poetry (3), in poetic form considered synchronically (4) and in poetic form considered diachronically with respect to historical art styles (5). Chapters 6–8 study the use of temporal numbers: first in renaissance critical theory and in the measure of the action, then in numerology at large, and finally in the numerology of the epithalamic genre. In sonnet sequences (9) temporal and triumphal forms are sometimes closely interwoven.

For the time in which much of this book was written I have to thank the Principal and Fellows of Brasenose College, Oxford, and the Board of the Faculty of English, for sabbatical leave. An invitation to the Institute for Advanced Study, Princeton, made it possible for me to work in almost ideal circumstances of quiet and scholarly companionship. My debt to generations of indulgent undergraduates is incalculable. Pupils and friends whom I have to thank for individual contributions include Maren-Sofie Røstvig, Douglas Brooks, Robert B. Cummings, Howard Erskine-Hill, John Peacock and Michael Wilding. Where my ignorance was particularly complete, I asked help of David R. Coffin, Ralph Giesey, Colin G. Hardie, Lewis H. Lockwood and John North, meeting with generous assistance to be remembered with pleasure.

In accordance with editorial principles I have set out elsewhere, spelling of post-medieval texts has been modernized throughout (except for proper names), but original punctuation has been retained. In the notes, omission of a place of publication implies London. Unless a specific English version is cited, I may be held responsible for translations myself. Acknowledgements are due to Penguin Books for quotations from Dorothy Sayers's translation of the *Divina commedia*, and to the University of Chicago for quotations from E. H. Wilkins's *The Triumphs of Petrarch*.

Brasenose College,   A.D.S.F.
Oxford

xii

least the imitator's belief in the existence of the device. All five types of evidence are hardly ever available for any particular device. Usually, though, it seems to be thought enough to have one or two types. Thus, for the sixteenth century there is some critical theory about rhyming, but practically no evidence of the other four types. Yet we never doubt that Elizabethan poets meant their rhyme words to rhyme. Similarly with ambiguity: there is no evidence of types 1, 3, 4 and 5; only the semantic 'fit' of the device with the theme, perhaps, of the poem, or with the tone of the context. In this instance, the evidence of contemporary critical theory actually counts against belief in the device, since ambiguity was generally dismissed by rhetoricians as a fault of style. But this does not make us view with scepticism all discussions of ambiguities in Donne. Why should it? We are used to the idea of ambiguity.

With numerological patterning, things are different. In a sense this device is better documented than many others, since all five types of evidence can be produced. It is rarely practised nowadays, however, so that we are not used to the idea that Elizabethan poets organized their poems spatially. Those of us without much historical sense may even, like Nelson, put a blind eye to the telescope and pretend that numerology never existed. For number symbolism is not quite respectable: we associate it with cranks or lunatics, not with great authors and serious scholars. It would be instructive to trace the interplay of belief, superstition and scepticism about number symbolism since the time of the Church Fathers. First, belief in number symbolism was general and often rational (St Augustine): later, some argued sceptically (Selden) while others were superstitious or believed rationally (Browne, Fludd): later still, rational belief grew more difficult and number symbolism became the domain of eccentrics such as Francis Webb: and finally a new superstitious prejudice arose—the pretence that rational belief had never existed.

Recent numerological studies have done a little to dispel this prejudice. But some readers may still wish to hear evidence for the bare existence of the device, before consenting to relearn its enjoyment.

AUTHORS' STATEMENTS

Authorial statements about numerological patterns occur, though seldom in connection with poetic works of the highest merit. Thus

1. Evidence

It is seldom possible to prove that a writer of a former age intended to use any particular literary form. All the same, we sometimes achieve a high degree of probability in our critical statements. Believing rhymes to be common in the eighteenth century and specifically in Pope's poetry, we can say that he very probably rhymed 'way' with 'Bohea' and 'mind' with 'join'd'. And our familiarity with puns makes some of us sure that Donne meant more than one word-play in 'We can die by it, if not live by love'. These convictions cannot quite be proved, but neither can they easily be dismissed. And it is the same with probable statements about the numerical or spatial organization of works by authors no longer living.

Evidence for the intentional character, even for the mere existence, of a device in past literature generally belongs to one or more of the following categories: (1) *authorial statement* or other explicit external sign of intention (always rare and not always trustworthy); (2) *internal consistency* of the device with other elements (usually too implicit to be persuasive, except to those familiar with the work); (3) *commentary* by critics more nearly contemporary than ourselves, showing the response once to be expected from readers (even if commentators are hardly ideal readers); (4) *contemporary theory* about the use of the device (patchy evidence, since theorists and poets share few interests); and (5) *imitation* in later literature, which, if close enough, proves at

The analytical study of works of music reached the point where musical themes were transformed into physico-mathematical formulas. Not long after this philologists began to work on the same lines, and to measure word pictures in the same way as the physicists measured the manifestations of nature: this brought the analysis of pictorial art into line with the long standing relationship between architecture and mathematics. Abstract formulas, relationships, analogies and correspondences were now discovered among those which had already been gained by following these paths.

Hermann Hesse, *Das Glasperlenspiel*, tr. Mervyn Savill as *Magister Ludi* (New York 1949) 33

Henry Constable prefaces one arrangement of his sonnets with a fairly elaborate account of 'The order of the book', beginning 'The sonnets following are divided into 3 parts, each part containing 3 several arguments, and every argument 7 sonnets',[1] and followed by cross-headings above each heptad of sonnets. But both Sidney and Drayton use the same climacteric number 63 in arranging their sonnets without advertising the fact (p. 176). Nevertheless, I shall touch on a few indiscretions of this type, committed by celebrated authors: notably Pico della Mirandola, Du Bartas and La Primaudaye.[2]

More frequently the author contented himself with a hint in the title of list of contents. The title of Spenser's *Shepherd's Calendar* describes it as 'containing twelve eclogues proportionable to the twelve months'. And anyone who cared to could list whole chiliads of works entitled Enneads, Decades, Centuries, Weeks, Pentamerons, Decamerons, Tetrachordons, Decachordons, Heptapli, Zodiacs, etc., all divided accordingly.[3] A late example is Gay's *Trivia* (1716) in 3 books. Sometimes the author or his printer could be quite laborious about numbering items numerically organized, as when verses pre-

---

[1] *The Poems of Henry Constable* ed. J. Grundy (Liverpool 1960) 114; also her Pl. facing 113 reproducing the relevant folio in the Todd MS. See further below, p. 176.

[2] Pp. 137, 138 and n. Patristic prose writers sometimes explain their book divisions very explicitly; see Vincent Foster Hopper, *Medieval Number Symbolism* (New York 1938) 87 and Maren-Sofie Røstvig, 'The Hidden Sense' in *The Hidden Sense*, Norwegian Studies in English ix (1963) 8, on St Augustine's division of the *De Civitate Dei*, as well as on Cassiodorus' explanation of his division of a book into 33 chapters on the ground that 33 is 'a number acknowledged to correspond with the age of the Lord when he offered eternal life to ...those who believed'.

[3] A few instances must suffice: Heinrich Bullinger, *Sermonum decades quinque* (1587) and *A hundred sermons upon the apocalypse* (1561); Owen Feltham, *Resolves, a duple century* (1628–9); Thomas Watson, *The Ἑκατομπαθία or passionate century of love* (1582); Thomas Traherne, *Centuries* (not published until 1908) and Barnabe Barnes, *A Divine Century of Spiritual Sonnets* (1595); Du Bartas, *Divine Weeks* tr. J. Sylvester (1605), with other hexaemeral works discussed in Ch. 7 below; Giovanni Battista Basile, *Il pentamerone* (50 stories told 10 per day); Boccaccio, *Decameron*, 'wherein are contained a hundred tales told in ten days by seven ladies and three young men'; William Watson, *A decachordon of ten quodlibetical questions* (?Douay 1602); Johann Saubert, Δυωδεκάς emblematum sacrorum (Nuremberg 1625); Pico della Mirandola, *Heptaplus* (1489); Marcellus Palingenius, *Zodiacus vitae* (Venice ?1535; over 60 Latin edns, the first in England being 1569; tr. Barnaby Googe 1565); R. Dodoens, *Stirpium historiae pemptades sex, sive libri xxx* (Antwerp 1583).

paratory to Drayton's *Polyolbion* have it that Prince Henry 'by that virtue in the treble trine'[1] will add to his own goodness

These several glories of the eight English kings;
Deep [1]knowledge, [2]greatness, [3]long life, [4]policy,
[5]Courage, [6]zeal, [7]fortune, [8]awful majesty.

Since what we are dealing with is properly an elegance, however, explicit authorial signposts are inevitably rare. They would be clumsy, even self-destructive. And it would be an improbable accident indeed that would preserve foul papers showing an author's numerical scaffolding. Nevertheless, such an accident has occurred, in the case of a prose history of England projected by the Elizabethan antiquary Henry Ferrers, which was to have been called 'The Enneads of England'. This is how Ferrers begins:

9 times 9 is 82 / The whole history nine enneads / every ennead nine books / every book 27 chapters that is thrice nine / 81 books / 2177 chapters.[2]

For Ferrers, at least, the planning of a work began with numerical divisions: these were subsequently filled in, like the spaces on a blank form. An interesting feature of the draft is the magnitude of the numbers involved. If the planning of a prose history could deal in numbers running into four figures, what arithmetical complexities may we not expect in the more highly organized world of poetry?

INTERNAL CONSISTENCY

The internal consistency of a spatial pattern with the subject or theme, a *sine qua non* from the critic's point of view, may also provide evidence of a kind. Such consistency can even sometimes be self-evident.

[1] Ed. J. W. Hebel iv p. iv (superscript figures in original). Numbering in text or margin was particularly common in accounts of pageants. See e.g. A. H. Thomas and I. D. Thornley, *The Great Chronicle of London* (1938) 161; also Alastair Fowler, *Spenser and the Numbers of Time* (1964) 239 n. on an example in Blennerhasset (1582).

[2] See Elizabeth K. Berry, 'Henry Ferrers, an Early Warwickshire Antiquary, 1550–1633', *Dugdale Society Occasional Papers* xvi (Oxford 1965) 30, from the volume of Historical Collections in the Archer MSS at Shakespeare's birthplace, fol. 85v. For this reference I am indebted to Dr R. W. Hunt of the Bodleian and to Mr R. B. Cummings. When Ferrers writes $9 \times 9 = 82$, we should not immediately conclude that his arithmetic is bad: totals just exceeding or falling short of an expected number were sometimes deliberate finesses. Professor Maren-Sofie Røstvig has drawn my attention to several discussions of this device in arithmological authors: on $999 = 1000 - 1$ see Francesco Giorgio, *Problemata* (Paris 1574) II iii 132, fol. 82r; on $53 = 54 - 1$, Fabius Paulinus, *Hebdomades* (Venice 1589) iii 2 and 4.

4

The line total of Chapman's 'A Hymn to our Saviour on the Cross', for example, obviously matches the subject, since 300 regularly symbolized the cross, being the number denoted by the cross-shaped Greek letter Tau.[1] Such inorganic, arbitrary and trivial organization, however, has little interest for the critic.

The more organic and complex forms with which this book is mainly concerned have more interest, I hope. On the other hand, being far from self-evident, they are not designed to convince sceptics. This is particularly true when the internal consistency is with another constituent, such as imagery or verbal ambiguity. In Chapman's 'The Amorous Zodiac', a verbal narrative of the sun's course round the ecliptic is so repeatedly and so closely related to the poet's progress through the poem that few sympathetic readers could miss his broad hints at a spatial organization (pp. 141–6). Certain phrases, in fact, almost amount to authorial statement. But to catch these hints the reader must be willing to listen for overtones in phrases customarily treated as crude or vapid. Self-referring passages generally seem empty when the structural patterns they refer to are not grasped, so that critics tend to ignore or deride rather than interpret them. Merely explaining such ambiguities would not necessarily make them good poetry; but at least it might protect them from automatically being dismissed as bad. And perhaps it would clarify something of the mannerist poet's preoccupation with formal style.

COMMENTARIES

Early commentaries drawing attention to spatial patterns are rare. But then, descriptive criticism of any kind is rare in the sixteenth and seventeenth centuries. Such commentaries as we have were mostly written by humanist scholars interested only in textual, mythological and rhetorical matters, or else by edifying allegorists using the literary work as a point of departure for moral generalizations. Nevertheless, more than one commentator on Virgil finds time to discuss the numerology of his book division. Writing in 1563, Sebastianus Regulus interestingly foreshadows Brooks Otis's analysis of the *Aeneid* into

[1] See Pietro Bongo, *Numerorum mysteria*, 'De numero CCC' (Bergamo 1591) 605: 'Tricentenarius numerus in Tau littera continetur, quae crucis speciem tenet, cui si supertransversam lineam, id quod in cruce eminet, adderetur, non iam crucis species, sed ipsa crux esset.' Both in Hebrew and in Greek, letters served orthographically as numbers.

two matching parts. Regulus is in no doubt that the book division had a basis in number symbolism:

> I think Virgil wished to divide this poem into 12 books, so that it would seem an absolute, perfect and complete work, even in its numerical aspect. For the ancients divided both the day and the night into 12 unequal hours; the heavens are divided into 12 signs; and a perfect year is completed in 12 natural years. Indeed, I even think that the poet recalled the esoteric Pythagorean philosophy of numbers. For by 6 the ancients meant a symbol of marriage, and in these books of the *Aeneid* nuptials are celebrated twice —first those of Dido and Aeneas, then those of Lavinia and Aeneas; from which the greatest part of the work is developed. On these grounds I am persuaded that Virgil chiefly wished by this number to show us the perfection of his whole work.[1]

With the first part of this interpretation, the later Jesuit commentator Jacopo Pontano (1542–1626) is broadly in agreement. As might perhaps be expected, however, he imparts a more pious tone to his own discussion of the book division, introducing Scriptural associations with the duodecad:

> The whole work is seen to be divided into 12 books. 12 for this reason, that by this very number its highest perfection may be judged, since we perceive that many other complete and perfect things are similarly contained in the duodecad. Let us imagine this by means of examples. There are 12 months: 12 hours of day and as many of night: the unit of measure is divided into 12 equal parts.[2] The same number is often used in Holy Scripture. Thus there are 12 tribes of Israel, 12 fountains, 12 apostles, 12 gates of the New Jerusalem in the Apocalypse, and a crown of 12 stars.[3]

The purpose here is more homiletic. But both commentators evidently start from the assumption that external divisions of a literary work are likely to have symbolic meaning.

Apart from Virgil, no secular poet seems to have attracted commentary of this kind—except that much of the early criticism of Dante, as of Spenser the English Virgil, dealt with number sym-

---

[1] Sebastianus Regulus, *In primum Aeneidos Virgilii librum ex Aristotelis De arte poetica et rhetorica praeceptis explicationes* (Bologna 1563) 20f. See the discussion of this and the following quotation in R. B. Cummings, 'Two Sixteenth-Century Notices of Numerical Composition in Virgil's *Aeneid*', *N & Q* CCIV (1969) 26f.

[2] Probably misunderstanding Regulus and taking *assis = axis*, the heavens, for *assis = as*.

[3] Jacopo Pontano, *Symbolarum libri xvii. Quibus P. Virgilii Maronis Bucolica, Georgica, Aeneis ex probatissimis auctoribus declarantur, comparantur, illustrantur* (Augsburg 1599) 9f. See below pp. 13, 136.

bolism in the content.[1] But with sacred literature it was different. In 1617 Hendrik Van der Putte published a whole treatise on the spatial symbolisms in a single verse by Bauhuis in praise of the Virgin.[2] More important than this *tour de force* was the ancient and normal practice of interpreting the Bible numerologically. Here I am not primarily thinking of cabalistic interpretation, which some Reformation and Counter-Reformation theologians already regarded as dangerously unsound. Less secretly, poetical parts of Scripture such as the *Psalms* were known from Patristic times to be arranged in symbolic spatial patterns. A good example is Vulgate *Psalm* cxviii, which consists of 22×8 verses, 8 for each letter of the Hebrew alphabet. Patristic, medieval and later writers might interpret this acrostic pattern variously (Hebrew the source of all wisdom, $22 = 10$ for the commandments $+ 12$ for the counsels of the gospel, etc.),[3] but its presence could hardly be ignored.

The occurrence of the alphabetic number here and elsewhere in the Bible was so well known that it came to be applied as a compositional device. St Jerome even cooked the book total of the Old Testament by grouping and subdivision until he got the required 24, the number of letters in the Greek alphabet.[4] Continuity of tradition extends from the Bible, through Patristic commentators and theologians, then through medieval and later commentators, encyclopaedists and arithmologists, to sixteenth- and seventeenth-century compositions on a numerological basis. It was well known, for example, that *Lamentations* is divided into 5 verse elegies, the first 4 of which consist each of 22 acrostic stanzas, arranged alphabetically. The third elegy has a more demanding form, the appropriate letter not only beginning each stanza but also each verse. (The fifth elegy, though in 22 verses, is not acrostic.) So Origen speaks of Jeremiah 'mourning the destruction of

[1] See Fowler 260 ff., citing Digby and Austin. Early commentators on the *Divina commedia* discussed the symbolic dimensions of the inferno, which they explained as based on the 11 of transgression.

[2] *Eryci Puteani pietatis thaumata in Bernardi Bauhusi e Societate Iesu Proteum parthenium, unius libri versum, unius versus librum, stellarum numero, sive formis M.XXII. variatum* (Antwerp 1617); see Fowler 238 and n.

[3] Røstvig, 'The Hidden Sense' 10 f.

[4] 12 minor prophets e.g. are treated as one. Bongo (446) notes that this numerological pattern was recognized by the Tridentine Council (whose decree on the canon is still prefaced to editions of the Vulgate). By a little manipulation he manages to square the book total also with the 22-letter Hebrew alphabet.

his city in quadruple alphabet': Cassiodorus quotes Origen's saying and arranges his own *De universo* in 22 parts: and St Augustine does likewise in his *De Civitate*.[1] In 1591 the arithmologist Pietro Bongo is still repeating Origen's saying, significantly with elaborations that account for more of the spatial pattern in symbolic terms: 'The *Lamentations* of Jeremiah, composed in Hebrew verse forms, number 4, and are divided by a fourfold alphabet, because in them Jeremiah mourns the sins not only of the Jews, but of the whole world.'[2] On the number 23, Bongo cites Cassiodorus' numerological explanation of *Psalm* xxiii: namely, that its number alludes to the language of eloquence (the Latin alphabet having 23 letters, as against the 22 of the Hebrew and the 24 of the Greek).[3] And in 1617 Van der Putte arranges his numerical commentary on Bauhuis in 24 chapters corresponding to the letters of the Greek alphabet.

Numerical composition might thus be an inspiration of the Christian Muse. Poets looked for a form analogous to that of Biblical poetry, and according to a main doctrine of Biblical Poetics the composition of the Bible followed the same creative method referred to in *Wisdom of Solomon* xi 20: 'thou has ordered all things in measure and number and weight.'[4] Biblical commentaries must be regarded not merely as evidence of a habit of numerological interpretation but also as an effective cause of the practice of numerological composition itself.

CRITICAL THEORY

At first sight the almost complete absence of contemporary critical theory about numerology counts very strongly against thinking the practice widespread. True, Minturno's *De poeta* asserts the poet's possession of mathematical and musical lore:

The doctrine and wisdom that flowed from the Orphic fount through to Pythagoras and then to Plato ordered the universe according to a musical principle. And since...the ordering of sounds is divided into numbers and melody, you will certainly find all the elements of music in the art of poetry.

[1] See Røstvig, 'The Hidden Sense' 8, 10f., who cites other patristic comments of a similar kind. Her own description of the pattern of *Lamentations*, however, is incorrect: the central chapter is not divided into 3, and the 'quadruple alphabet' does not refer to Chs. i, ii, iv and v, but to Chs. i–iv, the acrostic chapters.
[2] Bongo 644, 'De numero MDC'.
[3] *Ibid*. 442.
[4] See Harry Bober, 'In principio. Creation before time', *Essays in Honor of Erwin Panofsky. De artibus opuscula xl* (1961) 18, *cit*. Røstvig, 'The Hidden Sense' 8.

For it is beyond question that numbers have always been common to all poets together with musicians.[1]

Or again: 'The wise ancients believed that there is a great power in numbers, and that this must be familiar to poets.'[2] But probably Minturno means 'numbers' only in the sense of metre or rhythm. And it is no more conclusive when he proves Virgil's acquaintance with Pythagorean number symbolism by citing monads and dyads in the action of the *Aeneid*.[3] So with other renaissance critics. Either they apply the *Wisdom* text to poetic creation in such a way that they could be referring simply to metre—

L'invenzion, la favola, il poema,
e l'ordine e 'l decoro e l'armonia
. . . .
Seco il numero, il metro e la misura,
si prendon de la musica la cura.[4]

—or else, like Henry Reynolds, they talk so generally about Pythagorean secrets that they might mean mysteries concealed in the content. Reynolds' *Mythomystes* (1633) exhorts poets to steep themselves in the cabala and in the lore of Pythagoras the Master of Silence. But though he gives a useful list of arithmological authorities, he himself is a master of vagueness: he never quite explains how poets are to apply this number symbolism.[5]

On second thoughts, however, we see the situation to be much as we might have expected. The tone of Reynolds' *Mythomystes* shows, after all, that he thought number symbolism an esoteric mystery. It was hardly an aspect of the art of poetry lending itself to treatment in systematic prescriptive treatises: that would have spoilt the whole game of secrecy. (With numbers in renaissance architecture, as we know, it was much the same. No one now doubts that some at least of

[1] Antonio Sebastiano Minturno, *De poeta* ii (Venice 1559) 91; see Fowler 241 f., and n.
[2] *De poeta* 89.   [3] *Ibid.* 89 f.
[4] *L'Adone* v 123. Cf. Richard Wills, *De re poetica* (1573) tr. and ed. Alastair Fowler (Oxford 1958) 62–4: 'The origin of metrical form is from God the almighty creator, in that he created this universe and whatever is contained in its sphere with a fixed design, as it were by measure; to such an extent that Pythagoras has asserted that there is a harmony in celestial and in earthly things. For how could the universe exist, unless it were governed by a fixed order and established numbers (*certa ratione ac definitis numeris*)?'
[5] *Mythomystes* is reprinted in *Critical Essays of the Seventeenth Century* ed. J. E. Spingarn i (Oxford 1908).

9

the number symbolisms discovered by Professor Wittkower were intentional; but it would be hard to find contemporary theory that went beyond general sentiments about proportion.) A further reason for the absence of numerology from renaissance arts of poetry lies in the traditional range of their topics. It was not one of the conventional topics of a genre that had developed under exclusively rhetorical influences. As Curtius has remarked, rhetorical theory had little to say about the compositional arrangement of large units.[1] To put it in another way, rhetoricians were only interested in the verbal organization of poetry, whereas numerology depended on a spatial approach. Consequently the theorists left number to iconographers and arithmologists.

The silence of the theorists is thus less significant than at first appears. It is also to some extent illusory. When we read with sympathy and attention, we see that renaissance critics often imply numerological conceptions that could not form their direct subject. And, very occasionally, they will treat these conceptions more or less directly. Thus Francesco Patrizi devotes a volume (*Deca dogmatica universale*, 1587, MS Pal. 421) to the division of poetic form into 'parts'. His elusive conception of 'part' must to some degree be numerical, since he discusses the division of the *Divina commedia* 'into three "total" parts and one hundred "partial" ones'.[2] Moreover, the endless renaissance debate about the unity of time had, as we shall see, numerological overtones.[3]

In England, Puttenham's approach is strikingly spatial. His *Art of English Poesy* (1589) deals with poetic form in a book called 'Of Proportion Poetical', beginning with the usual allusion to *Wisdom*:

It is said by such as profess the mathematical sciences, that all things stand by proportion, and that without it nothing could stand to be good or beautiful. The doctors of our theology to the same effect, but in other terms, say: that God made the world by number, measure and weight: some for weight say tune, and peradventure better.[4]

[1] Ernst R. Curtius, *European Literature and the Latin Middle Ages* tr. W. R. Trask (1953) 501, *cit.* Gunnar Qvarnström, *Poetry and Numbers* (Lund 1966) 36.
[2] Bernard Weinberg, *A History of Literary Criticism in the Italian Renaissance* ii (Chicago and Toronto 1961) 779.
[3] See below, Ch. 6.
[4] George Puttenham, *The Art of English Poesy* ed. Gladys D. Willcock and Alice Walker (Cambridge 1936) 64.

Here he finds room for discussions of figure poems exhibiting various geometrical shapes.[1] These sections, often brushed aside as frivolous curiosities, should in some instances be seen rather as serious though fumbling attempts at a theory of numerical composition. As Maren-Sofie Røstvig has discerned, Puttenham's discussion of poems in the shape of a square, 'the figure of most solidity and steadfastness', is in a sense numerological.[2]

More significantly still, Puttenham's section on poems in the form of 'The Roundel or Sphere' (98–100) is true numerological criticism, since it deals not with shape poems but with poems whose structure is discernible only by counting lines. The examples given, in fact, have no visible resemblance to a circle at all. After praising the circle's perfection—'his indefiniteness having no special place of beginning nor end, beareth a similitude with God and eternity'—Puttenham gives a prescription for writing circle poems, which is almost impenetrably obscure:

This figure hath three principal parts in his nature and use much considerable: the circle, the beam, and the centre. The circle is his largest compass or circumference: the centre is his middle and indivisible point: the beam is a line stretching directly from the circle to the centre, and contrariwise from the centre to the circle.[3] By this description our maker may fashion his metre in roundel, either with the circumference, and that is circlewise, or from the circumference, that is, like a beam, or by the circumference, and that is overthwart and diametrally from one side of the circle to the other.

Fortunately two examples follow, making it clear that Puttenham has in mind a centralized numerological pattern, of a kind I discuss in Chapter 4. The second example of a circle poem, 'A special and

---

[1] As does Richard Wills in the *Poematum liber* to which the 'De re poetica' forms the Introduction. Both English critics follow in this respect J. C. Scaliger, *Poetice* Bk I, Ch. xxv; see Wills ed. Fowler 12 and n.

[2] Ed. Willcock and Walker 100: 'The square is of all other accounted the figure of most solidity and steadfastness, and for his own stay and firmity requireth none other base than himself, and therefore as the roundel or sphere is appropriate to the heavens, the spire to the element of the fire: the triangle to the air, and the lozenge to the water: so is the square for his inconcussable steadiness likened to the earth, which perchance might be the reason that the prince of philosophers in his first book of the *Ethics*, termeth a constant minded man, even egal and direct on all sides, and not easily overthrown by every little adversity, *hominem quadratum*, a square man. Into this figure may ye reduce your ditties by using no more verses than your verse is of syllables, which will make him fall out square.' See Maren-Sofie Røstvig, 'The Hidden Sense' 23 n.

[3] As often *circle* = 'circumference' (*OED* s.v. *Circle* I 1); *beam* = 'radius', a meaning common in mathematical contexts (*OED Beam* sb.[1] III 22).

particular resemblance of her Majesty to the Roundel' (see p. 206), begins according to prescription with the circumference ('circle'), treated in 2 couplets:

First her authority regal
Is the circle compassing all:
The dominion great and large
Which God hath given to her charge.

There follow 15 couplets, the first and the last of which share the same rhyme (*bound/round, ground/round*). This portion mimes the shape earlier referred to verbally, since the return to the opening rhyme imitates the true circle's ending where it begins. Moreover, it also follows Puttenham's prescription in being shaped 'overthwart and diametrally from one side of the circle to the other'. If the 15 couplets represented the diameter of a circle ('by [alongside] the circumference'), their bisection would correspond to the bisection of diameters at its centre. Now the central eighth couplet refers to the 'beams' of the queen's 'justice, bounty and might'—'And reflect not, till they attain / The farthest part of her domain.'—in a conceit whose force depends on the geometrical identity of a reflected 'beam' and a diameter (both twice the radius).[1]

There are a few other suggestions of numerological thinking in *The Art of English Poesy*. For example, Puttenham treats 'proportion in measure'—numbers in the prosodic sense—in terms of Pythagorean symbolism. Thus he disparages classical feet consisting of more than three syllables, on the ground that 'whatsoever foot pass the *trisyllable* is compounded of his inferior as every number arithmetical above three, is compounded of the inferior numbers as twice two make four, but the three is made of one number, *videlicet* of two and an unity' (68). And there may even be more than meets the eye in his comparison of the caesura to a midday halt: 'our poet when he hath made one verse, hath as it were finished one day's journey, and the while easeth him self with one bait [rest] at the least, which is a comma or caesura in the mid way.'[2]

[1] In Puttenham's other example, 'A general resemblance of the Roundel to God, the world and the Queen' (ed. Willcock and Walker 98f.), ll. 17f. are: 'The furthest part of all his sphere / Is equally both far and near.' Here the imitation of the circumference is more obvious, 2 rhymes being repeated instead of one (ll. 1–4, 29–32).

[2] Ed. Willcock and Walker 74f. Cf. Milton's numerological use of the same metaphor at *Paradise Lost* xii 1; see Milton, *Poems* ed. Carey and Fowler 1027.

Certain imitations that necessarily imply a numerological intention on the imitator's part offer the most conclusive evidence of all for the existence of numerical composition. The case of Virgil is again instructive. In his *Spectator* paper 632 (13 December 1714) Tickell, having given as instances of the irrational love of symmetry and order Homer's division of his poems 'into as many books as there are letters in the Greek alphabet' and Herodotus' adapting 'his books to the number of the Muses', continues:

> Several epic poets have religiously followed Virgil as to the number of his books; and even Milton is thought by many to have changed the number of his books from ten to twelve for no other reason; as Cowley tells us, it was his design, had he finished his *Davideis*, to have also imitated the *Aeneid* in this particular.[1]

And imitation of Virgil's form could go to more elaborately numerological lengths: The *Teseida* has 9896 lines, exactly the same number as the *Aeneid*.[2]

Cowley's imitation of a structural pattern in *Epithalamion* is less slavish and more interesting. It shows that Professor A. Kent Hieatt was not the first to see number symbolism in the form of Spenser's poem: though Cowley wrote no critical commentary, he yet left incontrovertible evidence of his understanding of the numerology of his model, and incidentally of the unexpected compositional methods of a seventeenth-century poet. He designed his lyric 'The Long Life' on a plan very similar to that of *Epithalamion*, but with certain departures of vital significance from our point of view. If he had used exactly the same plan, we would not know whether he was imitating a meaningful pattern, or just copying externals. But in fact he has used Spenser's pattern *reduced in scale*. Where *Epithalamion* has 24 stanzas to represent (as Hieatt argues[3]) the hours of day, 'The Long Life' has 24 lines:

[1] *The Spectator* ed. D. F. Bond v (Oxford 1965) 159.

[2] In the best manuscripts available to Boccaccio; see E. Hutton, *Giovanni Boccaccio* (1910) 79 and R. A. Pratt, 'Chaucer's use of the *Teseida*', *PMLA* LXII (1947) 599.

[3] A. Kent Hieatt, *Short Time's Endless Monument: the Symbolism of the Numbers in Edmund Spenser's 'Epithalamion'* (New York 1960). Hieatt's interpretation of *Epithalamion*—the first numerological interpretation of a renaissance poem in modern times—is discussed, supported and supplemented below, pp. 103-7 and 161-73.

1

Love from Time's wings hath stolen the feathers sure,
He has, and put them to his own;
For hours of late as long as days endure,
And very minutes, hours are grown.

2

The various motions of the turning year,
Belong not now at all to me:
Each summer's night does Lucy's now appear,
Each winter's day St Barnaby.

3

How long a space, since first I loved, it is?
To look into a glass I fear;
And am surprised with wonder when I miss,
Grey-hairs and wrinkles there.

4

The old patriarchs' age and not their happiness too,
Why does hard fate to us restore?
Why does love's fire thus to mankind renew,
What the Flood washed away before?

5

Sure those are happy people that complain,
Of the shortness of the days of man:
Contract mine, Heaven, and bring them back again
To the ordinary span.

6

If when your gift, long life, I disapprove,
I too ingrateful seem to be;
Punish me justly, Heaven; make her to love,
And then 'twill be too short for me.[1]

It will be remembered that, according to Hieatt's theory, the spatial position of nightfall in *Epithalamion* Stanza xvii represents the division of a 24-stanza-hour solstitial day into 16 stanza-hours of light and 8 stanza-hours of darkness. Cowley's poem similarly mimes the length of day and night at the summer solstice by the position of a mention of night. The brevity of the solstitial night and the long duration of the solstitial day are mentioned only in lines 7f., so as to divide the lines 8 + 16.

True, the pattern is complicated by a conceited hyperbole whereby the lover feels the shortest night of absence (the night of 11 June,

---

[1] *The Mistress* in *Poems* ed. A. R. Waller (Cambridge 1905) 93f.

St Barnaby's Day) to be as long as the longest night (that of 13 December, St Lucy's Day). This leads to inversion of *Epithalamion*'s pattern —8 LINE-HOURS + 16 LINE-HOURS instead of 16 STANZA-HOURS + 8 STANZA-HOURS. Also, since both solstices have been brought into play, there is an additional punning mention of the shortness of *days* at an appropriate distance from the end of the poem. Nevertheless, the pattern of 'The Long Life' remains close enough to that of *Epithalamion* to put Cowley's understanding of the latter beyond reasonable doubt. He perhaps hints at the connection in his opening line, 'Love from Time's wings hath stolen the feathers sure', since stolen feathers were a common image for literary borrowing; though the line may depend solely on the iconographical tradition that portrayed Time with 4 wings and 12 feathers to symbolize the seasons and months.[1] It is a happy chance that Cowley should thus be able indirectly to repay his debt to Spenser, by providing support for Hieatt's restoration of the form of *Epithalamion*.[2]

INFLUENCES: THE CONCEPT OF CREATION

Given this evidence[3] for the practice of numerology, we naturally wonder what climate of ideas could have fostered such a method of composition.

A prominent element of that climate may have been the principle of renaissance humanism already referred to: imitation of nature. For Elizabethan poets conceived a mode of imitation at once more formal and more literal than we might expect. Believing with Cristoforo

[1] Erwin Panofsky, *Studies in Iconology* (New York and Evanston 1962) 79 and Fig. 50. See below, p. 167, for an analysis of the seasonal pattern in *Epithalamion*.
[2] Cowley's love of Spenser's work from his earliest years is attested in his autobiographical essay 'Of My Self': 'There was wont to lie in my mother's parlour ... Spenser's works; this I happened to fall upon, and was infinitely delighted with the stories of the knights, and giants, and monsters, and brave houses, which I found every where there: (Though my understanding had little to do with all this) and by degrees with the tinkling of the rhyme and dance of the numbers, so that I think I had read him all over before I was twelve years old, and was thus made a poet as immediately as a child is made an eunuch' (*Essays, Plays and Sundry Verses* ed. A. R. Waller (Cambridge 1906) 457f.). His familiarity with *Epithalamion* is evinced elsewhere in *The Mistress*: with 'That all the woods may answer and your echo ring' (*Epithalamion* 36) cf. 'Then all the fields and woods shall with it ring; / Then Echo's burden it shall be' ('Her Name'; *Poems* ed. Waller 135).
[3] Further evidence from contemporary commentaries is advanced below; see e.g. pp. 66, 137 f.

Landino that the world was God's poem[1] and with Scaliger that the poet was almost like another God,[2] they set about the creation of fictive worlds in the same way that God created the universe, 'by measure and number and weight':[3]

God's poem, this world's new essay;
So wild and rude in its first draft it lay;
The ungoverned parts no correspondence knew,
And artless war from thwarting motions grew;
Till they to number and fixed rules were brought
By the eternal Mind's poetic thought.[4]

A seminal passage in Plato's *Timaeus* (35 A–36 C) confirmed this view, adding a number series as the means of generation, and pre-existence of numerical pattern. Consequently renaissance poets in their imita-

[1] *Dante con l'espositione de Cristoforo Landino* (Venice 1564) sig. ** 3v, the probable source of the *De re poetica* passage quoted above; see Wills ed. Fowler 30. The ultimate authority for both passages, however, was St Augustine, *De Civ. Dei* xi 18; see Curtius 397–401, and K. E. Gilbert and H. Kuhn, *A History of Esthetics* (1939) 135, 158, 183.

[2] Julius Caesar Scaliger, *Poetices libri septem* (Lyons 1561) 3: 'ac demum sese isthoc ipso perinde ac Deum alterum efficit.' The poet seems not to deal with existing things, like those practising other sciences, but to create: 'sed velut alter deus condere.' See also M. C. Nahm, 'The Theological Background of the Theory of the Artist as Creator', *JHI* VIII (1947) 363 ff. and his *The Artist as Creator* (Baltimore, Md 1956). Nahm stresses the difficulty of reconciling the notion with other more mimetic conceptions of poetry—a difficulty felt, one suspects, more by Nahm himself than by renaissance theorists.

[3] *Wisdom of Solomon* xi 20: the Latin *metro* admits the same ambiguity as the English *measure*. For architectural applications of the same text, see Rudolf Wittkower, *Architectural Principles in the Age of Humanism* (third edn, revised 1962) 119, 132.

[4] Abraham Cowley, *Davideis* i ed. Waller 253. In his own notes to the *Davideis*, Cowley traces the idea to St Augustine: 'I have seen an excellent saying of S. Augustine's, cited to this purpose, *Ordinem saeculorum tanquam pulcherrimum carmen ex quibusdam quasi antithetis honestavit Deus—sicut contraria contrariis opposita sermonis pulchritudinem reddunt, ita quadam non verborum sed rerum eloquentia contrariorum oppositione saeculi pulchritudo componitur.* And the Scripture witnesses, that the world was made in number, weight, and measure; which all are qualities of a good poem. The order and proportion of things is the true music of the world, and not that which Pythagoras, Plato, Tully, Macrobius and many of the Fathers imagined, to arise audibly from the circumvolution of the heavens. This is their musical and loud voice, of which David speaks, *Psalm* 19. *The heavens declare the glory of the Lord—there is no speech nor language where their voice is not heard. Their sound is gone out through all the earth, and their words to the end of the world*—or as our translation nearer the Hebrew (they say) renders it, Their *line* is gone out, *linea, vel amussis eorum*: to show the exactness of their proportion' (i n. 34, ed. Waller 276). Cf. *De Civ. Dei* xii 18, where the numerical character of creation is further treated.

tion of nature or aspiration to independent golden worlds would naturally have recourse to measure and numbers: they would build these into the physical form of their works, just as God built numerical proportion into the cosmic structure. Authors were even urged to have a numerical pattern of ideas in mind—as we saw that Ferrers had—before proceeding to material creation. Guy le Fevre de la Boderie (himself a poet) in the introduction to his French translation of Giorgio's *De harmonia mundi totius* (1579) recommends the invention of a preliminary numerical plan, to be applied subsequently in structural division. As an example he offers the method of Giorgio himself, who 'imitating the order of the world, almost imitating its artificer and architect, first of all divided this world harmony' into elaborate part and chapter divisions, whose musical symbolism le Fevre goes on to explain.[1]

A more pervasive but also more elusive element, whose bearing on literary forms we are only beginning to grasp, is the spatial character of renaissance thought.[2] I shall only touch one aspect of this: the tendency to order ideas in visual schemes (especially linear sequences). The dominance in the renaissance of the pseudo-Horatian doctrine *ut pictura poesis* has long been obvious.[3] But the application of the doctrine to literary structure, as distinct from texture or imagery, is far from obvious. We may understand some of the possibilities more readily, however, if we turn to a slightly different analogy, that between poetry and architecture. This subject has been pioneered in Per Palme's study of Elizabethan descriptions of festal architecture, '*Ut architectura poesis*'.[4] Palme shows that the conceptions of structural unity in poetry and in architecture were closely analogous: Ben Jonson, for example, more than once defines the organic integration of literary works in architectural terms. Thus he speaks of 'action...

[1] See Røstvig, 'Hidden Sense' 27 ff., where substantial passages from le Fevre's introductory chapters are quoted and analysed.

[2] This topic is brilliantly discussed by Fr W. J. Ong, in *The Barbarian Within* (New York 1962) Ch. v, 'System, Space and Intellect in Renaissance Symbolism'; see also the same author's 'From Allegory to the Diagram in the Renaissance Mind', *The Journal of Aesthetics and Art Criticism* xvii (1959).

[3] See e.g. R. W. Lee, '*Ut pictura poesis*: The Humanistic Theory of Painting', *Art Bulletin* xxii (1940).

[4] In *Idea and Form* ed. N. G. Sandblad, Acta Universitatis Upsaliensis, Figura Nova Series 1 (Uppsala 1959). See also J. R. Spencer, 'Ut Rhetorica Pictura', *JWI* xx (1957).

which answers place in a building; and . . . hath its largeness, compass and proportion.[1]

That Jonson meant exact numerical proportion such as the Pythagorean-Platonic musical ratios of Palladian architecture, is suggested by Palme's quotations from festal descriptions by Dekker and others. These give the dimensions of triumphal arches with astonishing particularity, in such a way as to bring out the 'proportionable measures' of the members.[2] Evidently a public with keen interest in architecture's numerical ratios existed. Jonson himself usually speaks in general terms: the parts of arches seem 'all, with that general harmony so connexed, and disposed, as no one little part can be missing to the illustration of the whole'.[3] But the analogy between poetry and architecture could be quite minute, as Drayton's defence of the eight-line stanza of his *Barons' Wars* shows:

I chose this stanza, of all other the most complete and best proportioned, consisting of eight lines, six interwoven and a couplet in base.

[1] *Ben Jonson* ed. C. H. Herford, Percy and Evelyn Simpson 11 vols (Oxford 1925–52) viii 645, *cit.* Palme 107, who also quotes viii 623.
[2] The Dutchman's arch at the Royal Exchange, for example, ascended '18 foot high, aptly proportioned to the other limbs, and 12 foot wide' (*Dramatic Works* ed. F. Bowers ii (Cambridge 1955) 267), and the Soper Lane entrance was 'a fair gate in height 18 foot. In breadth 12. The thickness of the passage under it, being 24. Two posterns stood wide open on the two sides, either of them being 4 foot wide, and 8 foot high' (ed. Bowers ii 275, *cit.* Palme 102). Stephen Harrison, who designed the arches and published the series of engravings on which Dekker's descriptions provided a commentary, invites readers to work out proportions for themselves: 'where mention is to be made of heights, breadth, or any other commensurable proportions, you shall find them left thus—with a blank, because we wish you rather to apply them to the scale your self, than by setting them down, to call either your skill or judgement in question' (*The Arches of Triumph Erected in Honour of the High and Mighty Prince James* (1604) sig. C).
[3] Ed. Herford, Simpson and Simpson vii 90, *cit.* Palme 100.

...The sestin hath twins in the base, but they detain not the music nor the close (as musicians term it) long enough for an epic poem. This of eight both holds the tune clean thorough to the base of the column (which is the couplet, the foot or bottom) and closeth not but with a full satisfaction to the ear for so long detention.

Briefly, this sort of stanza hath in it, majesty, perfection, and solidity, resembling the pillar which in architecture is called the tuscan, whose shaft is of six diameters, and bases of two.[1]

It would be at best a half-truth to say that the other arts shared ideas of musical proportion. Instead of a tendency to Anders-streben towards music taking place, we find renaissance music itself showing the impress of spatial thought. Not only was it organized symmetrically, but it even exhibited visual (and inaudible) symbolic patterns known as 'eye-music': sixteenth-century madrigalists would set words such as *night* in black notes, or imitate arches with arch-shaped melodic lines.[2]

Such phenomena in all the arts are to be seen as effects of the visual ordering of ideas that characterized the period. The art of memory itself, as Frances Yates has reminded us, inculcated the habit of referring data to places in a mnemonic spatial array—often a development of some astronomical system or architectural structure.[3] Moreover, the revived memory arts of antiquity sometimes used number as an *aide-mémoire*. Miss Yates herself discusses Metrodorus of Scepsis' 360 places of memory, and we might add the Pythagoreans' custom (according to Vitruvius[4]) of writing their rules 'cube fashion' in 216 lines, because of the number's stability: 'this number of verses, like a cube upon whatever sense it falls, makes the memory there stable and unmoved.'[5] In the renaissance, the enduring poetic ideal of memorability (*monumentum exegi*) may well have been taken to involve spatial or numerical disposition.

Besides these factors there is another, much simpler and more

[1] Ed. Hebel ii 3f. Drayton goes on to discuss the practice of the ancients, who were accustomed 'to distinguish works into books, and every one to bear the number of their order'. Puttenham's whole chapter 'Of Proportion by Situation' is similarly spatial in conception; but see especially the architectural analogy between rhyme and masonry bonds (ed. Willcock and Walker 89).

[2] See Gustave Reese, *Music in the Renaissance* (New York 1954) Index s.v. *Eye-music*; Alfred Einstein, *The Italian Madrigal* 3 vols (Princeton, N.J. 1949); John Shearman, *Mannerism* (1967) 100.

[3] Frances A. Yates, *The Art of Memory* (1966) Index s.v. *Planets, the seven*; *Zodiac*; and *Memory, art of, or artificial memory*; *architectural systems*.

[4] Bk V Pref. 3f.; see Fowler 243.   [5] i.e. $216 = 6^3$, the 'psychogonic cube'.

inevitable in operation: association of ideas. Numbers had certain symbolic meanings as integrally related to them as semantic fields to words. It goes without saying that some associations would be common (the mortality and mutability of 7, the heavenliness of 9), others arcane. But the volume of arithmological publication in the sixteenth and seventeenth centuries obliges one to suppose that even comparatively esoteric number symbolisms then aroused more interest than some modern writers unfamiliar with the period are willing to believe. Giorgio's *De harmonia mundi*[1] and Bongo's *Numerorum mysteria*[2] both went through several editions, the former being also translated into French. In English there was William Ingpen's *The Secrets of Numbers* (1624). And many popular encyclopaedic, hexaemeral, or magical treatises had sections on number symbolism: St Augustine's *De Civitate Dei*, Macrobius' *In somnium Scipionis*, Valeriano's *Hieroglyphica*, Du Bartas's *Semaines* (with Sylvester's translation and Goulart's vast commentary translated by Lodge), La Primaudaye's *French Academy* englished by Bowes and Dolman. In some cases the question of availability is settled for us: Cowley, for example, cites Kircher's *De arte magna consoni et dissoni* on the therapeutic value of harmony, number and proportion in *Davideis* i note 32. The prospect of a history of arithmology by Christopher Butler may excuse our neglecting the problem of direct individual accessibility. But I shall sometimes touch on the equally interesting question of general currency of ideas. Number symbolism was so common an ingredient in public arts and ceremonial that it must have been regarded almost as a necessary aspect of decorum. Some pageants and royal entries even attempted fairly sophisticated efforts in this direction, to judge by the evidence of programmes and *ex post facto* descriptions.

In the former category, a famous example is the Emperor Maximilian I's instructions for the painted version of his *Triumph*, dictated to his secretary in 1512. Maximilian's programme abounds with precise numerical instructions: '5 falconers abreast in good order...5 animals...5 chamois hunters...5 deer abreast. Then 5 deer hunters... 5 boars painted as wild as possible. Then shall follow 5 boar hunters ...5 bears...5 bear hunters...5 court offices.' There are to be 5

---

[1] Venice 1525, Paris 1545 and (in French trans.) 1579. See Frances A. Yates, *The French Academies of the Sixteenth Century* (1947), s.v. *Giorgi*.
[2] Bergamo 1584–5, 1585 and 1591, Venice 1585 and Paris 1618 (two issues).

triumphal cars filled with musicians—on the first, for example, 'shall be 5 lutenists and rybeben players'. After ranks of mummers ('5 men in each rank') should come the *Gefecht*, 'in groups of 5 men abreast in good order, as follows, all on foot: 5 men with flails. 5 men with staves. 5 men with lances...'[1] It seems needless to go on: the insistence on 5 throughout the programme stands out clearly enough (Pl. 2). Now 5 is an obvious choice of number for an emperor, in view of its connotation as the sovereign throned at the centre of the 9 digits.[2] But who is to say that Maximilian may not have wished to allude also to more pointed meanings of the number? Sir Thomas Browne notes that 5 appears prominently in several places in Scripture:

That five should put to flight an hundred might have nothing mystically implied: considering a rank of soldiers could scarce consist of a lesser number.[3] Saint Paul had rather speak five words in a known than ten thousand in an unknown tongue: that is as little as could well be spoken. A simple proposition consisting of three words and a complexed one not ordinarily short of five.[4]

On the eve of the Reformation these associations may have had a special significance.

PARAMETERS

Numerical and spatial constructivism is very widely distributed in Elizabethan literature. Most of the good poets and many of the less good seem to have practised the method. In fact, we should probably regard it less as an isolated device or *concetto* than as a general level of organization, intermediate between the prosodic and the internal structure. Historically constructivism goes back, as John Shearman

---

[1] *The Triumph of Maximilian I* tr. and ed. Stanley Appelbaum (New York 1964) 2f. The grouping in 5s continues through a large part of the written programme, as well as in the series of woodcuts by Hans Burgkmair, Dürer and others, which was intended as the public version of the *Triumph*.

[2] See Fowler 34f., citing Ficino, *Opera omnia* 2 vols (Basel 1576) ii 1451; also Sir Thomas Browne, *The Garden of Cyrus* v, in *Works* ed. G. Keynes i (1928) 221: 'five surnamed the number of justice; as justly dividing between the digits, and hanging in the centre of nine....'

[3] *Lev.* xxvi 8 'five of you shall chase an hundred'; *Exod.* xiii 18 marg. 'Israel went up five in a rank'.

[4] *Garden of Cyrus* v, ed. Keynes i 223f. The last allusion is to *I Cor.* xiv 19, 'Yet in the church I had rather speak five words with my understanding, that by my voice I might teach others also, than ten thousand words in an unknown tongue.' Note Maximilian's stress on the use of 5 vernacular synonyms for 'orders' in the choir pageant (ed. Appelbaum p. 6).

has noted, through medieval literature—particularly in the long poem —to antiquity.[1] In the forward direction, it survives in the eighteenth-century novel: Fielding, for example, has ordered the chapters of *Joseph Andrews* according to an elaborate symmetry, which is explored in a recent study by Douglas Brooks.[2] In poetry, there was a change after the Augustan period (but already in Pope) towards a looser, more subjectively impressionistic method of construction. Instances of numerical composition occur much later—Gray, D. G. Rossetti and Hopkins come to mind—but these can be accounted for as springing from traditionalism or bizarre exotic whim or eccentricity. By the early eighteenth century numerological composition had ceased to be a dominant form.

Much of the present book is inevitably occupied with description and analysis of formal patterns that have become obscure. These have a direct bearing on criticism, however. Numerological structure is of interest to the literary critic not only from a historical but also from a theoretical point of view. When he interprets numerically composed works numerological analysis is obviously a necessary stage in the critical process, if he is to appreciate the form with its structural and moral emphases. Moreover, a numerological approach will often assist the interpretation of self-referring passages. Theoretically, the interest of numerical composition lies in its strategic position on the borderline between form and content. On one side, it is unquestionably formal—continuous, in fact, with large-scale prosody, a dormant province offered new openings for development by access through it to substance and significance. On the other, it interpenetrates just as inextricably with content—so closely, at times, as to threaten the whole balance of power on which the present Intentionalist treaty is based. For numerology, however intrinsic and organic, always springs from an author's deliberate decision. We can hardly call formal patterns extraneous, like explicit verbal statements of intention. Yet these particular formal patterns are also intentional, unambiguous and resistant to posterity's efforts to remould and enrich. They can be ignored, but they cannot easily be misinterpreted or improved upon.

[1] *Mannerism* 96.

[2] 'Symbolic Numbers in Fielding's *Joseph Andrews*' in *Silent Poetry* ed. Alastair Fowler (1970) pp. 234–60. Emrys Jones discusses an even later instance of constructivism in prose fiction in 'The Artistic Form of *Rasselas*', *RES* n.s. XVIII (1967).

2. Triumphs

COSMIC CENTRALITY

An outstanding feature of triumphal motifs is their emphasis of the centre. This position once carried a generally recognized iconological significance: it was the place, if not for an image of sovereignty, at least for a 'central feature' (to use an idiom still current). The sovereign might occupy either the centre of a circle, such as the zodiacal border of an imperial coin, or the mid point of a linear array, as when a throne was placed at the centre of one side of a table. In the linear form, elaborate symmetries often surround the significant middle point.

Centralized motifs, both in the arts and in political ceremony, seem to have had an origin in the iconology of cosmic kingship. H. P. L'Orange, who has studied the microcosmic symbolism of kingship in the ancient world, describes Near Eastern capitals that were planned to mirror the rule of the sun in heaven by location of the king's palace at the centre of a circle divided into four quadrants.[1] Within the palace, the throne room might contain a smaller cosmic symbol—such as the splendid working model at Khusrau, so complete that horoscopes could be cast by it.[2] We have to think of Nero's cosmic

---

[1] *Studies on the Iconography of Cosmic Kingship*, Instituttet for sammenlignende kulturforskning, Serie A: Forelesninger xxiii (Oslo 1953) 13; cf. *Num.* xxxv 5, decreeing just such a city. See also Berta Segall, 'Notes on the Iconography of Cosmic Kingship', *The Art Bulletin* xxxviii (1956).

[2] L'Orange 21.

23

hall, and not merely of the rhetoric of panegyry, when we read Lucan advising him 'to choose his seat exactly in the middle of the universe, in case the cosmic system should lose its equilibrium'.[1]

Cosmic ruler often meant sun king. Informing most symbolism of the centre, ancient and renaissance alike, was an awareness of the macrocosmic sun's position in the midst of the planets. The Ptolemaic system, for example, made Sol 'lord of the middle sphere',[2] the central planet in linear order of proximity to earth.[3] This tradition, with the Ptolemaic system itself, remained viable in the sixteenth and seventeenth centuries, so that Du Bartas could still write of the sun as a king on progress, keeping his ceremonial middle place: 'Six heavenly princes mounted evermore, / Wait on thy coach, three behind, three before.'[4] Centuries of visual art, not to speak of cosmic memory systems such as Camillo's Theatre, had set the image of the sun at the centre of the planets deep in men's imaginations. The success of the Copernican system robbed the sun of its linear middle position, only to give it a more fundamental centrality. Copernicus himself describes the sun's place at the centre of his system as 'like the king's throne'. At times the position had an almost mystical significance: Cartari, explaining why Apollo is portrayed in the midst of the Muses ('Apollo perche nel mezzo'), writes that 'the central position is given to Apollo not only here but also in the universe, because he diffuses his virtue through all things—which is why he was called the heart of heaven'.[5] And everyone knows Nicholas of Cusa's Augustinian image of God as a circle whose centre is everywhere and the circumference nowhere.[6]

The idea of the sovereign mid point came down to the sixteenth century by two more or less distinct traditions. One of these was sacred and learned, though not necessarily esoteric. It depended on a

[1] *De bello civili* i 45 ff., *cit.* L'Orange 30. See *ibid.* Chs. vi and vii for discussions of the cosmic symbolism of 'Jahve's Cherub Throne' and of 'Astral Thrones, Temples and Palaces in the Ancient Near East'.
[2] Ptolemy, *Tetrabiblos* iv 10 ed. F. E. Robbins, Loeb edn (1948) 445.
[3] The Ptolemaic order is Saturn, Jupiter, Mars, sun, Venus, Mercury, moon.
[4] *Divine Weeks* tr. J. Sylvester i iv 561 f. (1613) 106. Cf. La Primaudaye, *The French Academy* tr. T. B[owes] (1586) sig. a 8r; Francesco Giorgio, *De harmonia mundi* Index s.v. '*Sol in medio planetarum rex*'.
[5] Vicenzo Cartari, *Imagini delli dei de gl'antichi* (Venice 1647), facs. ed. W. Koschatsky (Graz 1963) 30.
[6] *De docta ignorantia* ii 12; tr. Fr Germain Heron (1954) 54. On Kenelm Digby's adaptation of the idea in relation to a passage in Spenser, see Fowler 266 f.

literalistic and mystical interpretation of Biblical texts mentioning the location of certain important symbolic objects. The tree of knowledge, for example, was placed according to its status as a divine prerogative 'in the midst of the garden' (*Gen.* iii 3 Vulgate *in medio paradisi*). And medieval moral allegorizations of Paradise assigned the same position to the tree of life: as the *Somme le roi* has it, 'God set the tree of virtue and in the middle the tree of life, that is Jesus Christ'.[1] The temple of Solomon occupied the centre of the whole world, so that Francesco Giorgio could interpret its geographical location *in meditullio mundi* as a symbol of just centrality.[2] Similarly Jerusalem was 'set...in the midst of the nations and countries that are round about her' (*Ezek.* v 5)—a text that Dante remembered when he was constructing the geography of the *Divina commedia*. Through all these images of divine centrality, and others like them, runs the theme of the cosmic ruler's claim 'I am the Lord in the midst of the earth' (*Exod.* viii 22). The theme became so familiar to Scriptural commentators that they developed a habit of automatically looking for the central position, even in the Bible's physical form. Thus Alexander Gil, Milton's schoolmaster at St Paul's, admires the diligence of the Masoretes, who 'numbered in the whole Bible, the verses, the words, the letters; and of them, the common, and the final; and what verse, what word, and letter, was the midst of every book.'[3] The more attentive laymen must inevitably have been influenced by this habit of the commentators. As late as 1793, Ostervald's Bible indicated the central chapter of each book.

The other tradition communicating the significance of the centre was political and public: as a matter of court protocol, when the sovereign appeared in full majesty on any judicial or state occasion, he had to be placed centrally. In visual representations of such events, the linear centrality—in parliament, in council, or at table—strikes one with particular force (Pl. 8).[4] Naturally authors often took for

---

[1] Rosemond Tuve, *Allegorical Imagery* (Princeton, N.J. 1966) 109; cf. *ibid.* 24 and Fig. 7.

[2] Giorgio I vii 33, fol. 158v; cf. below, p. 66.

[3] Alexander Gil, *The Sacred Philosophy of Holy Scripture* 2 Pts. (1635) ii 141, a passage to which my attention was drawn by Professor Maren-Sofie Røstvig.

[4] See e.g. the well-known miniature of the trial of Robert d'Artois showing Philip VI in the midst of the court of peers, or the representations of Louis XII enthroned amidst his council and of Charles IX and Catherine centrally throned at the 1560 États généraux; illus. *Histoire de France* i (Paris 1954) 256,

granted an arrangement so obvious and familiar. But explicit statements about it are by no means lacking: Ogilby, for example, happens to note that at Charles II's coronation feast in Westminster Hall, the throne was at the centre of the table.[1] From ancient times domestic custom has observed a similar practice in respect of the senior or socially superior person present. Thus Ovid, discussing reverence, has Urania recall the place of honour once accorded to an older man *medius iuvenum*.[2] And in our own time the senior person presiding at a formal dinner may still follow tradition by occupying the centre of the long side of the table. But formerly the symbolism was more conscious, even in a children's game; Sir Thomas Browne, when he explains the meaning of 5 as the just divider of the 9 digits, suggests that this 'might be the original of that common game among us, wherein the fifth place is sovereign, and carrieth the chief intention. The ancients wisely instructing youth, even in their recreations unto virtue, that is, early to drive at the middle point and central seat of justice.'[3]

The growth of absolutist monarchy in the sixteenth and seventeenth centuries brought a specially heavy emphasis on the sovereign centre. Ernst Kantorowicz has shown detailed iconological connections between the imagery of ancient cosmic kingship and that of the revived solar cult drawing support for the ideal of the sun king from the new heliocentric planetary systems.[4] The latter cult, though practised in England,[5] reached its greatest brilliance only in the ceremonial of the Roi Soleil himself, Louis XIV (1643–1715). Through the medium of coins and medals, the ancient types of cosmic kingship— the *Sol oriens* between pairs of horses, the *Sol invictus*, the sun within

334 etc. Among numerous English examples, 'The Entrance of Queen Elizabeth' in George Carleton's *A Thankful Remembrance* (1627) and the 1642 medallion of Charles I in Parliament (E. H. Kantorowicz, *The King's Two Bodies* (Princeton, N.J. 1957) Fig. 2) are especially notable for their mathematically strict centrality, as is Renold Elstrack's engraving of Queen Elizabeth in parliament. For several of the above examples I am indebted to Mr Ralph Giesey.

[1] J. Ogilby, *The Entertainment of. . .Charles II in his Passage through the City of London to his Coronation* (1662) 187.   [2] *Fasti* v 67f.

[3] Ed. Keynes i 221. Browne possibly refers to the dice game *novem quinque*, mentioned in *Love's Labour's Lost* at V ii 538 (New Arden), in which the principal throws were 5 and 9. Cf. p. 21 n. 2 above.

[4] Ernst H. Kantorowicz, 'Oriens Augusti—Lever du Roi', *Dumbarton Oaks Papers* XVII (1963) 165 n. 264.

[5] *Ibid.* 164 n. See also E. C. Wilson, *England's Eliza* (Cambridge, Mass. 1939).

a zodiac ring (Pl. 3)—all were relearned and reapplied.[1] And in the ritual of the *lever du roi* Louis put to shade the ritual elevation of the Byzantine emperors by rising daily amidst his court in a bedchamber positioned at the centre of the vast palace of Versailles, facing eastwards across the *Cour de marbre* towards Paris and the rising sun.[2] Despite the temptation, it would be a mistake to regard such cults simply as orgulous blasphemies. Kantorowicz makes it plain that an earthly sun king might be associated with the divine *Sol oriens* or the Christian *Sol iustitiae* (himself portrayed as a *Sol oriens*) in an exquisitely complex theological relation, perhaps involving the invention of special doctrines (the divine *comes*: the Two Suns).[3]

TRIUMPHS AND TRIUMPHAL ENTRIES

Sovereignty of the centre found its most splendid expression in royal entries and other triumphal pageants. To call the triumph the dominant form of pageantry from the late middle ages until the eighteenth century is no exaggeration. It not only provided the physical model for both religious and civic processions and shows but also for court masques, theatrical grouping and stage design. Moreover, the triumph can be termed a dominant form in the sense that it enshrined characteristic and precious values of the age. A classical inspiration is obvious, for example, in its retrospective attempt to recover the greatest magnificence of the ancient world. Thus, during the Italian renaissance, secular *trionfi* carefully imitated historical processions of Roman imperators, so that antique ceremonial mingled with contemporary pageant. At Rome in 1500 a triumph of Julius Caesar was re-enacted before Cesare Borgia: at Florence, under Lorenzo the Magnificent, the triumph of Aemilius Paullus: again at Florence, 1515, on the occasion of Leo X's entry, the triumph of Camillus.[4]

With more lasting validity, the form embodied affirmation of the mutable glory of the mundane world. For, in spite of its religious origins, the triumph had from ancient times celebrated human glory. The tension between the religious parts of the ceremony (such as the sacrifice) and the visible honour, almost deification, paid to the

[1] Kantorowicz, 'Oriens Augusti' 119 ff., 128, 166–77.
[2] *Ibid.* 173 f. and, on the corresponding Byzantine cult, 155.
[3] *Ibid.* 127 f., 135 f., 144, 152–4.
[4] Paul Kristeller, *Andrea Mantegna* i (1901) 288. Cf. Jacob Burckhardt, *The Civilization of the Renaissance in Italy* (Vienna and London n.d.) 217 f.

triumphator must have been continual: it appears visibly in the soldier regularly posted by the triumphator's side to remind him of his mortality. The instance of the triumph of Camillus is instructive. It seemed irreverent because the imperator went on a chariot drawn by white horses, an attribute of solar deity: as Livy put it, 'in respect of his steeds the dictator was made equal to Jupiter and the sun god'.[1] The triumphal form was thus well adapted to express both a lofty ideal of the renaissance and its deep uneasiness about the presumption of earthly glory.

Though the idea of cosmic sovereignty is evident enough in the iconology of ancient triumphs, they did not display strict centralization in the sequence of parts of the procession. True, the triumphator occupied an approximately central place, in that he followed trophies of victory, to be followed in his turn by the army. But one hears of no symmetry of arrangement: written accounts, in fact, put the triumphator very nearly last, dismissing the army with a perfunctory mention. According to Appianus (*Punic Wars* ix 66), the order of the triumphal procession of Scipio Africanus was: *trumpeters* | *wagons with spoils* | *representations of victories and captured cities* | *captured gold* | *crowns presented to the imperator* | *sacrificial oxen* | *elephants* | *captives* | *lictors, harpists and pipers* | *incense bearers* | *the triumphator on a chariot, with his relatives* | *his army*. The triumph of Aemilius Paullus Macedonicus, fully described by Plutarch, lasted three days. On the first, captured statues were exhibited, on the second captured arms and armour. The procession on the third day followed the order: *trumpeters* | *sacrificial oxen and vessels of libation* | *vessels of captured coin* | *consecrated bowls* | *the chariot of the principal captive Perseus* | *Perseus' children with their servants* | *Perseus himself* | *wreaths* | *the triumphator* | *his army*.[2] Though similar in sequence, these processions are obviously far from identical. And we find the same with others. The most we can say is that certain items tended to form a fixed sequence: namely, *trumpeters* | *sacrificial oxen* | *captives* | *the*

[1] v 23: 'Maxime conspectus ipse est, curru equis albis iuncto urbem inuectus, parumque id non ciuile modo sed humanum etiam uisum. Iouis Solisque equis aequiperatum dictatorem in religionem etiam trahebant, triumphusque ob eam unam maxime rem clarior quam gratior fuit.'

[2] *Life of Aemilius Paullus* x 32–4. The incomplete account of Aemilius' triumph in Livy xlv 40 is in agreement: he tells us that the triumphator came last, followed only by his sons, by certain distinguished men and by his army.

28

triumphator | his army. Often a highly organized array preceded the triumphator: often a relatively disordered multitude came after him.

The fashion for antique triumphs declined in Italy during the *cinquecento*.[1] But farther north it continued well into the seventeenth century and reached a new height of popularity in England at the Restoration. There, however, pageantry had from the outset taken a distinct form. Whereas the Italian *trionfo* was essentially a procession —ordered movement—French and English royal entries laid more emphasis on static displays.[2] The northern triumphator reviewed series of elaborately prepared tableau pageants, or negotiated triumphal arch after triumphal arch. In these displays, the symbolic central accent of which northern art was fond received full employment. They commonly had a triadic *a B a* arrangement, as in a pageant for the royal entry of Louis XII at Paris in 1498, showing a king enthroned with Good Counsel on his right and Justice on his left.[3] Or the symmetry might be more elaborate. When Henry VI returned from his coronation in Paris he was met at London Bridge by three empresses, Nature, Grace and Fortune, with 7 maidens on the right hand offering each a Gift of the Holy Spirit and 7 on the left presenting secular virtues desirable in a prince.[4] And at the reception of the Emperor Charles V in London (1522) a pageant at the Gracious Street Conduit showed a complex tripartite array with Charlemagne in the centre offering imperial crowns to Charles and Henry, on the left Charlemagne, again, receiving the crown of thorns and on the right Charlemagne setting the Pope in his see. Farther on, at the Cornhill Conduit, another pageant represented King Arthur (wearing a crown imperial) flanked by 7 princes on either hand.[5]

Central focus in pageants, entries and theatrical design generally has been brilliantly treated by George Kernodle. His classic work *From Art to Theatre* traces accent in art and stage design from the

[1] Josèphe Chartrou, *Les Entrées Solennelles et Triomphales à la Renaissance 1484–1551* (Paris 1928) 60.

[2] A contrast developed in George R. Kernodle, *From Art to Theatre: Form and Convention in the Renaissance* (Chicago 1944) 44 f., 59 *et passim*.

[3] Robert Withington, *English Pageantry* i (Cambridge, Mass. and London 1918) 164: cf. 145 f. Similar arrays are common in literature. One obvious example, Mercilla's enthronement between the prince of Grace Arthur and the knight of Justice Artegall at the trial of Duessa (*The Faerie Queen* v ix 37) perhaps reflects the actual physical arrangement at the trial of Mary Queen of Scots; see Fowler 197 n., citing Camden's *Annales*.

[4] Withington i 44.   [5] *Ibid.* i 176f.

centre pavilion, central 'Royal Door' and centralized arcade screens of the Greek theatre, through Byzantine and gothic paintings with central thrones backed by arcades, to Italian renaissance paintings and stage designs (such as the Teatro Olimpico of Vicenza) using the same principles of organization.[1] In particular, the centralized arcade of honour of the sixteenth-century street theatre, often used as backing for a throne, exhibited elaborate symmetries (Pl. 6).[2] It sometimes had a structure of several storeys, with a throne set on high like the niche of honour above the central doorway in ancient stages, or the divine throne in medieval Last Judgements.[3] Kernodle's purpose is to explore the origins and symbolism of the Elizabethan stage, but the evidence he has amassed could be regarded more simply as establishing the iconological significance of the central accent.

A huge output of contemporary publications, both general treatises and occasional descriptions of individual events, catered for the enthusiasm for triumphs and the keen interest in precise details of their form. These works illustrate all the points made above. The most important early work is Roberto Valturio's *De re militari* (Verona 1472), which devotes several chapters to the proper conduct of triumphal ceremonies. According to Valturio, the processional sequence should be: *standard bearers | spoils | tributary crowns | trumpets | captives, with the most prominent last | the triumphator in a chariot drawn by four white horses | freed captives | the army, by legion, cohort and maniple.*[4] (He omits sacrificial oxen, perhaps in the interest of secularization, perhaps because of a limit even to renaissance Italian imitation of paganism.) The *De re militari* was to carry authority for nearly two centuries. Sir William Segar, writing in 1602, alters little in Valturio's account of the order of ancient triumphs; though he adds an interesting description of 'The triumphal going of Darius to meet Alexander', which makes very evident the cosmic kingship of the triumphator riding a chariot consecrated to Jupiter and drawn by 4 white horses called 'horses of the sun'.[5]

In Italy, many descriptions of individual triumphal processions

[1] *From Art to Theatre* 18f., 22, 32f., 36, 38f., and Figs. 3–5, 50.
[2] *Ibid.* 85f., 88f., Figs. 28–31.
[3] *Ibid.* 29, 86, Figs. 11b, 17, 19. Among countless central thrones, several are to be found in the tapestries at Hampton Court Palace alone (e.g. *The Deadly Sins*, No. 1035 and *Music*, No. 1036).   [4] *De re militari* xii 6 (Paris 1532) 356f.
[5] *Honour, Military and Civil* (1602) iii 24.

were produced by Vasari and others,[1] while in England a similar abundance of publications appeared, concentrating on the details of static pageants and triumphal arches, for example Dekker's *The Magnificent Entertainment* (1603) and Stephen Harrison's closely related *Arches of Triumph* (1604), James Shirley's *Triumph of Peace* (1633) and John Tatham's *Aqua triumphalis* (1662).[2] Evidence exists of an interest in the geometrical proportions of the arches (Pl. 9).[3] At last John Ogilby, to whom we owe the most historically informed of the English accounts of the triumph, showed awareness of a distinctive subgenre of the triumph. His *The Entertainment of. . .Charles II, in his Passage through the City of London to his Coronation* (1662) begins, not with a history of processions—except for a brief note on processional order, drawn from Plutarch and Appian—but of 'the custom of erecting triumphal arches among the Romans'. Most of the work is devoted to description of the elaborately symmetrical temporary arches erected for the royal entry. Though he usually explains their decorative details by reference to classical precedent, he shows pride in the magnificence of the English achievement: the ancient Romans' arches of marble 'we, by reason of the shortness of time, could not equal in materials, yet do ours far exceed theirs in number, and stupendious proportions'.[4]

The influence of triumphal processions and royal entries on the arts is incalculable. Themselves inspired by the seminal masterpieces *Purgatorio* xxix, Petrarch's *Trionfi*, the *Hypnerotomachia* and Mantegna's *Triumph of Caesar*, which recreated the vision of the triumph for the renaissance,[5] the triumphal entries in turn had repercussions both on the visual arts and on literature.

[1] See e.g. Vasari's *Vita di Pontormo, Vita di Piero di Cosimo* etc., *cit.* Burckhardt n. 849; also Franciscus Modius, *Pandectae triumphales*, 2 vols (Frankfort 1586). Many other references are given by such modern authorities as Chartrou; Werner Weisbach, *Trionfi* (Berlin 1919); Émile Mâle, 'L'art symbolique à la fin du moyen âge: Les Triomphes', *Revue de l'art ancien et moderne* xx (1906); and Christiane Lorgues-Lapouge, 'Triomphes renaissants', *L'œil* xxxv (1957). Kernodle (226–38) catalogues several hundred royal entries by countries, listing contemporary and later literature on each.

[2] See also Bulstrode Whitelocke, *Memorials* (1732); J. Nichols, *The Progresses and Public Processions of Queen Elizabeth*, 3 vols (1823) and *The Progresses Processions, and Magnificent Festivities of King James the First*, 4 vols (1828); and Withington, *op. cit.*   [3] Palme, '*Ut architectura poesis*'.

[4] *The Entertainment* 1 f.

[5] Chartrou 62; see also A. Venturi, 'Les triomphes de Pétrarque dans l'art représentatif', *Revue de l'art ancien et moderne* xx (1906).

In architecture, for example, even in the south, the antique model of the tripartite triumphal arch played a vital role in the development of the neoclassical styles, from Alberti's S. Francesco at Rimini to Palladio's Loggia del Capitanio at Vicenza.[1] Sometimes its use can even be related directly to particular triumphal occasions.[2] The *a B a* triumphal arch motif informs pyramidal renaissance, mannerist and victoriously upswirling baroque façades alike. More generally, we may regard the majority of neoclassical façades as influenced by the iconology of the triumphal entry. For the Vitruvian theory of proportion was limited to a non-significant symmetry of bisection,[3] whereas renaissance and later façades usually went beyond equal division to a positive emphasis of the centre. Filarete, San Gallo and above all Palladio designed elaborately symmetrical plans.[4] But linear centralization of the façade was more widespread and more consciously symbolic. Palladio takes it for granted that 'the ensigns or arms of the owners...are commonly put in the middle of the front'.[5] Such centralization—to whose influence on poetic form I shall return—often attains considerable complexity. Thus, in Antonio da San Gallo's design for the façade of the Palazzo Farnese at Rome (1530) [Pl. 10], the scheme of the *piano nobile* may be expressed: *a b a b a b C b a b a b a*.

In the masque, symmetrical arrangements with a central accent were exceedingly common, as a glance at the designs of Parigi (*Il Giudizio di Paride*, 1608, *La Flora*, 1628 and *Le Nozze degli Dei*, 1637) or Inigo Jones (*The Triumph of Peace*, 1634) will show. Ben Jonson, who often indicates the grouping with some care, specifies the central

[1] Rudolf Wittkower, *Architectural Principles* 37 ff., 54, 87 f., 92 f. There was also an obvious continuity with the design of west fronts of medieval cathedrals, which often had a low–high–low arrangement, with Christ the Judge enthroned above the central door of three. Everywhere in the art of the Middle Ages one finds Christ the apocalyptic judge placed at the centre of heaven and earth.

[2] *Ibid.* 87 f. The design of architectural triumphs often embodied literary allusions. Ogilby's *Entertainment*, for example, is full of literary parallels and illustrations, as at 59–65, where he quotes a long passage from Drayton's *Polyolbion* xv as comment on a marriage of Thames and Isis portrayed over one of the triumphal arches for Charles II's entry.

[3] *De architectura* I ii 4.

[4] Wittkower 70. Cf. also Michelangelo's *a b c d c b a* façade scheme for the Palazzo Senatorio.

[5] The whole passage justifying the use of the pediment for private buildings, *cit.* Wittkower 74, is relevant.

position of sovereignty verbally in at least one masque, *Love's Triumph through Callipolis* (1630):

The triumph is first seen afar off, and led in by Amphitrite, the wife of Oceanus, with 4 sea-gods attending her: Nereus, Proteus, Glaucus, Palaemon. It consisteth of 15 lovers, and as many Cupids, who rank themselves 7 and 7 on a side, with each a Cupid before him, with a lighted torch, and the middle person (which is his Majesty,) placed in the centre.

1. The provident.		2. The judicious.
3. The secret.		4. The valiant.
5. The witty.		6. The jovial.
7. The secure.	15. The heroical.	8. The substantial.
9. The modest.		10. The candid.
11. The courteous.		12. The elegant.
13. The rational.		14. The magnificent.

It is perhaps an impossible task to separate these reciprocal influences and counter-influences; certainly impossible in so brief a survey as this. Still, comparisons with pageantry and with the visual arts seem worth making: already they have given us a clue to the puzzling absence of discussions of central symmetry from Italian literary criticism. No doubt Aristotle's not having written on the triumphal genres (as Salviati noted) partly explains this.[1] But it may also in part be due to the relative unimportance of the centre in Italian triumphs.[2] Significantly it was left to a northern critic, Puttenham, to discuss centralized patterns in poetry.[3]

[1] Weinberg, *A History of Literary Criticism* i 611.
[2] Kernodle 44 f.
[3] See p. 11 f. above.

3. Fictional triumphs

The earliest fictional triumph of the renaissance is perhaps the triumph of the sacrament in *Purgatorio* xxix. This tremendously dramatic and yet liturgical masque almost certainly resembled actual Corpus Christi processions:[1] it begins with 7 candles, like the processional torches used at the Bishop's Mass in allusion to the candlesticks of *Revelation* i. The 7 lights paint the air with splendid *liste*, bands of colour 'like the rainbow', which remain behind, farther than the eye can see. Next come 24 elders representing the books of the Old Testament in St Jerome's arrangement, followed by the triumphal chariot in the midst of the 4 living creatures of *Ezekiel* (here identified with the beasts of the Apocalypse and the emblems of the Evangelists). The 3 Theological Virtues dance on the right of the chariot: the 4 Cardinal Virtues on the left. Finally the procession closes with 7 men representing the rest of the New Testament books.

The masque as a whole is not numerically symmetrical, though there is some correspondence between the 7s that begin and end it. But analysis of the content shows a centralized array of groups:

	THEOLOGICAL VIRTUES	
OLD TESTAMENT BOOKS	TRIUMPHAL CAR AND GOSPELS	OTHER NEW TESTAMENT BOOKS
	CARDINAL VIRTUES	

[1] The feast of Corpus Christi was promulgated in 1264. For a description of a later procession, see Burckhardt 213.

A central accent falls on the triumphal car drawn by a griffin whose composite form—part eagle, part lion—symbolizes Christ's two natures. And where the griffin's wings rise out of sight, passing through the 7 *liste*, exact centrality is emphasized:

And he stretched up the one and other wing
Between the mid band and the three and three,
Not cleaving them nor marring anything.

(*Purgatorio* xxix 109–11)

The 7 bands of light have been variously interpreted. Benvenuto Rambaldi da Imola and Cristoforo Landino took them to symbolize the 7 sacraments, the fourth in the centre being the Eucharist. But why should the sacraments precede the books of Scripture? Lombardi understood the *liste* as virtues and explained the griffin's alignment with the centre one as an allusion to *Psalm* xcii, *indutus est Dominus fortitudinem*. But why, then, the separate representation of the virtues as dancing beside the chariot? More recently Grandgent, followed by Dorothy Sayers, has offered a more plausible interpretation: the Gifts of the Holy Ghost (Wisdom, Understanding, Counsel, Might, Knowledge, Piety and Fear of the Lord). This interpretation can accommodate the allusion Lombardi saw, since the fourth Gift of the Spirit happens to be *fortitudo*.[1]

Obviously the figures of the pageant are drawn from *Revelation*. There we find the 4 living creatures and 24 elders—not, it is true, in procession, but round a stationary throne. The candles and *liste* have their types in the same passage: 'there was a rainbow round about the throne' (*Rev.* iv 3) and 'seven lamps of fire burning before the throne, which are the seven Spirits of God' (*Rev.* iv 5). But these verses do not explain Dante's elaborate account of the griffin's spatial relation to the rainbow. His stress on the centrality of the Christ-griffin depends on a separate tradition, though one that stemmed originally from a common Scriptural source. The idea of a divine throne 'set in heaven' (*Isa.* lxvi 1, *Rev.* iv 3) combined with that of Christ's coming in judgement at a central place 'in the midst of the nations' (*Ezek.* v 5) to produce a vision of a sovereign judgement-seat at the astronomical zenith. This tradition interacted with that of the *Sol*

[1] On the Gifts of the Holy Ghost, see R. Garrigou-Lagrange, O.P., in *Enciclopedia Cattolica* iv (1950) cols 1861–5; Rosemond Tuve, *Allegorical Imagery* Index s.v. *Gifts of the Holy Spirit*.

3 2

iustitiae (*Mal.* iv 1 f.): Panofsky notes an astronomical version of the type of Christ as judicial sun god in Pierre Bersuire's popular theological encyclopaedia, the *Repertorium morale* (1489):

Further I say of this sun that he shall be inflamed when exercising supreme power, that is to say, when he sits in judgement, when he shall be strict and severe... because he shall be all hot and bloody by dint of justice and strictness. For, as the sun, when in the centre of his orbit, that is to say, at the midday point, is hottest, so shall Christ be when he shall appear in the centre of heaven and earth, that is to say, in judgement.[1]

Another Scriptural source for the griffin's coincidence with the fourth *lista* may be *Revelation* xvi, where 7 angels 'pour out the vials of the wrath of God upon the earth'. For these 7 vials contain the plagues that obsessed medieval apocalyptic artists—the sores, the blood, the frogs from the dragon's mouth, the hail at Armageddon. And the fourth, central plague is heat: 'the fourth angel poured out his vial upon the sun; and power was given unto him to scorch men with fire' (*Rev.* xvi 8).

The solar sovereignty of Dante's griffin accords implicitly with his central position, his association with the fourth plague and the fourth angel lamp. And it is stated overtly in the description of the chariot. Such a chariot was never conferred on Scipio Africanus or Caesar Augustus:

Nay, but the sun's own car were poor, compared:
  The chariot of the sun, that when it drave
Awry was burned at Earth's most instant prayer,
When Jove in secret court just judgement gave.[2]

The elaborated image of the solar chariot, associated as it is with those of a Roman imperator and emperor, unambiguously alludes to the imperial sun cult. That cult, originally a pagan cult of cosmic kingship, had since the time of Constantine been assimilated to a Christian solar theology of the *Sol oriens* (*Luke* i 78, *Zach.* iii 8) and *Sol iustitiae*.[3]

[1] *P. Berchorii dictionarium seu repertorium morale* (Nuremberg 1489) s.v. *Sol*: 'Sicut Christus quando in medio coeli et terrae, sc. in iudicio apparebit'; *cit.* Panofsky, *Meaning in the Visual Arts* (Garden City, N.Y. 1955) 262.

[2] *Purg.* xxix 117–20: 'Ma quel del Sol saria pover con ello: / quel del sol, che sviando fu combusto, / per l'orazion della Terra devota, / quando fu Giove arcanamente giusto.'

[3] The adjustment between the Christian *Sol iustitiae* and the imperial *Sol invictus comes Augusti*, discussed in A. Alföldi, *The Conversion of Constantine and Pagan Rome* (Oxford 1948) is related to Dante's political thought in Ernst H. Kantorowicz, 'Dante's "Two Suns"', *Selected Studies* (New York 1965) 325–

Guelf as he was, Dante (1265–1321) had himself contributed to this ancient veneration of the emperor's sun-likeness: in an earlier canto of the *Purgatorio* he had developed the idea of pope and emperor as twin suns.[1] Against this background, the meaning of the climactic sequence of vehicles in *Purgatorio* xxix is plain. The griffin chariot's superiority to the triumphal and solar chariot implies the relations emperor-sun : sun : : sun : Christ-sun.[2]

This interpretation is confirmed by the position of the mundane sun amidst the planets in the Ptolemaic order of proximity to earth. For commentators commonly identified the 7 candles of *Revelation*— from which the *liste* shine forth and in the 'midst' of which Christ appears (*Rev.* i 13)—with the 7 planets.[3] Thus the centre light in line with the griffin and chariot of the divine sun is from one point of view the planetary sun. The candles derive ultimately from a Jewish ceremonial tradition that had its classic expression in Josephus' description of the Tabernacle: 'By making the candelabrum to consist of 70 portions, [Moses] hinted at the ten-degree provinces of the planets, and by the 7 lamps thereon the course of the planets themselves, for such is their number.'[4] Dante's symbolism has come far from cosmic description. His whole procession is apocalyptic in character, as the sequel makes clear, when a divine judgement destroys Antichrist in the ecclesiastical chariot (Canto xxxii). Nevertheless, *Purgatorio* xxix shows the iconology of sun-rulership determining the arrangement of an early renaissance triumph.

PETRARCH'S 'TRIONFI'

In Petrarch's own time, his Latin poem *Africa* and his *Trionfi* enjoyed equal favour with the *Rime*. The first of these works culminates in the

---

38. When the sun rises at *Purg.* xxxii 17f. it is the light of the divine *Sol oriens* that mingles with that of the lamps. For a history of the *Sol oriens* image from classical times to the seventeenth century see Kantorowicz, 'Oriens Augusti— Lever du Roi' 119–77.

[1] *Purg.* xvi 106–8, the subject of Kantorowicz's 'Dante's "Two Suns"'.

[2] Canto xxxii develops a historical allegory of the relation between various emperors and the Church. The metaphor of the Church as a vehicle carrying souls to heaven seems to have been based on allegorical exegesis of *Song of Solomon* iii 9f.; see e.g. G. Foliot, *Expositio in Canticum Canticorum* (1643) 174f.

[3] On the basis of *Rev.* i 20: 'The mystery of the seven stars which thou sawest in my right hand, and the seven golden candlesticks. The seven stars are the angels of the seven churches: and the seven candlesticks which thou sawest are the seven churches.' [4] *Jewish Antiquities* iii 182f.; cf. Philo, *De vita Mos.* ii 9 (102).

military triumph of its hero Scipio Africanus.[1] As for the *Trionfi*, as
the title suggests it is given over entirely to a series of triumphs, in
which exemplary historical figures mingle with allegorical abstractions. A triumph of Chastity, in the person of Laura, follows a triumph
of Love and turns Love's victory into defeat. But Chastity gives way
in turn to Death: her subsequent vindication by Fame's triumph is
effaced by Time's: and she only finds redemption in the triumph of
Eternity. In short, the series of 6 triumphs—those of Love, Chastity,
Death, Fame, Time and Eternity—constitutes a search for some ultimate value impossible to undercut. It is the deep seriousness of this
search, quite as much as the splendid pomp with which it is conducted, that accounts for the early success of the *Trionfi*. We exagger-
ate the secularity of renaissance aspiration for fame, forgetting that it
might take for granted a religious frame of reference. In England the
Trionfi was used by Stephen Hawes for the solemn conclusion of his
Pastime of Pleasure (1509) and by Spenser, less obviously, for the
series of peripeteias underlying the *Mutability Cantos*.

The overall structure of the *Trionfi* is uncertain. Petrarch (1304–
1374) left it incompletely revised: we cannot even be sure that all
the surviving *capitoli* would have found places in the finished poem.[2]
I shall confine myself, therefore, to the *Trionfo della Pudicizia*, in
which the procession not only is symmetrical but even finesses the
sovereign centre.

Well-ordered virtues to the number of 16 accompany Laura against
Love, who cannot withstand the sight of them. Wresting the palms of
victory from him they free his captives. Now attention turns to the
chaste victrix herself and her 'lesser friends': *a la mia donna | vengo ed
all'altre sue minor compagne* (166f.). Laura wears a Minerva shield, in
which the poet sees reflected Love, chained to a column of ardour-
cooling jasper and beaten. The famous chaste of history follow in a
list that turns into a triumphal procession from Cyprus to Baia, Lin-

---

[1] *Africa* ix 324–86; ed. Nicola Festa (Florence 1926) 273–5. The procession is too
vast and too loosely described to have any clear order of details, but its rough
(and incorrect) sequence runs *Triumphator/Captives/Trophies and spoils/Horses
and elephants*.

[2] For various speculations as to the final structure intended for the *Trionfi*, see
Renato Serra, *Dei 'Trionfi' di Francesco Petrarca* (Bologna 1929) ii 17, who
proposes a finished scheme of *capitoli* 4 / 1 / 1 / 4 / 1 / 1. A brief survey of
more recent and less decided views is given in *I Trionfi* ed. Paolo Lecaldano
(Milan 1956) 5.

terno and finally the Temple of Chastity at Rome, where Love is left under close guard. These friends of Laura's are too numerous to put into verse (*chiudere in rime*) but Petrarch will enumerate some in the forefront (*in su la cima*). In fact he names 14. If we add the triumphator herself with her captive Love the procession numbers 16 and exactly matches the sixteen-strong army of virtues: the whole array is symmetrical, with the triumphator at, or next to, the centre. What seems stranger still, the sequence *army/triumphator/captive/ procession* reverses the order of historical Roman triumphs.

In matters of detail, the distance from ancient triumphs is still more remote. For the allegorical army has an appropriately rationalized arrangement. Thus the 16 virtues are linked hand in hand (*teneansi per mano a due a due*) and ordered with moral decorum. A column of 4 mutually dependent pairs—Honour and Modesty in the van, Prudence and Moderation, Habitual Welldoing and Gladness of Heart, Perseverance and Glory bringing up the rear—comes in the centre. The other 4 pairs[1] are drawn up *fuori* or *intorno*, round the sides. This emphasis on pairing and four-square arrangement alludes clearly enough to symbolic properties of 16. As with all square numbers, its geometrical rectitude symbolized virtue; moreover, it was susceptible to repeated equal (and therefore just) divisions.[2]

This suggests a reason for the symmetrical division of Chastity's triumph: namely, to manifest even division and hence virtue. Significantly the participants total 32, a number whose Pythagorean epithet Justice arose from the fact that it is repeatedly divisible by 2 without remainder.[3] The aptness of division as a triumphal motif is obvious if one recalls the former economic importance of spoils and their consequent prominence in triumphal processions: 'just division crowned the soldier's toils.'[4]

The second half of the *Trionfo*, containing the procession, belongs to a subgenre now usually passed over as mere catalogue. But in fact it is an ordered array and conveys meaning by its spatial arrangement:

---

[1] Bella accoglienza, Accorgimento; Cortesia, Puritate; Timor d'infamia, Desio d'onore; Beltate, Castità.
[2] See Fowler 39, 278.
[3] Bongo 486: 'Ceterum Pythagorici hunc numerum Iustitiam appellarunt, quia semper ad unitatem divisibilis est in partes aequales; in aequalitate autem, omnis servatur Iustitiae ratio atque integritas.'
[4] Pope's Homer, *Il.* i 481.

LOVE CONQUERED IN CYPRUS

1 Laura
2 Love
3 Penelope
4 Lucretia
5 Virginia
6 Virginio

German women

7 Judith
8 Hippo

TRIUMPH OF LAURA

9 Tuccia
10 Hersilia

Sabine women

11 Dido
12 Piccarda Donati
13 Scipio Africanus
14 Spurina
15 Joseph
16 Hippolytus

LOVE IMPRISONED IN ROME

A division into 'these' (*queste*, Penelope to Hippo) and 'certain others' (*certe altre*, Tuccia to Piccarda Donati) gives verbal notice of the symmetry of the array about lines 145–8. Between the 2 groups, at the centre of the procession, the poet again sees Laura's triumph:

> With these and other souls illustrious
> I saw my lady triumph over him
> I had seen triumph over all the world.
> Among the others was the vestal maid.

Immediately before and after this central mention of Laura's triumph come 2 individual examples; then in each case a large unnumbered group (the wives of the Germani, who committed suicide upon Marius' refusal to dedicate them to the Vestals:[1] Hersilia's Sabine women); then 6 more individuals.[2] In brief, the array has the form *6/group/2/2/group/6*.

---

[1] Valerius Maximus VI i 13 iii.

[2] The English translation of the *Trionfi* by Henry Parker Lord Morley (1554, ed. Stafford Henry Earl of Iddesleigh, 1887) is of interest, in that it alters Petrarch's scheme, while preserving the central symmetry: *14 virtues / Laura and Love / 14 exemplary figures*. Parker apparently failed to grasp the spatial arrangement of the virtues, for he presents them as a column of 8 pairs, thus ruining the square array. He mistranslates the virtues as (1) Honesty and (2) Shamefast-

Within this array, however, the procession proper strictly speaking excludes the guard at the Temple of Chastity, Spurina, Joseph and Hippolytus. It would conclude with Piccarda Conati *al fin* (160), were it not that when it passes Linterno, Scipio Africanus (as censor of Masinissa's love of Sophonisba) readily joins 'a triumph not his own'. Thus even the hero whose historical triumph crowns *Africa* contributes to the glory of the vernacular poems' heroine. But where does he come in the procession? Inevitably last, in the triumphator's place, where an ancient Roman would expect one born 'only for triumphs and imperial might' (177).

We conclude that two triumphal forms were available to Petrarch. One, seen in the subsidiary pattern of the moving procession, derives historically from the Roman triumph. In this form the last place, here occupied by Scipio, is principal. The other form, seen in the pattern of the whole array (and repeated in its second half), is static, symmetrical and elaborately centralized. Its central place of sovereignty makes Laura a divine representative and solar surrogate. In the following canto, this is explicit: when her company returned from the triumph,

Bright stars they seemed, and in their midst a sun
Adorned them all, and made them brighter still.[1]

In devising the symmetry of the *Trionfo della Pudicizia* (which extends to imagistic and verbal echoes[2]) Petrarch would be aware of the ceremonial tradition traced in the previous chapter, as well as of Dante's example. But he had also a more specific literary model—or anti-model, since from one point of view his own poem refutes it. This is the triumph of Cupid in *Amores* I ii. Before Ovid's Cupid go 3 captives: the poet himself 'a recent spoil', *Mens bona* and *Pudor*. After him follow his army represented by *Blanditiae*, *Error* and *Furor*. It must have seemed an obviously symmetrical array to anyone familiar with monarchic protocol. And, in the event, Ovid's poem was to join with Petrarch's in exerting a powerful influence on the literary triumph.

ness; (3) Wit and (4) Soberness; (5) Perserverance and (6) Fair entreating; (7) Clemess and (8) Courtesy; (9) Purity of heart and (10) Fear of shame; (11) Old wise thoughts and (12) Gracious concord; (13) Beauty and (14) Chaste clean thought.

[1] *Trionfo della Morte* i 25 f.: 'Stelle chiare pareano, in mezzo un sole / che tutte ornava e non togliea lor vista.'

[2] E.g. the allusion to Hannibal's overthrow by Scipio (98 f.), answered by Scipio's triumph; or the mention of Dido (10), answered by the appearance of Dido in the procession.

Petrarch's *Trionfi* stimulated a copious production of more or less illustrative visual representations: easel paintings, *cassoni*, ivories, book illustrations and separate engravings.[1] These made common property many motifs of the triumph, including the roughly central chariot of the principal figure. But the greatest triumphal composition of the renaissance, *The Triumph of Caesar*[2] by Andrea Mantegna (1431–1506), who himself painted a *Triumphs of Petrarch*,[3] belongs to a more directly classical tradition.

It consists of 9 large paintings designed to be fastened on a long wall between pilasters, to give the illusion of a procession continuing behind interruptions. The subjects are: (1) Trumpeters and standard-bearers, (2) Car-bearing statues, (3) Litter-bearers with armour and vessels of coins, (4) Vase-bearers, trumpeters and votive bulls, (5) Elephants bearing candlesticks, (6) Corselet-bearers, (7) Captives, (8) Musicians and (9) Triumphator on chariot. Begun about 1484, the paintings (or some of them) were by 1486 at the Castello di corte at Mantua. It seems probable that Mantegna planned more than 9 paintings and that when he went to Rome on a Papal commission he left *The Triumph of Caesar* incomplete. So, at least, says Equicola; adding that Lorenzo Costa was commissioned to implement the scheme. On 7 April 1494 Teofilo Collenuccio informs the Marquis that the parts of the hall left empty by 2 missing triumphs have been filled up with crimson satin. And an engraving survives, probably after a drawing by Mantegna, showing the van of an army in procession.[4] Considerations of scale must have precluded more than a token force, however: probably only 1 or 2 paintings. In any case, the procession up to the triumphator has its own logic.

The first impression Mantegna's *Triumph* gives is of solemnity and magnificence. Kristeller (i 296) draws attention to the enthusiasm

---

[1] See Weisbach, *Trionfi*; Victor Masséna, Prince of Essling, and E. Munz, *Pétrarque. Ses études d'art, son influence sur les artistes*...(Paris 1902); and A. Venturi, 'Les Triomphes de Pétrarque dans l'art représentatif' 81.

[2] Now at Hampton Court. There is evidence of Mantegna's own special regard for the work: see Paul Kristeller, *Andrea Mantegna* i 272f.

[3] Now lost. Mantegna's so-called *Triumph of Scipio* is not a triumph in the formal sense.

[4] Kristeller i 290–2. The documents are reprinted, somewhat uncritically, in Alessandro Luzio and Roberto Paribeni, *Il Trionfo di Andrea Mantegna* (Rome 1940) 9, 12–6.

displayed by certain figures, such as the youth looking up at Caesar admiringly. He sees this as pointing beyond renaissance style to the idealistic manner that followed. But perhaps the religious intensity of *The Triumph of Caesar* would be unusual in any period. Certainly the procession represents far more than a military triumph. Only occasionally does Mantegna follow Valturio, as in the late placing of trumpeters and the prominence of standard-bearers—and even here a religious sense imbues the details of the standards, so that they suggest attributes of deities (Pl. 7 (*a*)). Yet his restoration of the votive bulls Valturio omitted is by no means mere servility to an ancient source (Appianus, who provided the musicians of the eighth painting): as Kristeller (i 289) rightly stresses, Mantegna is never merely 'correct' but recovers the spirit of the antique in freedom. The votive bulls (Parts 4, 5) have a sacrificial inference that confirms our general impression. Similarly with the winged Victory crowning the triumphator and ending the procession. This figure had a classical precedent in the first tablet of the Arch of Titus; but Mantegna's spiritualized Victory far more resembles an angel than the perfunctory emblem on the Arch. In the series as we have it, no mortal follows Caesar, only the rewarding angel.

The gravity of *The Triumph of Caesar* is expressed to an extraordinary degree through symbolic objects—standards, bulls, enormous urns and vases.[1] Most striking of all are the gigantic candlesticks carried by elephants in the fifth painting (Pl. 7(*b*)), which has been regarded as Mantegna's finest work (Kristeller, i 296). These form a high point in the procession, the flames from the candles leaping in silhouette against the sky with a sombre and mysterious affect. Mantegna had authority for the candles in Suetonius, who mentions 40 elephants bearing lamps in a triumph of Caesar's (*Iulius* xxxvii). But the candlesticks are so obviously anachronistic that their ecclesiastical character must be intended deliberately. The allusion is again to the Arch of Titus, this time to the second tablet, where the spoils of the Temple include a candelabrum:[2] the same candelabrum

---

[1] On the hieroglyphic content of the *Triumph*, see K. Giehlow, in *Jahrbuch der kunsthistorischen Sammlungen in Wien* (1915).

[2] William Knight, *The Arch of Titus and the Spoils of the Temple* (1867) 84 ff. relates this tablet to Josephus' account of the triumph of Titus and Vespasian in *Bell. Iud.* VII v 4 f. The inclusion of lamps in triumphs was without other classical precedent; see Kristeller i 289.

that Josephus interprets as signifying the seven planets. True, Mantegna's candles number 9, not 7. But their arrangement may still suggest a cosmic meaning. The highest light of the 9 is the central fifth, to which a youth draws attention by the gesture of his outstretched arm. Did Mantegna intend here a revised equivalent of Josephus' seven-branched candelabrum? If so, the 9 lights would symbolize the 9 heavenly spheres and the fifth's exaltation the sovereignty of the fifth digit, associated with Jupiter. Seen in this way, the central painting of the series of 9 portrays the sovereign glory of the king of heaven, glory that earthly triumph reflects without rivalling. In the completed scheme, the lights would have been central only to the part of the procession up to the triumphator—the ordered part. As it is, the centrality has acquired a contingent emphasis that Mantegna was perhaps not discontented to leave, when he interrupted his work after the ninth term of the series.

COLONNA'S 'HYPNEROTOMACHIA'

Francesco Colonna (1432/3–?1527) adapted the triumphal procession to the purposes of a complex, esoteric and often obscure allegory expressed in terms of alchemical symbolism. In the processions and tableaux he describes in his *Hypnerotomachia Poliphili* (Venice 1499) the fictive mode is further interiorized. Even the narrative implication of a victory almost disappears: the triumph becomes simply a way of manifesting a cosmic power, simply a 'show'.

At *Hypnerotomachia* I xiv Colonna's dreamer views a series of triumphs. The first 4 represent each a love of Jupiter's, the chariots being carved with reliefs illustrating divine amours—the rape of Europa, Leda and the swan, Danae and the shower of gold, Semele and the cloud. The triumphs also show different aspects of Cupid, from a selfish destructive Cupid who wounds Gods and men in the first, to a Cupid himself hurt by Psyche's lamp in the fourth. Then a fifth procession, with Vertumnus and Pomona on mobile thrones, circumambulates an altar dedicated to a Saturnian Priapus. In this rite—challenging to the promiscuous Polifilo—we can see beneath the alchemic symbolism of the *prima materia* a triumph of sexuality oriented to generation.[1] Next, Polifilo and the nymph he hopes is his

---

[1] Cf. Linda Fierz-David, *The Dream of Poliphilo: Related and Interpreted* tr. Mary Hottinger, Bollingen Series xxv (New York 1950) 123.

Polia enter a temple of Venus and Mercury. There the torch of the nymph's virginity is extinguished and sacrifices of love performed to the accompaniment of terrifying divine manifestations, such as a whirlwind. Finally the lovers sail in Cupid's boat, across a sea filled with the hosts of Nereus, Neptune and Oceanus, to Cythera.

On that island the sixth and most elaborate of Colonna's triumphs is celebrated (i xxii). Heading a procession come minutely described trophies of Mars, Jupiter, Hercules, together with others of obscurer symbolism.[1] The young Cupid is greeted by a queenly Psyche, Polia by Imeria (ἵμερος, desire) and Polifilo himself by Erototimoride (ἔρως and τιμωρέω, avenge or assist). Then follow 12 nymphs, arranged in 3 columns of 4. Of these, the centre column forms a progressive sequence of phases in the symbolic wounding and death of love: *Bow-giver/Arrow/Blindness/Consummation*. The outer columns, however, are composed of psychological abstractions that personify the accompanying stages of experience more explicitly. One of each external pair represents a state of mind, the other a state of feeling. Thus Ennia (Love Thoughts) is associated with Philedia (Delight), Omonia (Concord) with Diapraxe (Physical Expression), Asynecha (Incontinence) with Aschemosyne (Shamelessness).[2] Now Love ascends his mobile throne of gold: Plexaura and Ganoma (Joy) fetter the couple with roses: and Synesia (Union, or Conscience, or both) ties them behind the triumphator's chariot.[3] In front go 2 satyrs and 3 nymphs carrying mysterious symbolic objects, so that the immediate attendants on Cupid form a group symmetrical about the triumphator very like that in Ovid's triumph of love. Polifilo and Polia occupy the place traditionally reserved for captives to be freed after the triumph; yet he is apprehensive enough to need all the assurances of the smiling nymphs.

When the procession arrives at the centre of the island, Cupid descends and enters an ampitheatre with Psyche, Polia and Polifilo, who stumbles on the verge of the lustrous black obsidian floor because of his fear of falling into what seems a dreadful abyss. The stone reflects the sky: opposites merge within it. At its centre is a fountain of Venus, between whose columns a curtain hangs. To part this

---

[1] *Hypnerotomachia Poliphili*, ed. Giovanni Pozzi and Lucia A. Ciapponi, 2 vols (Padua 1964) i 320–3.
[2] *Ibid.* i 322–4.   [3] *Ibid.* i 335, 338.

hymeneal curtain of virginity concealing the goddess, Cupid first of all transmits his favourable golden arrow through Synesia to Polia. But she timidly declines the weapon; whereupon the smiling god passes it *via* Philedia to Polifilo. The latter, eager to behold Venus, is consumed by a blind flame; he tears the curtain and discloses the goddess. By so doing he enacts the experiences symbolized by the nymphs in the triumph. Thus the arrow given him by Philedia corresponds to Velode and his blind desire to penetrate the divine presence to Typhlote. And now Cupid wounds each lover to the heart.

In the sexual act following defloration, the lovers almost lose themselves to the divine roles they assume. As Linda Fierz-David has observed,[1] Polia becomes a vessel of Venus, just as Polifilo is externalized in the Mars united with Venus at the fountain. But in a later episode—which was to fascinate Spenser, Shakespeare and Marino in turn—Polifilo finds a remedy for self-loss at the tomb of Adonis, the transient body of corruption.[2] That episode falls outside our subject however, except for its treatment of death subsequent to a triumph: a formal sequence whose significance is only fully apparent when we recall the custom of killing the principal captives after the triumphal procession had arrived at the Capitol. It is only a seeming contradiction that Polifilo and Polia, captives to be freed, should behave with reverent insouciance at the tomb. For by then they know that the death of sexual initiation need not be feared, that love can revivify Adonis' body.

Colonna's triumphs partly depend for their iconography on Petrarch's, as in their use of the same animals to draw the chariots. But their inner content is far removed from the moral allegory of the *Trionfi*. The chariots of Jupiter, for example, represent the four elements and play their symbolic parts in an adumbration of the alchemic *opus magnum*.[3] This alchemic work, however, is itself a metaphor, serving the end of a larger psychological action. The dreamer watches the triumphs as one who marvels at the creative processes of nature. But each show brings a further initiation: each

[1] *The Dream of Polifilo* 175 f.
[2] Miss Fierz-David discusses the tomb of Adonis as a symbol of individuation at 182–4.
[3] Scholars disagree over the detailed correspondences between Jupiter's loves and the elements, however. With Miss Fierz-David's interpretation cf. Pozzi and Ciapponi ii 137.

discovery of a more ultimate secret of nature means self-discovery. It is this inner direction, indeed, that accounts for the prevailing impression of mystery and half-disclosed profundity. With consummate skill Colonna adapted triumphal motifs to the purposes of psychological allegory and by so doing added a new metaphorical possibility to the idea of the triumph. In the *Hypnerotomachia* a procession is for the first time a vehicle for introspective exploration of natural forces.

SPENSER'S TRIUMPH OF LOVE

The Faerie Queen (1590, 1596) represents a high point of the triumph in one art as Jonson's masques do in another. Spenser not only fills his poem with processions but calls whole books of it pageants.[1] But the best of his triumphs is perhaps the masque of Cupid, which comes in an episode that exemplifies his art at its subtlest and most magnificent. The triumphal character of the masque is so primary a feature of it that it has proved hard to interpret from any other starting-point.

The episode begins with Britomart's finding Scudamour in a wood of perplexity and error, abjectly bemoaning his marital difficulties. A tyrant Busyrane, it seems, has 'by strong enchantments and black magic lear' (III xi 16) imprisoned his wife Amoret and tortures her day and night 'because to yield him love she doth deny'. Britomart encourages Scudamour to attempt a rescue; but only the knight of chaste love can pass the fire in Busyrane's porch. Inside she finds a room hung with tapestries showing deeds of love:

And eke all Cupid's wars they did repeat,
And cruel battles, which he whilom fought
'Gainst all the gods, to make his empire great;
Besides the huge massacres, which he wrought
On mighty kings and caesars, into thraldom brought. (III xi 29)

Of the great set piece that follows, a description of love's transformations beginning with 12 metamorphoses of Jupiter, Thomas Roche has observed that the splendour of the writing tends to disguise 'the fact that it is a picture of love as bestiality'.[2] While Jupiter 'these pageants played' Cupid usurped his throne and vaunted his victory over the gods: 'Lo now the heavens obey to me alone, / And take me

[1] *Faerie Queen* II i 33; see C. S. Lewis, *Spenser's Images of Life* (Cambridge 1967) 3.
[2] Thomas P. Roche, Jr, *The Kindly Flame: A Study of the Third and Fourth Books of Spenser's 'Faerie Queen'* (Princeton, N.J. 1964) 84.

47

for their Jove, whiles Jove to earth is gone' (xi 35). Moreover, all the tapestry gods are debased, or destroy the mortals they love. Their loves are tragic—defeats for the lovers, victories for 'cruel Cupid' (xi 38)—so that, as Spenser himself puts it, it would be impossible to tell all 'the mournful tragedies, / And spoils' (xi 45). Clearly the tapestries represent a triumph of Love, or rather of erotic passion in its most destructive form.

At the end of this first room, on an altar to Cupid, stands a golden idol trampling a dragon of chastity[1] irremediably wounded by an arrow through its eyes. Below, an inscription: UNTO THE VICTOR OF THE GODS THIS BE (xi 49). The people of the house, we are told, commit idolatry before this image. But Britomart enters a second room decorated this time with gold reliefs, life-like 'wild antics [grotesques], which their follies played' (xi 51). Hanging (or represented as hanging) on the walls are spoils of heroes destroyed by love:

And all about, the glistering walls were hung
With warlike spoils, and with victorious preys,
Of mighty conquerors and captains strong,
Which were whilom captived in their days
To cruel love, and wrought their own decays:
Their swords and spears were broke, and hauberks rent;
And their proud girlands of triumphant bays
Trodden in dust with fury insolent,
To show the victor's might and merciless intent. (III xi 52)

It would be wrong to say with Roche (p. 85) that 'in contrast to the bestial transformations of the first room these conquerors conquered represent the effects of love as destruction not only of personal but also of political power'. For dereliction of duty and loss of power figure just as much in the first room, where Jupiter lost his throne and Apollo fondly ceded the sun-chariot. Conversely, the second room is not lacking in bestial transformations: the description of its relief reads like a demythologized version of the tapestries:

A thousand monstrous forms therein were made,
Such as false love doth oft upon him wear,
For love in thousand monstrous forms doth oft appear. (III xi 51)

In fact the rooms are not contrasting but complementary. They treat the same subjects differently, the second room being conceived on a

[1] For the iconographical reasons for this interpretation, see Lewis 22–4.

48

more human and personal scale (Scudamour himself, we recall, conquered 20 knights to win Amoret). The first room was populous, but this is appropriately deserted, the scene of the ritual of a private, inner tragedy.

After a long vigil in the second room, Britomart hears 'a shrilling trumpet sound aloud, / Sign of nigh battle, or got victory' (xii 1). Two hours of earth-shaking storm ensue, then at midnight an inner wicket of iron blows open and the masque of cruel passion appears. Its prologue, Ease, is distinguished from the Idleness who gives access to Love's realm in the *Roman de la Rose* by being a 'grave personage...fit for tragic stage' (xxi 3). First to come on are 6 pairs of masquers, personifications like those of medieval love allegory, all fully described. Amoret follows in her own person, 'called by strong charms out of eternal night' (xii 19), her face deathly and frightening from the consuming pain of her heart, which is drawn out from her deeply wounded breast into a silver basin and transfixed with a dart. Behind her, on a ravenous lion, 'the winged god himself' unbinds his eyes to rejoice 'in his cruel mind' at 'his proud spoil', Amoret (xii 22). Cupid is succeeded by Reproach, Shame and Repentance, and finally by a confused rout of more perfunctory personifications.

The masquers return to the inmost room, where Britomart cannot follow, the iron wicket having blown shut. But she lies in wait until the following night, spending the time in contemplation of erotic images, and when the wicket next opens she boldly enters—to find the triumph a vanished illusion. The inner reality is only Amoret, the lady of the masque, bound to a pillar like Love in the *Trionfo della Pudicizia*, and her tormentor the magician Busyrane. Despite his charms he has failed to make her love him; now he seeks revenge. There is a scuffle during which he wounds Britomart (in the same part of the body as Amoret); she strikes him down, spares him at his victim's request, makes him undo the enchantments and binds him in turn with his own chain. When Britomart and Amoret leave, the porch fire is quenched.

Older interpretations of the episode assumed that Busyrane represented adulterous lust: his abduction of Amoret was an allegory of temptation to break marriage vows: the masque traced the tragic course of an *affaire*. But all such interpretations foundered on recalcitrant details, particularly the odd romantic simultaneity of abduction and wedding. On the older assumption, this must mean that adulterous temptation began on the wedding day—a coincidence hardly probable enough for fiction. Yet Spenser emphasizes the representativeness: Amoret is conveyed away as 'oft in masques is known' (IV i 3). Current interpretation, on the other hand, takes its starting-point from Roche's refusal to identify Busyrane with adulterous passion. For him, Busyrane 'is the image of love distorted in the mind, distorted by lascivious anticipation or horrified withdrawal'. Far from merely lusting, the tyrant

> is literally trying to kill Amoret. His love is not sexual but destructive—destructive of the will to love within Amoret herself. Amoret is afraid of the physical surrender which her marriage to Scudamour must entail. The wedding mask crystallizes this fear, and she turns from a joyful acceptance to a cold rejection of the claims of the physical. (Roche 80 f.)

Busyrane is Chastity's enemy because he is a false chastity; the negative force to which chaste love opposes a positive ideal.

We may accept much of Roche's sensitive interpretation, even if we reject such flaws as the notion that Busyrane does not desire Amoret (Scudamour explicitly says he torments Amoret 'because to yield him love she doth deny'[1]) and the uncertainty about the fictive status of the tyrant. Is Busyrane Amoret's emotional state, or its objective cause? Sometimes Roche presents him as a false love, sometimes as a perverse chastity, sometimes—more abstractly and perhaps oversubtly—as a false conception of love (p. 83).

One support of the newer theory is the allusion in *Busyrane* to *Busiris*, the cruel Egyptian tryant.[2] Roche cites Ovid's ironic advice to the lover to trifle with girls as a matter of poetic justice: 'Deceive the deceivers...let them fall into the snare which they have laid' (*Ars amatoria* i 643–58). Busiris exemplifies such justice: when Thrasius told him a drought could be relieved by propitiating Jupiter-Osiris with a stranger's blood, the tyrant made Thrasius himself the first victim. 'There is no juster law than that contrivers of death should perish by their own contrivances. Therefore...let the woman feel the smart of a wound she first inflicted.' Spenser's allegory cer-

---

[1] III xi 17; cf. III vi 53, also Letter to Raleigh: 'Busirane had in hand a most fair lady called Amoretta, whom he kept in most grievous torment, because she would not yield him the pleasure of her body.'

[2] See Roche 81–3 with refs. Cf. Kathleen Williams, *ELH* XXVIII (1961) 114 and Fowler 20 n., 150 n.; both independently.

tainly makes Amoret feel the smart of a love-wound. Moreover, the name *Busiris* was separately known as the location of a famous temple of Isis, a fact that Roche rightly connects with Britomart's Isis role in Book v. Perhaps we are even to see the House of Busyrane as a false Temple of Isis and Osiris, an antitype to the true Isis Church of v vii. In both Britomart spends the night, in both she sees visions of sexual experience, in both she feels the tempest of wind that symbolized, for Plutarch and Colonna, the divine presence.[1]

Another approach to Busyrane is through his masque of Cupid, the same masque that he put on for Amoret's wedding (IV i 3). The power of the masque, according to Roche, 'lies in the essential ambiguity of its figures, an ambiguity that allows three interpretations, that of the wedding guests, that of Amoret, and finally that of Britomart' (p. 73). Despite its sinister horror to our eyes, the wedding guests would have viewed it neutrally as a conventional allegory of courtship, such as 'might have been taken from any sonnet sequence'.[2] But one may doubt if a masque containing such horrors would have been acceptable at any wedding, even in an age of mannerist oddities. Figures such as Shame, Disloyalty, Dread of Heavenly Vengeance and Death with Infamy—not to speak of the heart in the dish—must surely have been too tasteless to pass muster (as they had to, for Busyrane's plot to succeed). Indeed, the unsuitability of the masque is precisely the discrepant feature that leads us to seek a deeper meaning, to reflect that its performance at Amoret's wedding and every night thereafter can be probable only as metaphor. In other words, the masque represents allegorically an experience beginning with marriage. Thus Amoret's abduction is 'unknown to living wight' in two senses: (1) she is carried off without anyone noticing; (2) she experiences Busyrane's captivity inwardly, without anyone knowing.

Many features of the masque itself and the events that led up to

---

[1] III xii 3, 27; v vii 14f.; see Fowler 209n. citing Plutarch *De Iside* 375 F ('the power assigned to the wind some call Osiris').

[2] Roche (74f.) compares the wedding masque in John Fletcher's *A Wife for a Month* (1624), in which Cupid claps his wings and calls for a dance from his 'servants the effects of love': Fancy, Desire, Delight, Hope, Fear, Distrust, Jealousy, Care, Ire, Poverty and Despair. The later masque, certainly modelled on Spenser's, offers a useful analogue; but the differences are as striking as the resemblances. Fletcher's Cupid is under the control of the Graces and 'bound' by them: he is unbound not to enjoy victory but only to view the spectators' beauty.

it seem triumphal. In consequence, worshippers of Cupid will tend to connect the tapestry wars with the spoils in the second room and the shrilling trumpet, and see the masque as celebrating another victory for the god. But Britomart, though long subjected to the influence of false representations of love, can penetrate to the truth that there is no battle and no victory. Even the triumphal procession is an illusion of Busyrane's art.

The procession has an artful triumphal pattern, with symmetry about a central place of sovereignty: *Ease* / *Fancy* and *Desire* / *Doubt* and *Danger* / *Fear* and *Hope* / *Dissemblance* and *Suspect* / *Grief* and *Fury* / *Displeasure* and *Pleasance* / / *Amoret*, led by *Despite* and *Cruelty* / *CUPID* / *Reproach* / *Repentance* / *Shame* / / *Strife, Anger, Care, Unthriftihead, Loss of Time, Sorrow, Change, Disloyalty, Riotise, Dread, Infirmity, Poverty* and *Death*. In short, *13* / *3* / *Cupid* / *3* / *13*. The travesty of the *16*/*16* scheme of Petrarch's *Trionfo della Pudicizia* is particularly interesting in view of Roche's characterization of Busyrane as perverted chastity. Busyrane's Cupid thrusts into the centre and changes the virtuously just division of 32 into a triumph of 17, the *infaustus numerus*.[1]

But the echo of the triumph in *Amores* I ii is stronger still, the *3* / *Cupid* / *3* array at the centre of Busyrane's masque recalling Ovid's sequence *lover* / *Conscience* / *Shame* / *Cupid* / *Caresses* / *Error* / *Madness*. In Ovid, Cupid's foes (*castris quidquid Amoris obest*) go before as captives, while behind follow the rout (*turba*) of his companions, the manner and consequences of sexual passion. So, in Spenser, the first part of the procession includes such traditional obstacles to love as Doubt and Danger, while the last is a 'confused rout' of 'maladies'. We are tempted to speculate that Busyrane's procession may also resemble Ovid's in following the sequence *opposition to love* / *submission to love* / *love's consequences*. Here we meet a difficulty, however. The triumph of Ovid's Cupid has a definite sense: namely, the yielding of the lover to passion. (Like other ancient authors, he sees falling in love as a madness.) But Amoret never returns Busyrane's love, so that the masque cannot celebrate her submission to him. On the other hand, her love for

[1] On the similarity of the pattern of the tapestries, see Fowler 150–2. The number 17 was evil, according to Pythagorean theory, because it came between 16 and 18, interrupting the harmony of their sesquioctave proportion, the 8 : 9 ratio of a single tone interval (Bongo 416 f.).

Scudamour is socially too acceptable—at court she is 'the ensample of true love' (III vi 52)—to have such evil consequences.

Comparison with yet another triumph of Cupid, Colonna's, may clarify the problem.[1] We recall that in the last triumph of the *Hypnerotomachia*, Cupid is preceded by 12 allegorical figures,[2] more overtly sexual than Spenser's 12, and representing a less interrupted movement to satisfaction as they progress swiftly from Love Thoughts and Agreement through Act to Abandonment and Consummation. Even so, fear is not absent from Colonna's triumph either. Polifilo fears the abyss of absolute self-loss; Polia, the rending of the curtain that symbolizes her maidenhead.

The inference is clear. Even if sexual penetration appears less unambiguously in Busyrane's masque, the 'horror' (xii 19) that begins for Amoret on her wedding day has surely a similar focus in physical surrender. Hence the displaced symbolism of the whirlwind penetrating 'throughout the house' and blowing open the iron gate of life 'as it with mighty levers had been tore'; hence the horrific wound involving physical exposure ('Her breast all naked...Of her dew honour was despoiled quite') and dyeing 'in sanguine red her skin all snowy clean' (xii 20). The overtones of 'honour' and 'clean' are unmistakable, as is that of the heart 'quite through transfixed' drawn out into a basin. The wound shocks precisely because of the eversion through a 'wide orifice' of organs normally internal and concealed: later, it is described still more suggestively as 'riven bowels gored' (xii 38). We conclude, as Roche does on other grounds, that Amoret's horror is occasioned by sexual penetration.

Nevertheless, though her fears focus on the actions of physical sex, they have also complex motivations. At one extreme, the most unparticularized, she fears like Colonna's lovers that sexual abandonment means abandonment of identity. Reared in the Garden of Adonis, she shares its involvement with Chaos, its vulnerability to Time and its dead god. At the other extreme, Amoret's fears have a

[1] The connections between Colonna's allegory and Spenser's are numerous but unobtrusive: the material borrowed has been thoroughly assimilated. Thus the Cythera of the *Hypnerotomachia* becomes the Temple of Venus on an island in *Faerie Queen* IV x, far apart from the triumph of Cupid, while the loves of Jupiter in Colonna's first 4 triumphs are transposed as tragedies in the tapestries of Busyrane's first room.

[2] Two of these, Ennia and Phileda, correspond to figures in the first phase of Busyrane's masque (Fancy and Pleasance).

more individual motivation. Her upbringing has taught her shame-fastness and modesty (IV x 50), so that Scudamour's wooing had to overcome many obstacles, including at least two—Doubt and Danger—that figure in the first part of Busyrane's masque (xii 10 f.; IV x 12–17). Here they represent aspects of a courtship resulting in captivity and outward surrender to physical mastery and torture; not, however, in self-surrender. The later stages of the courtship are charged with aggressive or negative feelings (Suspect, Grief and Fury): Roche cannot be far wrong when he says that Amoret fears 'the vengeance of male sexuality on the chastely reticent female' (p. 76).

Amoret does not know and cannot imagine what form vengeance will take. Consequently the figures before the procession's centre are described each at some length, but the 'confused rout' after the triumphator are only listed briefly, characterized by perfunctory epithets—'unquiet Care', 'faint Infirmity'. This contrast is only partly a reflection of Ovidian precedent and of the historical disorder of armies in triumphal processions. It also renders the vagueness of Amoret's fears. For the maladies at the end are as many 'as there be fantasies / In wavering women's wit. . . Or pains in love' (xii 26). She can only see the ghastly surgical operation that a triumph of physical passion would entail: nothing beyond that is distinct. Perhaps, if she surrendered, Scudamour, having got what he wanted, would be unfaithful (Disloyalty), perhaps pleasure would meet with divine punishment (guilty Dread). She is not going to surrender to find out. How can she trust the victor, surrounded as she is by images of bestial or 'false love' (xi 51)?

According to Roche's theory, Busyrane is absent from the masque because he himself created it: a morbid perversion of chastity, he generates illusions about love, such as the idea that it means cruel sacrifice. But Busyrane's connection with Cupid seems to me closer and more organic than this theory allows. He is bent on conquering Amoret, completely, like the illusory Cupid of his masque. Thus, when Britomart enters the inmost room to find the masquers vanished, 'that same woeful lady' Amoret remains wounded and Busyrane figures charms 'with living blood. . .Dreadfully dropping from her dying heart' (xii 30 f.). If we ask who inflicted the wound, the answer can only be, the magician. He carries a 'murderous knife' (xii 32) like the 'knife accursed keen' that wounded Amoret (xii 20):

he causes 'all' Amoret's suffering, 'all perforce to make her him to love' (xii 31). But the wound seemed also to be inflicted by Amoret's captor, Cupid; and this is not denied in the third room where her heart is still 'transfixed with a cruel dart' (xii 31).[1] Evidently Busyrane bears an intimate relation to Scudamour. For it is her husband who has her heart, who subjects her to the captivity of marriage, who makes her undergo the ordeal of penetration on the wedding night, who has the physical strength[2] and tyrannical mastery of a Busiris sacrificing for fertility, who conjures up sexual passion (Cupid), who tries vainly to conjure a reciprocal passion in her.

This is not to say that Busyrane 'is' Scudamour, any more than either 'is' the Cupid he experiences in passion. Scudamour may bear Cupid's arms—may even become, in the sexual act, a divine vessel (as Colonna's Polifilo becomes a vessel of Mars)—but he should not be confused with the god. And Busyrane, far from being the same with Scudamour, is the obverse. He replaces Scudamour in Amoret's eyes on their wedding day, as any masterful husband replaces an erstwhile lover: so long as Amoret belongs to the one, she does not belong to the other.

Hence one reason why Scudamour fails to enter Busyrane's house. If he were once in Amoret's presence, Busyrane would not be: the story would end. (Similarly, when Amoret is freed and Busyrane disappears from the poem, Scudamour returns.[3]) The narrative reason for Scudamour's incapacity, however, is a fire in the porch:

> A flaming fire, ymixed with smouldery smoke,
> And stinking sulphur, that with grisly hate
> And dreadful horror did all entrance choke,
> Enforced them their forward footing to revoke. (III xi 21)

This is no mere physical fire, since Amoret's rescue quenches it. Whether as a fire of Vulcan (xi 26) it symbolizes sexual lust or jealousy,[4] Scudamour fails through a moral defect: like all Gloriana's

---

[1] In the masque, Amoret's heart is 'quite through transfixed with a deadly dart' (III xii 21); cf. xii 23, 'the darts which his right hand did strain, / Full dreadfully he [Cupid] shook'.

[2] On Busiris' physical strength as an explanation of his name, see Valeriano, *Hieroglyphica* 41.

[3] In the 1590 version, Amoret and Scudamour are immediately reunited to form a hermaphroditic image of the one flesh (1590 III xii 43–7).

[4] Guy de Tervarent, *Attributs et symboles dans l'art profane 1450–1600* (Geneva 1958) s.v. *Flamme* i, ii; col. 183. Scudamour later enacts his jealousy of Amoret

heroes he has to face faults in his own character. Thus he attempts the flames 'with greedy will, and envious desire' and 'fierceness' (xi 26). And the flames for their part are 'stubborn'; 'cruel Mulciber would not obey / His threatful pride'.

In other words, the fire symbolizes not only Scudamour's passions, but also Amoret's. Scudamour's fierce attempts *provoke* the flames and cause hatred—'grisly gate / And dreadful horror'. Like the entry of the Temple of Venus, this allegorizes a relation involving both lovers. Resemblances with the later episode are numerous; except that here, in the absence of Dame Concord, access is more difficult. Within, the masque of ill-assorted couples applies to Scudamour almost as aptly as to Amoret: Roche comments that 'Amoret's main tormentors are those very qualities which have preserved her chastity during her courtship' (p. 75). Doubt and Danger (xi 10 f.) clearly belong to each partner's experience, as the latter will again at the Temple of Venus; while Care (xi 25), here primarily a wavering woman's fantasy, will torture Scudamour in IV v. The double application perhaps even continues in the sinister suggestion of cruel sacrifice. For when the sexual act was imaged as sacrifice the husband usually took the priestly role, his wife the victim's (as in Donne's Lincoln's Inn 'Epithalamium'). But here, though the principal victim is Amoret, Spenser may intend a subsidiary allusion to Busiris' association with sacrifice of the male Osiris. Certainly Danger's rusty blade is in one sense meant for Scudamour. And the whole masque, though generated from Amoret's blood, remains an invention of Busyrane's, whose house allegorizes Scudamour's problem. Amoret is a form of love, no less than he who bears Love's arms: their impasse the inner torture of love imprisoned by love.

Escape comes through yet another form of love, Britomart, who enters the house and resolves the problem. Her ability to get in depends not on her femininity (as Roche has it) but on her virtue. In contrast to Scudamour's greedy wilful desire, Britomart's attitude throughout is characterized by reverence—'we a god invade'—and by a discretion without which she would think it bestial to attempt Danger (ll. 22 f.). Thus she makes no move to force the iron wicket:

in more obvious narrative terms; see e.g. IV vi 7, 'Tho gan he...gnaw his jealous heart'. More broadly considered, the fire in Busyrane's porch is a fire of love (see e.g. many examples in Mario Praz, *Studies in Seventeenth-Century Imagery* (Rome 1964) Index s.v. *Flame, Fire*).

'It vain she thought with rigorous uproar / For to efforce, when charms had closed it afore' (xii 27). Hers is the form of love that succeeds where mere passion fails. Patient, yet prepared to risk all, she embodies the episode's positive ideal, so that even before its denouement her role is more than a spectator's. Her readiness to await the chosen occasions of Cupid's triumph, for example, abounds in moral and psychological implications recalling the *festina lente* theme of the *Hypnerotomachia*.

A vital strand of the allegory is Britomart's progress from room to room. If she had remained in the first, or even the second, the lovers' difficulty would have been unresolved. Yet the meaning of the sequence of rooms is left unclear in the ostensible narrative, and only revealed through progressions in the mode of imagery. The outer room, hung with tapestries showing Cupid's victories, contains a free-standing statue of the god, last to be described: the inner, hung with three-dimensional trophies, is the scene of a magical illusion of a masque of his triumph over Amoret: the inmost finds the real Amoret. Instead of the second room's 'thousand monstrous forms' of love (xi 51), this last has the 'thousand charms' (xii 31) that Busyrane attempts Amoret with and that symbolize—Spenser hints —the forms of love as she experiences it.[1] As for the 'strange characters' figured by Busyrane in her blood and imagination, they are none other than the characters of the masque. The dynamic movement through this sequence mimes a growing self-realization and a growing realization of love on the part of Britomart. At first flat, two-dimensional and remotely literary, the experience is subsequently imagined in more lively modes. Two dimensions give way to three, static to moving images, perfunctory forms to more detailed and subjective personifications. Eventually the divine image of passion comes to life, though in a false, idolatrous and cruel guise. Accompanying this movement rises a parallel crescendo of fear: if the second room seems so much more ominous than the first, what can lie behind the iron gate?

Sex may occasion a frightening tempest of emotional forces. But Britomart, though she feels awe, though her hair stands on end with terror, contemplates the apparent victory of passion without giving

---

[1] III xii 26; cf. the 'thousand thoughts' fashioned in Britomart's mind as she imagines Artegall at III iv 5.

way: she presses steadily on to further realization, 'neither of idle shows, nor of false charms aghast' (xi 29). It is this attitude that will enable her—even after Artegall's struggle for mastery—to imagine sexual intercourse with him as a divine 'game' (v vii 16). A boldness characterizes her love, an outgoing wholeness determined to penetrate beyond fantasies to the reality. Busyrane significantly puts BE BOLD legends everywhere except on the inner door: he encourages lovers to imagine boldly, not to be bold in fact.

The contrast between the conclusion of the episode and the *Trionfo della Pudicizia* is striking. Petrarch's Chastity binds Love to a column: Spenser's frees Amoret, a form of love, from a column. And the would-be conqueror Busyrane is bound, not like Petrarch's Love with an amethystine chain of virtue, but with his own 'great chain'. What Spenser proposes, as a moral ideal, is another form of sexual love.

SPENSER'S TRIUMPH OF TIME

Among Spenser's other processions, that in the *Cantos of Mutability* bears the most interesting relation to earlier triumphs. Establishing her claim to universal sovereignty, the Titaness Mutability first cites the Elements. She considers verbal demonstration sufficient to prove these subject to change, without calling them as witnesses. At the end of her review of the four elements in conventional upward sequence *Earth/Water/Air/Fire* she concludes:

> So, in them all reigns Mutability;
> However these, that gods themselves do call,
> Of them do claim the rule and sovereignty:
> As, Vesta, of the fire aethereal;
> Vulcan, of this, with us so usual;
> Ops, of the earth, and Juno of the Air;
> Neptune, of seas; and nymphs, of rivers all.
> For, all those rivers to me subject are:
> And all the rest, which they usurp, be all my share. (vii 26)

Though nothing is said to refute this claim, Mutability's demonstration proves in an odd way self-refuting. For her contemptuous list of gods ruling the elements puts them in a highly unusual order[1] exhibiting marked symmetry:

[1] There are analogues for the dichotomy of Fire (see *Variorum Spenser*) but not for that of Water, which is clearly an *ad hoc* device of Spenser's.

FIRE		EARTH	AIR	WATER	
AETHEREAL	USUAL			SEAS	RIVERS
Vesta	Vulcan	Ops	Juno	Neptune	Nymphs

The division is just, with Juno queen of heaven in one of the places of sovereignty, a disposition Mutability unwisely leads us to notice, by her remark about Air being 'of all sense. . .the middle mean'.[1]

Mutability next asks for 'the rest [i.e. other fundamental aspects of existence] who do the world in being hold' to be called as witnesses. Whether these are subject to mutability or not, Nature is to judge by the evidence of her eyes. A solemn procession of temporal emblems follows, dazzling in the copiousness of its astonishingly rich visual particularity. Spenser's rhetorical *varietas* seems to serve Mutability's forensic purpose by finding and varying her witnesses, until an overwhelmingly strong case emerges. The procession is a Triumph of Time.

First come 4 Seasons, then 12 Months, Day and Night, and 12 Hours. These temporal units in descending order of magnitude form a series with a point of disappearance in the momentary experience of time: Life 'like a fair young lusty boy, / Such as they feign Dan Cupid to have been' (vii 46). The sequence, which has the sanction of Nature's own Sergeant Order (vii 27), moves from relatively detached perception of long-term seasonal change to involvement in the phenomenal flux of the present moment of desire and joy. Mutability's conclusion is a grim one. The end of being, in this narrow sense, is 'lastly Death': Death 'unbodied, unsouled, unheard, unseen' negates the life of the passing moment. Only one answer to Mutability's challenge is possible:

For, who sees not, that Time on all doth prey?
But times do change and move continually.
So nothing here long standeth in one stay:
Wherefore, this lower world who can deny
But to be subject still to Mutability? (VII vii 47)

Nature concedes the justice of her case, while reminding her that the Triumph of Time will bring on a Triumph of Eternity.[2]

[1] vii 22. The surface meaning of this line is false: Air was considered the means of Hearing, but not of Touch or of Taste.

[2] Petrarch's sequence of 6 triumphs—*Cupid / Chastity / Death / Fame / Time / Eternity*—is thus condensed into the progressions *Life* (resembling Cupid) / *Death* and *Time / Eternity*.

In a less obvious sense, however, Mutability's witnesses give her only ambiguous support. Contrary to her purpose they disclose an underlying order that reaffirms Jupiter's challenged sovereignty. (Even Death, who is supposed to occupy the pagan triumphator's final position, fails to be last in the poem's actual portrayal of the procession: Life, mentioned earlier but described later, has the last say.) Thus, the images of changeable times and seasons allude again and again to Jupiter and hence to *necessitas*. The bull April rides is not only the zodiacal sign but also a form of Jupiter, 'the same which led / Europa floating through the Argolick floods'; May rides on the shoulders of 'the twins of Leda', Jupiter's children; Leo died by the hand of 'the Amphytrionide', that is, the son of Jupiter in Amphitryon's disguise; even the 'shaggy-bearded Goat' Capricorn turns out to be 'the same wherewith Dan Jove in tender years, / They say, was nourished' (vii 33–41). Most emphatically of all,

Then came the Hours, fair daughters of high Jove,
And timely Night, the which were all indued
With wondrous beauty fit to kindle love;
But they were virgins all, and love eschewed,
That might forslack the charge to them foreshowed
By mighty Jove; who did them porters make
Of heaven's gate (whence all the gods issued)
Which they did daily watch, and nightly wake
By even turns, ne ever did their charge forsake. (VII vii 45)

Unnecessarily, and from Mutability's viewpoint unfortunately, this stanza introduces the notion of Jupiter as equal distributor.[1] For the 12 unequal hours can be assigned diurnal and nocturnal watches by *even* turns only because each is as much longer by day at one season as it is longer by night at a season exactly 6 months later.[2] In this long and intricate process of seasonal compensation—hinted at also in the image of Day and Night riding 'with equal pace'—apparent mutability serves the purpose of a larger regularity or 'justice'.

[1] On Jupiter's distributive justice elsewhere in *The Faerie Queen* see Fowler 202–7.

[2] Unequal hours were twelve-part divisions of the time of light (diurnal hours) or of dark (nocturnal hours). Mythologically considered, the Hours of the day —as distinct from the 3 or 4 seasonal *Horae*—numbered 12 rather than 24; see the examples listed in Hieatt, *Short Time's Endless Monument* 111 f. Spenser's reference to gods issuing forth from the hourly gate clinches the identification, since the only hours assigned in turn to the planetary deities were unequal hours. See further p. 135 n. 5, p. 165 n.

But the extent of God's secret sovereignty is best grasped by considering the procession as a symmetrical triumph and looking for its central figure:

Seasons	Months		Day and Night	Hours	Life and Death
4	12		2	12	2
	16			16	

One of the figures at the point of equal division, the sovereign deity Day, bears 'upon his sceptre's height, / The goodly sun' (vii 44). As Upton perceived, Day in such a shape is again a form of Jupiter. The next stanza makes this clear: after Day and Night, from whose interaction the unequal hours are generated, come their children the 'fair daughters of high Jove, / And timely Night'. Just as in Petrarch's *Trionfo della pudicizia*, moreover, the figures evenly divided total 32, the number of Justice.

However much Nature may seem to concede in her verdict, therefore, the procession of Mutability is far from being a simple Triumph of Time, or even a dualism of light and dark, life and death. The balance, as Spenser presents it, is a just division by a supreme ruler: 'The sons of Day he favoureth, I see.'

4. Numerology of the centre

From central sovereignty in poetry's content it is a short step to central emphasis in the form. So far, all the triumphs discussed have been substantive, that is, actually represented in the action. But the triumphal pattern was also imposed on poetic form, producing symbolic arrangements very like those we found in historical pageants. For the spatial tendency of renaissance thought facilitated direct control of formal organization by ideas; and conventions of centralized symmetry naturally carried over from political protocol into poetry, as they did into architecture. Poets developed the habit of distributing matter through the metrical structure with careful regard to the centre's sovereignty. Almost as a regular practice, they would devote the central place to some principal figure or event, or make it coincide with a structural division of the poem.

Renaissance poets may have found models for such numerology in ancient authors. True, emphasis of the precise centre was by no means a convention of classical literature. But there were instances, real or imagined, in authors enjoying special favour. For example, the centre lines in the generally accepted text of Virgil's *Aeneid*, vii 193 f., find 'Latinus seated on the throne of his fathers'[1] greeting the embassy of

---

[1] 'Tali intus templo divum patriaque Latinus / *sede sedens Teucros ad sese in tecta vocavit, / atque haec ingressis placido prior edidit ore*' (vii 192–4: the italicized central lines are 4948f. out of 9896). Against Virgil's intending this, there is

Aeneas, the man predestined to be called to 'equal sovereignty' with him (vii 257). Though this confrontation has its thematic significance in the poem's action, it is hardly so prominent as the central images in certain renaissance poems. Nevertheless, it would be difficult to overemphasize the importance of the *Aeneid* as a literary model. And those who counted Virgil's lines—as we know Boccaccio did[1]— would hardly miss noticing the position of Latinus' throne.

Horace, too, occasionally puts a sovereign figure at the exact centre, such as the Jupiter *pater et rex* of *Satires* II i. A more striking instance is *Satires* I x, where the numerological centre comes at the culmination of a review of successful exponents of various kinds of poetry. After the recent successes of Fundanius, Pollio, Varrius and Virgil, the only genre left unconquered is satire. This Varro Atacinus has tried; but Horace himself can do it better, though 'falling short of the inventor Lucilius; nor would I dare to wrest from him the crown that clings to his brow with so much glory'. All the same, the subsequent lines (50–71) argue that even Lucilius' poetry lacks finish: he has much to correct by the higher standards of the present. Just as Homer nodded, just as Lucilius himself criticized Accius' and Ennius' faults, so his own should be criticized by a more polished age. For Lucilius was undisciplined, a little like Cassius Etruscus. These 4 older poets (5 with Lucilius) balance the 5 living poets Fundanius to Varro, to form the scheme *4 contemporaries/3 satirists/4 predecessors*, or alternatively *5 contemporaries/Horace/5 predecessors*. The centre poet of each array is Horace himself, who boasts his superiority to Varro in the satire's centre lines (italicized):

hoc erat, experto frustra Varrone Atacino
atque quibusdam alliis, melius quid scribere possem,
inventore minor; neque ego illi detrahere ausim
haerentem capiti cum multa laude coronam. (46–9)

Thus the crown renounced is tacitly reappropriated through the poem's arrangement. By putting himself at the centre of both arrays Horace not only claims to be better than Varro, but aspires to excel Lucilius. (The succeeding passage implies as much, though some

some evidence that the ancient corpus of his works may have had a smaller line total than the medieval and modern; *Carmina Vergiliana* 182 gives a total of 12,847, compared with our 12,913. See also John Sparrow, *Half-lines and Repetitions in Virgil* (Oxford 1931).

[1] For Boccaccio's imitation of the line total of the manuscript *Aeneid*, see p. 13.

critics have taken the modest disclaimer of 48 f. at face value.) Moreover, the numerological device makes a point against Lucilius simply by its existence, since it is precisely in respect of architectonic deficiencies that Horace criticizes him:

> sed ille,
> si foret hoc nostrum fato delapsus in aevum,
> detereret sibi multa, recideret omne quod ultra
> perfectum traheretur... (67–70)

Even in Virgil and Horace, however, such instances are isolated. Most of their symmetries are numerically inexact, the result merely of balanced thought.

Late antiquity provided further examples, among them Sidonius' triumphal epithalamium for Ruricius (*Carm.* xi). Gaius Apollinaris Sidonius (*c.* A.D. 430–80), a Gallo-Roman Christian, enjoyed high esteem in the sixteenth century.[1] His *Carmina* xi is an epithalamium of the narrative mythological type: it tells how Venus and her marine entourage arrive at a Temple of Love, and are joined by Cupid, who comes with the good news of Ruricius' capture. Cupid panegyrizes the bridegroom, listing the dowries that in an age of myth might have been paid for his love, and Venus replies that the bride is quite a catch, too, listing hypothetical suitors she might have had. The poem concludes with a lusciously described procession to the wedding. Now Cupid's catalogue of 10 mythological dowries occupies the numerological centre, so that he pays homage to the bridegroom at the place of sovereignty both formally and substantively. The first and last dowries are explicitly regal: Hypsipyle (l. 66) would have given her own *imperium*, Helen the *corona* (l. 69) with which she crowned Menelaus. That one of the two central dowries, Calypso's, comes in the central line (67: 'Alceste vitam, Circe herbas, poma Calypso') will not seem accidental, if one recalls the position of Calypso's isle at the navel or centre of the sea.[2] But, while Calypso's apt centrality pleases well enough, it does little for the poem as a whole, which is after all not about Calypso. The placement is a mere superficial felicity, of the sort Sidonius' formal verse specializes in.

---

[1] He was imitated by Spenser, e.g., in the description of Busyrane's tapestries. Cf. *Faerie Queen* III xi 29–46 with Sidonius' *Carm.* xv 158–84, another epithalamium, in which Araneola embroiders tales of ancient marriages and mythological amours, including metamorphoses of Jupiter.

[2] Homer, *Od.* i 50.

Illustrations

See also the list of illustrations on page vii

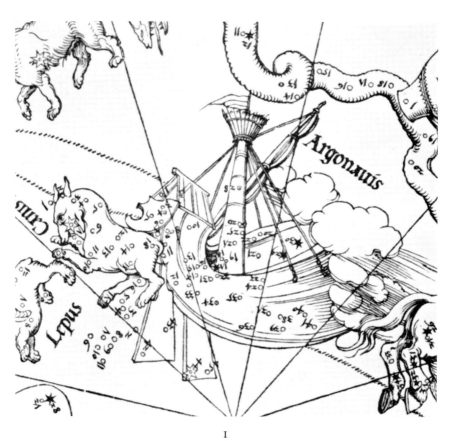

I

2 (a)

2 (b)

2 (c)

2 (d)

SONNET XXXIIII.

But when in *May* my worldes bright fierie sunne
　　Had past in Zodiacke with his golden teame
　　To place his beames which in the twynnes begunne,
　　The blazing twynne starres of my worldes bright beame
My mistresse eyes, mine heauens bright sunne, and moone,
　　The starres by which poore shepheard I am warned
　　To pinne in late, and put my flockes out soone,
　　My flockes of fancies as the signes me learned:
Then did my loues first spring beginne to sproute,
　　So long as my sunnes heate in those signes rayned.
　　But wandring all the Zodiacke throughout
　　From her mayes twynnes, my sunne such heate constrained,
That where at first I litle had complained,
　　From signe to signe, in such course he now posteth
VVhich dayly me, with hotter flaming tosteth.

SONNET XXXV.

Next when my sunne by progresse tooke his hold
　　In Cancer of my mistresse craftie minde,
　　How retrograde seem'd she, when as I told
　　That in his clawes such torches I did finde,
VVhich if she did not to my teares lay plaine
　　That they might quenched be from their outrage,
　　My loues hot Iune should be consum'd in payne
　　Vnlesse her pittie make my greefe asswage.
Oh how she frownes, and like the Crabbe backe turnes

　　　　　　　　　　　　　　　　　　　　　When

Or layd great bafes for eternity,
Which proues more fhort then waft or ruining?
Haue I not feene dwellers on forme and fauor
Lofe all, and more by paying too much rent
For compound fweet; Forgoing fimple fauor,
Pittifull thriuors in their gazing fpent.
Noe, let me be obfequious in thy heart,
And take thou my oblacion, poore but free,
Which is not mixt with feconds, knows no art,
But mutuall render. onely me for thee.
  Hence, thou fubbornd *Informer*, a trew foule
  When moft impeacht, ftands leaft in thy controule.

126

O Thou my louely Boy who in thy power,
  Doeft hould times fickle glaffe, his fickle, hower:
Who haft by wayning growne, and therein fhou'ft,
Thy louers withering, as thy fweet felfe grow'ft.
If Nature (foueraine mifteres ouer wrack)
As thou goeft onwards ftill will plucke thee backe,
She keepes thee to this purpofe, that her skill.
May time difgrace, and wretched mynuit kill.
Yet feare her O thou minnion of her pleafure,
She may detaine, but not ftill keepe her trefure!
Her *Audite* (though delayd) anfwer'd muft be,
And her *Quietus* is to render thee.
    (   )
    (   )

127

IN the ould age blacke was not counted faire,
  Or if it weare it bore not beauties name:
But now is blacke beauties fucceffiue heire,
And Beautie flanderd with a baftard fhame,
For fince each hand hath put on Natures power,
Fairing the foule with Arts faulfe borrow'd face,
Sweet beauty hath no name no holy boure,
But is prophan'd, if not liues in difgrace.

H 3   Therefore

4

5

6

7 (a)

7 (b)

6

8

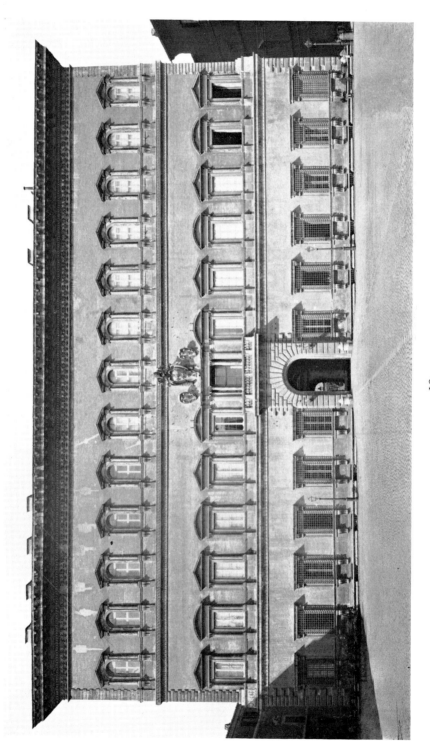

11

12

Other numerological poems by Sidonius include *Carmina* xxii, 'Burgus Pontii Leontii', which also has a triumphal procession. Its middle line accomplishes a re-establishment of Roman sovereignty (118, 'cum Latius patriae dominabitur') that the whole looks forward to. Here the formal pattern of the *Aeneid* is already imitated in a nostalgic attempt to conjure an empire receding into the past and the future.

During the Middle Ages monarchic symbolism, and with it the significance of the central place, assumed new importance. Numerological applications of the motif were often attempted, particularly in the architectonic organization of longer poems, so that by the early renaissance very elaborate effects were possible—as in the *Divina commedia*, discussed in the next chapter. For a simpler instance, consider Chaucer's *Troilus*, whose central stanza comes in a prayer exalting the god of love:

And for thow me, that leest koude disserve
of hem that noumbred ben into thi grace,
Hast holpen, ther I likly was to sterve,
And me bistowed in so heigh a place
That thilke boundes may no blisse pace,
I kan namore; but laude and reverence
Be to thy bounte and thyn excellence![1]

It is conformable to the irony of the poem that Troilus should in his innocence put himself, as a numbered (elect) lover, in a place triumphantly 'heigh': later he will discover his elevation to have been akin, more precariously, to the high point of Fortune's wheel. I do not suggest that this prayer constitutes the only or indeed the main imaginative 'centre' of *Troilus*. My more limited assertion is merely that Chaucer activates the sovereign and triumphal associations of the central place in such a way as to mime Troilus' statement in numerological terms. However, the thematic value of the passage thus emphasized formally should not be underestimated, in view of Troilus' subsequent vantage point in the eighth sphere (v 1809).

An equally important legacy of the Middle Ages from the numerological point of view, however, was the theological tradition of Biblical

---

[1] The centre line iii 1271 (my itals.) is 4119th of 8239. I am indebted here to Douglas Brooks. The poem's large-scale metrical structure is to some extent symmetrical, since only the 3 central books have formal proems.

exegesis.[1] That tradition taught the habit of regarding the most serious literature as numerically constructed, and of giving special attention to the centre verses of chapters, in the search for types of Christ.[2] Sardo, listing a series of manifestations of Christ's cosmic centricity, sums up the line of thought: 'Est itaque Christus, utriusque testamenti centrum.'[3] Out of this preoccupation with central types— the tree in the midst of Paradise, Jerusalem in the midst of the world, Solomon's temple *in meditullio mundi*, Christ in the Temple *in medio doctorum*, Christ in the midst of the candlesticks of the Apocalypse, Christ crucified between the thieves—emerged the numerological form of the Christocentric Biblical epic. An early instance is the *De Triumpho Christi* (Venice 1499) of Macarius Mutius, a poem that the *cinquecento* critic Antonio Possevino admired and even reprinted as an example to be followed.[4] The centre of this epic, which perhaps provided Milton with a first model for Messiah's central ascent of a chariot, finds Christ in triumph after harrowing hell and freeing the pre-Christian righteous. Near the numerological centre, as in *Paradise Lost*, comes Aaron's mystical breastplate, with its sovereign gold in the centre line of the poem (159 out of 317); and the chariot of the sun detained by Joshua follows almost immediately:

Dum litat et flavo limbus circumsonat auro   159
Monstratique haeres sacri cultusque paterni: [Heleazar
Et volucres Phoebi potuit qui sistere currus.   [Iosue

In the same tradition, De Sousa's *De miseria hominis deque reparatione humana carmen* (Lisbon 1615), though it most obviously divides into *4 books on the Fall | 4 books on the birth of the Virgin Mary and Christ | 4 books on the Atonement*, also forms 2 groups of 6 books each, with a central pause at the birth of the Virgin.[5] On the Protestant side, Alexander Ross's *Virgilii evangelisantis Christiados libri xiii* (1638) is representative: its central book treats the eternal reign of Christ. Thus, when Milton designed the intricate central sym-

[1] Discussed at length in Maren-Sofie Røstvig, 'Structure as Prophecy: The Influence of Biblical Exegesis Upon Theories of Literary Structure' in *Silent Poetry* ed. Alastair Fowler (1970).
[2] See p. 25 above.
[3] A. Sardo, *De arcanis* (Rome 1614) 391, *cit.* Røstvig, 'Structure as Prophecy'.
[4] *Tractatio de poesi et pictura* (Rome 1593), discussed in Bernard Weinberg, *History of Literary Criticism* i 337.
[5] Watson Kirkconnell, *The Celestial Cycle* (Toronto 1952) p. xxii f.; Røstvig, 'The Hidden Sense' 73.

metries of *Paradise Lost*[1] he could assume his readers' familiarity not only with the central types of exegesis but with earlier triumphal epics.

ELIZABETHAN DECORUM

Among Elizabethan poets attempting a neoclassical closeness of construction, numerological emphasis of the centre became a regular convention. In another book I discussed centralization in *The Faerie Queen*:[2] here we are mainly concerned with instances in short poems. These occur with particular frequency in epithalamia, a genre grouped by Puttenham with 'triumphals' and genethliaca (natal songs) as festal poems or 'poetical rejoicings'.[3] Some of the best Elizabethan epithalamies contain triumphal processions. Spenser's all do—not only *Prothalamion* and *Epithalamion* but also the spousals of Thames and Medway (*Faerie Queen* IV xi), which from one point of view are an inset epithalamy of the narrative-mythological type.[4] Many other festal poems, even if they do not feature a triumph in the narrative, nevertheless have the form of a symmetrical tableau.

Centralization is simple and obvious in the nuptial song that concludes Jonson's *Haddington Masque* (1608) for the wedding of John Viscount Haddington and Lady Elizabeth Radcliffe, daughter of the Earl of Sussex. This song has special interest, however, because of its extensive use of triumphal motifs. Throughout, the variable part of the refrain refers to the consummation of the marriage as Hymen's war —'Sound then to Hymen's war', 'Speed well in Hymen's war', etc. The newly wedded couple are captives of the triumphator Hymen, a god 'whose bands pass liberty' (l. 5); but simultaneously they belong to his band and 'are now waged to his war'. Jonson's pun carries the bonds of marriage beyond mere liberty to the 'long perfection' of the sweetened war that the exemplary true lovers are to enjoy. The fourth and central stanza imagines the marriage politically as a triumphal establishment of Love's empire:

[1] See below, pp. 116–9 and 131 f.
[2] *Spenser and the Numbers of Time* 45 f., 220; see also Michael Baybak, Paul Delany and A. Kent Hieatt, 'Placement "In the Middest" in *The Faerie Queen*' in *Silent Poetry* ed. Alastair Fowler (1970).
[3] *The Art of English Poesy* I xxiii; ed. Willcock and Walker 46.
[4] On central accent in *Epithalamion*, see p. 105. The central stanza of the spousals of Thames and Medway canto, IV xi 27, honours the bridegroom with his coronet of towers.

Love's commonwealth consists of toys;
His council are those antic boys,
Games, Laughter, Sports, Delights,
That triumph with him on these nights;
To whom we must give way,
For now their reign begins, and lasts till day.
They sweeten Hymen's war,
And in that jar,
Make all that married be
Perfection see.
Shine, Hesperus, shine forth, thou wished star.[1]

What is more, the reign of Love and his council, with that of the lovers, begins 'now' in the long central line, 'For now their reign begins, and lasts till day', the poem's only explicit mention of sovereignty.

Many epithalamies of the period have a rudimentary central accent of this type. One that preserves the original political significance of the device is Thomas Heywood's 'A Nuptial Hymn' from *A Marriage Triumph Solemnized in an Epithalamium in Memory of the Happy Nuptials betwixt the High and Mighty Prince Count Palatine and the Most Excellent Princess the Lady Elizabeth* (1613).[2] Of its 15 eight-line stanzas the central 3 develop the idea of the bride's queenliness. Stanzas vii–viii in Sidonian vein represent her as a fit consort for Jupiter (if she had lived in the old time 'Io had never been / The great Egyptian queen'); Stanza ix compares her in virtue with the queen from whom she received her name, Elizabeth.

Henry Peacham's *Nuptial Hymns* (1613) are more elaborately symmetrical. Published in honour of the same royal marriage, the whole sequence preserves a centralized decorum: it is the third of 5 hymns that invokes the 'chaste marriage sovereign' with its triumphal refrain 'Io, Hymen, Hymenaeus!'[3] Moreover, the sequence has an *a b c b a* metrical structure: I *Not couplets* / II *Couplets* / III *Couplet stanzas* / IV *Couplets* / V *Not couplets*.[4] Hymn IV has also an em-

---

[1] Ed. Herford, Simpson and Simpson vii 262. The stanza's numerical position is underlined by the composition of Love's council, which includes 4 'antic boys'. Together with Love, these make up the nuptial pentad (on which see pp. 148–51).

[2] Reprinted in Robert H. Case, *English Epithalamies* (Chicago and London 1896) 44.

[3] All the *Hymns* except the fifth are reprinted in Case 54–65.

[4] This would be clear to readers accustomed to analysing rhyme schemes as spatial patterns. See e.g. Puttenham's diagrams illustrating 'plain compass' and

phatic central emphasis of its own. It is a mythological-narrative epithalamium in imitation of Sidonius' epithalamium for Ruricius and (more closely) of Claudian's for Honorius and Maria. In Peacham as in Claudian Cupid reports the bridegroom's capture to Venus as she sits in a splendid palace peopled with allegorical fictions: in Peacham as in Claudian a procession follows 'of sea-gods, tritons, nymphs, who equal strove / The foremost who should aid the queen of love'. But the processions differ strikingly in arrangement. The order of Claudian's gods and nymphs seems unimportant, if, indeed, it is determinate at all. Peacham's, by contrast, form definite series, whose terms are always ordered distinctly—'First Neptune' (99); he has composed the elements of his source into a highly wrought formal pattern. The Jacobean procession is of 9 gods and nymphs, with the triumphant Venus riding 'a shelly chariot' drawn by dolphins (primates of the fish hierarchy) in the sovereign fifth position: *Neptune / Palaemon / Nereus / Glaucus / VENUS / Cymothoe / Spathale / Clotho / Galatea*. Not content with placing Venus medially between gods and nymphs, Peacham also contrives to put her at the metrical centre of the poem. The 107th of its 212 lines is 'Next Venus comes, with all her beauteous crew'. And he reinforces this accent on the sovereign fifth place by organizing the poem's images in groups of 5.[1] Thus Venus recounts the legends of 5 faithful women (Dido, Lucretia, Camilla, Hero and Thisbe) and the bride is worthy of a wider kingdom than that watered by the Rhine, Moselle, Maine, Nahe and Neckar.

The number 5 was always appropriate for royal weddings, which united its symbolisms of marriage and sovereignty; and on this occasion there was the accidental felicity of the Count Palatine's being the fifth Frederick of the line. Consequently Peacham's Fifth Hymn, celebrating the marriage as a political union, enjoys a special prominence formally, dignified by the use of the learned language and the abandonment of rhyme. Under the veil of its Latinity, number symbolism becomes substantive, almost explicit: the gods vote Elizabeth

'intertangle' rhyming, and the different 'proportions' or distances of rhymes (ed. Willcock and Walker, 85–8). In Puttenham's terms, Hymns II, III and IV have 'first distance' rhymes, Hymn I 'second distance'. Hymn I rhymes ababcdcd: Hymn III, aabr (where *r* indicates a refrain line).

[1] Perhaps taking a hint from Sidonius, *Carm.* xi 17 ff., where Venus' temple is built of stone from 5 regions and shines with 5 colours.

ter...quaterque amata and at the sovereign centre (l. 23 out of 44) Frederick is *quintus ille dives*.[1]

Discussing the multifarious forms of the triumphal procession in the Italian renaissance, Jacob Burckhardt remarks that 'all the festive processions, whether they celebrated any special event or were mainly held for their own sakes, assumed more or less the character and nearly always the name of a "Trionfo". It is a wonder that funerals were not also treated in the same way.'[2] If funerals were not, elegies and epitaphs were. Ben Jonson's 'To the Memory of My Beloved', for example, consists in effect of a triumphal procession of authors, with overgone ancients and moderns figuring as the captives, Shakespeare as the national triumphator. One of its two central lines exclaims: 'Triumph, my Britain, thou hast one to show.'[3] And even Surrey's epitaph 'Wyatt resteth here',[4] though its content is far from triumphal, does not omit observance of the central place. It comprises 9 stanzas and a final couplet, of which the 7 middle stanzas mourn 7 parts of the mortal body, each endowed with a Gift of the Spirit.[5] The central part, in the fifth stanza, recalls Wyatt's ambassadorial mission—'A tongue that served in foreign realms his king'— thus occasioning the sole mention of sovereignty.

In the poems we have been considering, recognition of the central accent was not usually essential to interpretation: numerological structure accompanied meaning rather than expressed it. Venus would seem central to Peacham's marine procession, even if we had not counted gods and nymphs and lines. Indeed, spatial symmetries are sometimes merely incidental effects of decorum. This certainly seems to be the case with Chapman's *A Hymn to Hymen* (1613,

---

[1] See F. G. Waldron's 1792 reprint, p. 47. Waldron notes that *Dives pace* 'interprets Frederique, in old English or Dutch'. Another numerological device is that the 16 *ordines* of Jupiter's council are mentioned in l. 16: 'Consulti simul ordines bis octo.' Waldron comments: 'It is trivial [commonplace] how *thrice and four times*, express a superlative. But also it here respects the name of our *Princess Elizabeth*, which together may signify the *Septenary of God*. The number withall includes *Virginity*, and by the ancients was titled *Pallas*.' For other instances of sovereign and nuptial 5s in triumphs, see pp. 20 f., 44.
[2] *The Civilization of the Renaissance in Italy* 218.
[3] Ed. Herford, Simpson and Simpson vii 391; l. 41 out of 80.
[4] Ed. E. L. Jones (Oxford 1964) 27 f. See further below, p. 102.
[5] On 7 as the number of man's mortal bodily nature, see Fowler 269–72, with references. There were 7 phases of the embryo, 7 ages, 7 inner members, 7 alimentary members, 7 tissues, 7 visible parts, 7 openings, 7 motions, etc.

another epithalamium for Princess Elizabeth), in which the centre is acknowledged by only the most casually republican of salutes: 'Sings, dances, sets on every foot a crown.'[1] The line contains the only reference to sovereignty; yet its location at the centre obviously has no thematic or structural importance.[2]

ORGANIC SYMMETRY: DONNE

Central accents may be essential to the poetic structure, however. No one can fully understand Donne's 'Nuptial Song'[3] for the wedding of the Earl of Somerset and the Countess of Essex, for example, without reference to its central pattern. It consists of 11 numbered and titled eleven-line stanzas, of which the first begins:

Thou art reprieved, old year, thou shalt not die,
Though thou upon thy death-bed lie,
And shouldst within five days expire,
Yet thou are rescued by a mightier fire,
Than thy old soul, the sun,
When he doth in his largest circle[4] run.

The occasion being 26 December, the old year-phoenix might have expected to burn out in 5 days' time. Instead, it receives new life from a fire greater than that of its soul the sun, even at his summer height. This is 'joy's bonfire' in the lovers' united soul, to which Donne's concluding stanza circularly returns. Their triumphant renewal of the old sun's life after the last 5 days of the year is mimed

[1] *The Poems of George Chapman* ed. Phyllis B. Bartlett (1941) 366; l. 42 of 84. To the initiate, certain key words must have become associated with triumphal sovereignty and with just division, so that their medial placing in a poem would be enough in itself to constitute decorum. Such words would include *triumph*, *sovereign*, *centre*, *balance*. E.g. 'Their rich triumphal arcs [arches] which they did raise, / Their huge pyramids, which do heaven threat' at the centre of Spenser's sonnet 'Upon the history of George Castriot', *Poetical Works* ed. J. C. Smith and E. de Selincourt (1912) 603; 'And the well-balanced world on hinges hung' at the centre of Milton's hymn *On the Morning of Christ's Nativity* (122nd of 244 lines).

[2] Except that the first 2 lines are repeated as the last 2, according to Puttenham's prescription for circular poems; cf. the substantive reference to Hymen's circle. The main division of the poem, however, is asymmetrical: it comprises 2 flower similes, of 56 and 28 lines respectively. The parts thus form an octave concord, in the numerical proportion 2 : 1.

[3] In *Eclogue. 1613. December 26*; ed. H. J. C. Grierson, 2 vols (Oxford 1912) i 135–40.

[4] For the commonplace that the sun's 'largest circle' was in summer and its least in winter see e.g. Horace, *Sat.* II vi 26.

formally in the sixth and central stanza–day, when it is the new sun of the lovers that rises:

VI. *Going to the Chapel*
Now from your easts you issue forth, and we,
As men which through a cypress see
The rising sun, do think it two,
So, as you go to church, do think of you,
But that veil being gone,
By the Church rites you are from thenceforth one.
The Church triumphant made this match before,
And now the militant doth strive no more;
Then, reverend priest, who God's recorder art,
Do, from his dictates, to these two impart
All blessings, which are seen, or thought, by angel's eye or heart.

A change in the variable refrain signalizes the new era. Each of the first 5 stanzas has a refrain mentioning the 'inflaming[1] eyes' of the lovers, whereas none of the second 5 has.[2] Moreover, the refrain line of the last stanza reverts to the earlier formula, to complete another circle like that of the sun. This pattern also, however, mimes the recapitulative relation between decad and monad. Out of 2 groups of 5 stanzas comes the higher unity of the last, which is concerned with the one flesh and the fire that may 'equal the divine'. In it love's arts and the poet's 'make of so noble individual parts / One fire of four inflaming eyes, and of two loving hearts'. This 10 + 1 pattern of stanzas is replicated microcosmically by the metrical pattern of individual stanzas.[3]

The central refrain is the only one that speaks not of the lovers' but of an angel's eyes and heart. This variation further emphasizes the central accent and at the same time explains it: the triumphal rites of marriage carry the poem to a new, supernatural level. Characteris-

---

[1] Burning with ardour of passion.

[2] Thus 'The fire of these inflaming eyes, or of this loving heart' (i), 'Since both have both the inflaming eyes, and both the loving heart' (ii) etc.; but 'With any west, these radiant eyes, with any north, this heart' (vii), 'A sunset to these weary eyes, a centre to this heart' (viii), etc.

[3] More exactly, $2 \times 5 + 1$. The rhyme scheme repeats this pattern, each stanza consisting of 5 rhymes arranged aabbccddee(e). The refrain rhyme *heart* is distinguished by its constancy throughout the poem. Besides their structural self-reference the lines quoted from the final stanza may also allude to the Neoplatonic doctrine that 2 lovers each transformed into the other may be considered either as 1 or as 4; see Leone Ebreo, *The Philosophy of Love* tr. F. Friedeberg-Seeley and Jean H. Barnes (1937) 260.

tically, Donne's use of the triumphal motif shows awareness of its significance. For 'the rising sun' of the central stanza surely alludes to the ancient types *Sol oriens* and *Sol iustitiae*—Christ's rising, after all, is the very victory that 'the Church triumphant' celebrates. On the other hand, the double sun primarily offers a similitude for the wedded lovers. They share the triumph, since—as Donne obscurely hints in 'The Church triumphant made this match before, / And now the militant doth strive no more'—married lovers' unity resembles the unity of Christ with his Church. As *Ephesians* v (a chapter used in the marriage service) puts it,

Husbands, love your wives, even as Christ also loved the church, and gave himself for it...that he might present it to himself a glorious church....For this cause shall a man...be joined unto his wife, and they two shall be one flesh. This is a great mystery: but I speak concerning Christ and the church.

The union of the wedded lovers anticipates the heavenly union with God for which the Church militant strives. Consequently it is worthy to occupy the central line of the poem: joy's fire burns as the soul and centre of the universe.

The metrical centre of 'The Ecstasy' also enthrones an image of sexual unity; though in a subtler and more organic, less lapidary manner.[1] Of its 19 stanzas, the first 7 describe from an external point of view the attitudes of lovers lying with their souls in *ecstasis* between them, negotiating union. The remaining 12 stanzas form a distinct section, a 'dialogue of one', clearly set off from the introductory section by a difference of grammatical form. For the 12 stanzas are in direct speech—'(we said)'—and purport to record the actual words of the combined single soul, as a sufficiently spiritual eavesdropper would overhear them. The 12 stanzas of the dialogue of one, however, also fall into distinct parts, through a substantive division in the argument which most critics have remarked. A first part of 5 stanzas (viii–xii) meditates on love's mystery, whereby a 'new concoction' of the 'mixture' of elements in the individual souls forms a single pure remixed quintessential soul. Then a final part of 7 stanzas (xiii–xix) turns to the body and its role as love's book. The transition between

---

[1] Cf. also Abraham Cowley, 'Platonic Love', *The Mistress* in *Poems* ed. Waller 75 f., which has the 'one' formed by the union of the 2 lovers' souls in the centre of each of its central stanzas. The subjects of Cowley's and Donne's poems are closely related.

the two parts is strongly marked: 'But o alas, so long, so far / Our bodies why do we forbear?' Thus to an external structural point of view the poem presents a symmetrical[1] stanzaic array of the form 7 / 5 / 7. It is appropriate that the central part dealing with the union of two souls into one should consist of 5 stanzas; since not only was 5 a 'nuptial number' combining the first masculine and the first feminine numbers, but also denoted the fifth, purer, quintessential element.[2] (We recall that in alchemy the hermaphroditic transmutation was an apex of the *magnum opus*.) The centre stanza of all, Stanza x, develops a condensed image of union: the five-petalled 'single violet transplant'. This numerologically central image of the two-in-one doubled violet brings to a focus the whole meditation on union, which indeed began with the same flower. For the poem takes its start from the violet, emblem *amantis unius solius*,[3] growing from a bank that will support 'the violet's reclining head' of the united lovers. In the present context, the link between the first and tenth stanzas recalls the return of the decad to the unity of the monad in Donne's 'Nuptial Song'.

THE WITTY CENTRE: COWLEY

Abraham Cowley (1618–67) contributed to spatial construction new delicacy, neatness and wit: qualities somewhat soberly present in his 1647 poem of retirement 'The Wish'.[4] About the third of its 5 eight-line stanzas—

3
Oh, fountains, when in you shall I
My self, eased of unpeaceful thoughts, espy?
Oh fields! Oh woods! when, when shall I be made
The happy tenant of your shade?
Here's the spring-head of pleasure's flood;
Here's wealthy nature's treasury.
Where all the riches lie, that she
Has coined and stamped for good.

[1] See further below, p. 107.
[2] On the union of odd (masculine) and even (feminine) numbers in 5, see p. 148. Donne himself uses the same symbolism substantively in 'The Primrose': 'all / Numbers are odd, or even, and they fall / First into this, five'. The last part of 'The Ecstasy', on the soul's descent, is in 7 stanzas, a number whose symbolism of body and subjection to change was very familiar; see n. 24 above.
[3] Filippo Picinelli, *Mundus symbolicus* (Cologne 1681) XI 242.
[4] In *The Mistress* in *Poems* ed. Waller 87 f.

74

—the matter is distributed symmetrically. Thus the fear expressed in Stanza v that others may be attracted to 'make a city here' returns to the rejection of the worldly city in Stanza i, and the descended gods making retirement a way to heaven (iv) correspond to the earlier guardian angels and thoughts of the grave (ii). Within Stanza iii itself, moreover, the fountains of the first half reflect 'the spring-head of pleasure's flood' in the second. Between, in a central line,[1] 'the happy tenant of your shade' reigns in anticipation at the centre of a syllabic arrangement *3 | tenant | 3*, re-enacting the pattern of solar sovereignty. The pattern sharpens the poem's paradox: not only does the virtuous man enjoy in retirement stoic sovereignty, but he is sun king, even in the shadow.

For delicacy of spatial arrangement it would be hard to match Cowley's 'Dialogue' (*The Mistress*, 1647) between a successful lover and the girl he has 'ruined'.[2] They speak the 9 stanzas alternately, the girl being assigned the odd-numbered, including the central fifth:

Thou first perhaps who didst the fault commit,
Wilt make thy wicked boast of it.
For men, with Roman pride, above
The conquest, do the triumph love:
Nor think a perfect victory gained,
Unless they through the streets their captive lead enchained.

In reply the lover promises secrecy, protesting ''Tis you the conqueror are, 'tis you | Who have not only taken, but bound and gagged me too.' Much of the poise of this confession depends on the delicious neatness of its structure. The girl, who feels conquered while seeming victorious to her lover, is given the central speech—but uses it to regret what she thinks of as submission. As for her conqueror, he follows after the defeated triumphator, bound, in the position of a captive spared. We are left as uncertain how to apportion victory and defeat as Cowley meant us to be: 'Thou hast this day undone me quite; | Yet wilt undo me more shouldst thou not come at night.'

A sharper wit characterizes 'The Waiting-Maid',[3] in which a lover,

---

[1] In the 1647 edn of *The Mistress*. The 1656 and 1688 edns omit the line 'Here's wealthy nature's treasury', whether by accident or design, so that a metrical irregularity has the effect of further distinguishing Stanza iii and increasing the central emphasis. The overall line arrangement becomes symmetrical (*8 | 8 | 7 | 8 | 8*) and the line arrangement within iii echoes the syllabic arrangement of the central line. [2] Ed. Waller 148.
[3] In *The Mistress, ibid.* 138.

suspected of attentions to his mistress' attendant, sophistically argues that he only prays to the saint in order to worship the goddess. The lady is being a tyrant: even her beauty is needlessly cruel. As the central Stanza iii puts it:

Three hours each morn in dressing thee,
Maliciously are spent;
And make that beauty tyranny,
That's else a civil government.

Extra lines in the last stanza make the line centre fall between the alternative sovereignties 'tyranny' and 'civil government'. So much is unambiguous. But in what sense would the lady's government be more civil if she did not augment her beauty's power? Is it only that fewer cosmetic additions would poison less a dart 'too apt before to kill'? Or are the hours of toilet spent maliciously in another sense, by keeping the maid from her lover?

Cowley's use of the central accent could also be solemn, as in 'The Ecstasy' (*Pindaric Odes*, 1656).[1] Though he usually chose to take advantage of the metrical licence of what he called 'this free kind of poetry',[2] several of the *Pindaric Odes* are structured spatially, among them 'The Ecstasy'. The 11 stanzas of 'The Ecstasy' describe a visionary flight above mortality in a whirlwind (i), up where the 'Great' Britain for which civil wars were fought seems a mere 'northern speck' (ii), through the 'arched magazines' of the elements (iii), past the upper fire (iv) and the starry firmament (v) in which 'the joint eyes of night make up a perfect day', to the height of heaven itself, reached in the central Stanza vi. Here, above contradictions, above even paradox, reigns the undifferentiated bliss of the divine vision, the only direct mention of God:

Where am I now? Angels and God is here;
An unexhausted ocean of delight
Swallows my senses quite,
And drowns all What, or How, or Where.
Not Paul, who first did thither pass,
And this great world's Columbus was,
The tyrannous pleasure could express.
Oh 'tis too much for man! but let it ne'er be less.

[1] *Ibid.* 204–6.
[2] *Ibid.* 200, in a note on the 'incorrect' rich rhyming in 'To Dr Scarborough'.

Cowley avoids anticlimax after this central eminence by declining to narrate the ecstatic's descent. Instead he turns to another ascent, Elijah's. Thus he devotes 2 stanzas in the second half to the mystical chariot in which the prophet mounted 'with much of pomp and show / (As conquering kings in triumph go)'. In Stanza viii the fiery chariot, made 'of essences of gems, and spirit of gold' by 'chemic angels' art', has an alchemical significance, so that it echoes the elemental fire of the corresponding Stanza iv in the first half. The same suggestion of a scientific cosmic vehicle is developed in the final stanza's prophecy that Elijah's unknown destination will be revealed at the last: then all nature will aspire to a better being 'and mount herself, like him, to eternity in fire'. In short, the ode has two upward movements. One, visionary and individual, ascends to the poem's mid point; the other, cosmic and general, to its conclusion. Elijah's chariot belongs to the same tradition of Christian mystical exegesis as Messiah's chariot at the centre of *Paradise Lost*. But Cowley in part also reverts to the ancient triumph's glorification of the ultimate place, though only after he has reverently devoted the centre to God.[1]

THE CENTRE FINESSED: MARVELL

The convention of central accent invited finesses surpassing expectation. A symmetrical pattern might be left ambiguous, for example, or shared between two centres, or even ironically inverted so as to dignify a figure unfit for the place of honour. When such effects focused a poet's energies, their interpretation is vital to any full critical response. This is especially often the case with the satiric and political poetry of the later seventeenth century,[2] from which Andrew Marvell's (1621–

---

[1] Cowley's 'On the Death of Mr William Harvey' (ed. Waller 32) has a similar pattern, comprising 19 stanzas of which the central tenth rises to heaven: 'Large was his soul; as large a soul as e'er / Submitted to inform a body here. / High as the place 'twas shortly in heaven to have, / But low, and humble as his grave. / So high that all the virtues there did come / As to their chiefest seat / Conspicuous, and great; / So low that for me too it made a room.' The conclusion returns once more to Harvey, now installed in his place in heaven.

[2] Comparable finesses on political iconography occur in the graphic art of the period. Displacement of the sun in propaganda against Louis XIV, e.g., is discussed in Kantorowicz, 'Sol Oriens' 176. When Louis was negotiating with the Ottoman Sultan, the Bey of Algiers and the refugee King James II, his opponents of the League of Augsburg issued a medallion that lampooned the Sun King and the unholy alliance of 4 by showing, where the sun might have been expected, a devil IN FOEDERE QUINTUS, 'the fifth of the alliance'. See

78) stands out as the most subtle and elusive. It was a characteristic of his poetry, as Ruth Wallerstein has remarked, 'to reflect the complex elements of his attitude to the full'.[1]

Marvell could on occasion handle a centre almost simply. It is the third of the 5 stanzas of 'The Picture of Little T.C. in a Prospect of Flowers' that looks apprehensively forward to the nymph's future triumph:

O then let me in time compound,
And parly with those conquering eyes;
Ere they have tried their force to wound,
Ere, with their glancing wheels, they drive
In triumph over hearts that strive,
And them that yield but more despise,
Let me be laid,
Where I may see thy glories from some shade.[2]

Even this, however, has some subtlety of suggestion. Little T.C. will be so far above emotional involvement that she will celebrate a triumph over, as well as a triumph of, Love: her contempt for lovers presupposes a preliminary conquest of wanton Love, who will 'under her command severe, / See his bow broke and ensigns torn'. If the poem recalls Petrarch's *Trionfo della Pudicizia*, however, it is no less suggestive of the following *Trionfo della Morte*. Marvell's last stanza warns T.C. not to kill the buds, in case Flora, offended, 'nip in the blossom all our hopes and thee'.

A more typically Marvellian central accent is that of *An Horatian Ode upon Cromwell's Return from Ireland* (1650).[3] It is not the triumphant Cromwell who occupies the place of honour, as we might expect the ruler and triumphator to do. On the contrary, that place is restored to Charles. At the centre we find the royal actor magnani-

Fr Claude-François Menestrier, *Histoire du Roi Louis le Grand par les médailles*...(Paris 1689) Pl. xl. A different finesse is seen in a satirical print from Romeyn de Hooghe's *Aesop in Europe*, which shows the Sun King flanked by 3 zodiacal signs on either side, but losing control of his chariot to the *Stella vespertina* Mme de Maintenon; see Charles Boost, 'Cartoonist in the Lowlands', *Delta* (Amsterdam autumn 1958) 79–81 with illus.

[1] *Studies in Seventeenth-Century Poetic* (Madison and Milwaukee, Wis. 1965) 278.

[2] *The Poems and Letters of Andrew Marvell* ed. H. M. Margoliouth, 2 vols (Oxford 1927) i 38. In another simple instance, 'Upon the Death of Lord Hastings' (i 4 f.), the central passage develops a simile of a politic prince entertaining his ally's thought 'with richest triumphs': the prince is on one side of the central line, Hastings on the other.

[3] *Ibid*. i 87–90.

mously adorning the scaffold-stage and earning applause even from the soldiers' bloodguilty hands. But what implication should we see in this? That sovereignty is the king's *de iure*,[1] or that Cromwell nobly renounces sovereignty, surrendering the spoils of his triumph 'to lay them at the public's skirt'? That Charles achieved a moral victory by his regal comportment ('He nothing common did or mean'), or that his sovereignty was mere decorum, an actor's, devoid of substance?[2] The positioning of the king's execution evidently focuses a complex range of ideas and feelings about Cromwell's triumph.

This is not to deny that the complexity of the *Horatian Ode* has been exaggerated.[3] Some critics have found irony easily assimilable, but failed to sympathize with the seventeenth-century fondness for simple surface incongruities ('A Caesar he ere long to Gaul, / To Italy an Hannibal'). Others have doubted that Marvell means what he says, because what he says is so Machiavellian. Professor Mazzeo's achievement is to have made a Machiavellian *Horatian Ode* credible, by showing it consistent with a single political system, in which Cromwell figures as 'the man of virtù who creates a state from chaos, the central figure of *Il Principe*, and the legally self-binding new ruler of the *Discorsi*, who, having consolidated his power, tries to establish the rule of good laws and good customs enforced by good arms'.[4] This view may overestimate the directness of Machiavelli's influence, underestimate the difference between Italian self-assertive statehood and English theocracy,[5] and miss certain reluctances or qualifications in Marvell's admiration of Cromwell. But at least Mazzeo has succeeded in ruling out, once and for all, the possibility that the *Ode*

[1] A conclusion that would be conformable to the view put forward by L. W. Hyman in 'Politics and Poetry in Andrew Marvell', *PMLA* LXXIII (1958) 475–9, which stresses the poem's distinction between rightful and necessary governments.

[2] Joseph Anthony Mazzeo, 'Cromwell as Machiavellian Prince in Marvell's "An Horatian Ode"', *JHI* XXI (1960) 1–17, esp. 12.

[3] An extreme example of this tendency is L. D. Lerner's 'Marvell: *An Horatian Ode*' in *Interpretations* ed. John Wain (1955) 59–74.

[4] Mazzeo 17.

[5] He is surely wrong (9) to deny religious meaning to '"Tis madness to resist or blame / The force of angry heaven's flame.' And '. . . Much to the man is due' means little unless it marks a transition from providence to Cromwell's personal qualities. Prof. Mazzeo places a truer emphasis in 'Cromwell as Davidic King' in *Reason and the Imagination* ed. J. A. Mazzeo (1962), an essay with which the present argument, in drawing attention to a formal iconography of kingship often associated with the Biblical priest-king, is in full accord.

satirizes the Protector. We see now that Marvell was trying for a Horatian impartiality far removed from the partisanship disrupting the nation. He wanted to find a morally respectable attitude to Cromwell's government that would allow him to serve it honestly and loyally.

The *Horatian Ode* is far from being a simple poem, and we can even agree with Miss Wallerstein that it expresses ambivalence—strange if the unquestionably divided sympathies of the poet had found no expression in it.[1] Nevertheless, Marvell firmly decided to support Cromwell's government on rational grounds. And this decision energizes the Ode and informs its structure. Even the central accent, which seems so ambiguous, proves on closer examination to work in Cromwell's favour. The pattern is so balanced that both Charles and Cromwell are linked to Caesar; but one is a Caesar blasted by lightning (ll. 23 f.), the other a Caesar climacteric to servile states (101–4). At the centre, Charles's supremacy seems unrivalled—

He nothing common did or mean
Upon that memorable scene:
But with his keener eye
The axe's edge did try: 60

Nor called the gods with vulgar spite
To vindicate his helpless right,
But bowed his comely head,
Down as upon a bed.

This was that memorable hour
Which first assured the forced power (57–66)

—until we notice, more precisely, that the axe's edge bisects the *Ode's* 120 lines and exactly marks the 'memorable hour' of 60 line-minutes. Marvell's implication is ineluctable: the axe was directed with equal justice. Similarly when the image of the edge or line is carried on in the allusion to Pliny's anecdote:

So when they did design
The Capitol's first line,

[1] Cf. the attitude of Fairfax, who could express a wish that the day of Charles's execution 'from time be blotted quite... That so the credit of our nation might be saved', yet in the next line accept the event as providential: 'But if the power divine hath ordered this, / His will's the law, and our must acquiesce' (B.M. 11744, fol. 42). For a full discussion of Marvell's political attitude see John M. Wallace, *Destiny His Choice: The Loyalism of Andrew Marvell* (Cambridge 1968). With many of the conclusions reached in this book I am in agreement; though it unfortunately appeared too late to be given here the attention it deserves.

A bleeding head where they begun,
Did fright the architects to run;
And yet in that the state
Foresaw its happy fate. (67–72)

The allusion can only mean that Marvell's own country should like-wise fearlessly conclude that the line beginning the British Capitol was rightly placed.

Yet Marvell would not be Marvell unless he added a further quali-fication: Charles, himself tried, also in a sense 'the axe's edge did try'.[1] *Edge* has resonance here, hinting at a common use of *acies* to mean 'sharpness of eyesight',[2] and consequently implying that Charles tested his judges' justice before deciding not to call on the gods. In other words, the regime in power is always under judgement and known by its fruits.[3] At the end of the Ode a triumphant Crom-well in the alternate position of dignity holds the same blade of justice that at the centre was tried—experienced and judged—by Charles.

It has been said that in *The First Anniversary of the Government under O.C.* Marvell expresses a less complex attitude to Cromwell than in the *Horatian Ode*.[4] So far as central accent is concerned, how-ever, the later poem is just as unpredictable: Cromwell may now figure at the centre among triumphal motifs, but he does so in a manner far, it seems, from triumphant. As the chief event of 1654 Marvell has selected Cromwell's September 29 coach accident,[5] so that in the centre line, instead of a triumphator riding high on his pro-cessional chariot, we find 'Cromwell falling'.[6] The normal triumphal pattern appears to be grotesquely inverted. Yet this is no random effect, for the reader has been led to expect a triumph. The allegory of the Commonwealth as an 'animated city' develops notions of

---

[1] The surface meaning perhaps refers to an actual incident at the execution, when Charles may have sighted with one ('keener') eye along the blade of the axe; see Wallerstein 178 f.

[2] Occasionally also in English. *OED* s.v. *Edge* 1 5 b cites Sir Thomas Browne: 'The wise contriver hath drawn the pictures and outsides of things softly and amiably unto the natural edge of our eyes.'

[3] Consequently the pears grown by the private Cromwell in St. viii are made to correspond structurally with the laying of a kingdom, 'his first year's rents', at the 'public's skirt' in the eighth and ninth stanzas from the end (85–90).

[4] E.g. Wallerstein 164.

[5] The coach, drawn by 6 horses that were a present from the Count of Oldenburg, overturned in Hyde Park; see Margoliouth's note, i 252.

[6] Ed. Margoliouth i 108; l. 201 out of 402.

architectural symmetry and centrality through several paragraphs:[1] Cromwell is portrayed in the role of a sun ruler running with superhuman vigour '(sun-like) the stages of succeeding suns' (l. 8) through various temporal and astronomical images: and even mentions of planets, Saturn (16), Jupiter (38), Mars (59), form a sequence in Ptolemaic order that builds up expectation of the fourth and central planet Sol. But at the metrical centre the coach overturns. Though the expected manifestation of the sun ruler occurs, it assumes an unnatural form: 'It seemed the earth did from the centre tear; / It seemed the sun was fallen out of the sphere' (205 f.).

The continuation shows that we misinterpreted the accident, however. It was wrong to think in natural selfish terms; even if Cromwell had died, his fall would have been a triumphal ascent:

> thee triumphant hence the fiery car,
> And fiery steeds had borne out of the war,
> From the low world, and thankless men above,
> Unto the kingdom blest of peace and love:
> We only mourned our selves, in thine ascent,
> Whom thou hadst left beneath with mantle rent. (215–20)

The Protector is more than a king, and the divinely directed events of his rule cannot be judged by ordinary criteria. Marvell brilliantly combines the chariot of Elijah with the Platonic soul-chariot, imagining the forces of extremism as irrational drives that impede the political ascesis of the nation under the guidance of mind to the heavenly kingdom. Cromwell himself, who gave up his privacy 'to turn the headstrong people's charioteer', figures as the national intellect.

Miss Wallerstein (p. 165) rightly sets Cromwell's solar role in *The First Anniversary* against the background of Neoplatonic cosmology —particularly the sun's part in the Platonic myth of the work of the divine mind. But Cromwell is a *declarator temporis* in a more specific sense also: his era marks a new temporal cycle, a constructive cycle after the previous cycle of deterioration. He realizes, in fact, the *Politicus* myth of the Great Year. Ordinary monarchs, even 'though they all Platonic years should reign' (l. 17), would accomplish nothing;

[1] Especially at ll. 79 f. ('No quarry bears a stone so hardly wrought, / Nor with such labour from its centre brought'), 87 f. ('The common-wealth does through their centres all / Draw the circumference of the public wall'), 91–3, 244–8, 312 and 363.

but Cromwell 'the force of scattered time contracts, / And in one year the work of ages acts' (13 f.). Like the later image of 'foreshortened time' (139), this alludes to the idea of the Platonic year as a large-scale year of 'days' each equivalent to a natural year.[1] That Cromwell inaugurates a new Platonic era is confirmed by the frequent temporal images, as well as by the terrene motion and disturbance of the sun's course at the accident, which thus figures as the *anacyclesis* marking transition between cycles.[2] Millenarian and apocalyptic passages[3] express the same enthusiastic sense of a new age. Altogether, Marvell's fervour about the 'mysterious work' Cromwell could effect under divine guidance expresses the sense of liberation characteristic of early revolutionary phases. Such bliss was it in that dawn that a magnificent epic simile of unexpected sunrise after man's first night in Eden (325–42) can illustrate the recovery of Cromwell, who 'does with himself all that is good revive'. This non-monarchic application of the *Sol oriens* must once have had a devastating effect: it marks an era too.

Besides its central accent, *The First Anniversary* has an independent pattern of equal division. The 'mysterious work' of renovation is symbolized by elaborate architectural and musical *allegoriae*, for example the one that makes the Commonwealth a 'harmonious city' raised by a 'sacred lute' like Amphion's: 'Such was the wondrous order and concent,[4] / When Cromwell tuned the ruling instrument' (67 f.). Now the common element linking architecture and music— together with the harmony of the spheres from which these arts took their origin[5]—was the principle of proportion. Thus, Cromwell raises the new temple by finding a mean between war and peace, destruction and construction, 'founding a firm state by proportions true' (248). His political 'contignation' makes even contentious factions strengthen the structure: in the democratic senate 'the

---

[1] See *The Republic of Plato* ed. James Adam, 2 vols (Cambridge 1929) ii 202, 301. The Platonic Year is the interval that elapses before the planets all return to their original positions.   [2] *Politicus* 268 E; see Adam ii 298.

[3] On these, some of the best critical comment is to be found in James F. Carens, 'Andrew Marvell's Cromwell Poems', *Bucknell Review* VII (1957) 41–70.

[4] Harmony; punning between 'concent in music and consent of minds' (*OED* s.v. *Concent*), as *instrument* in the next line puns between 'lute' and 'legal document granting the Protector his title'.

[5] Cf. 47 f.: 'Learning a music in the region clear, / To tune this lower to that higher sphere.'

resistance of opposed minds, / The fabric as with arches stronger binds' (95 f.), under the crowning pun 'knit by the roof's protecting weight'. These ideas have a formal correlate in the paragraph structure, itself built by 'proportions true'. For there are 32 paragraphs, evenly divided into 2 portions of 16 each at the line describing the mourners left Elisha-like behind at Cromwell's supposed Elijah-like ascent.[1] The significance of this arrangement lies in the aptness of equal division to the 'mantle rent'; Elisha expressed his grief at Elijah's departure by dividing his robe: 'he cried, My father, my father, the chariot of Israel, and the horsemen thereof. And he saw him no more: and he took hold of his own clothes, and rent them in two pieces.'[2] Marvell's wish is that the spirit of Cromwell, charioteer of the new Israel, should rest on his 'mourners' as the fallen mantle of Elijah was assumed by Elisha. If

> a seasonable people still
> Should bend to his, as he to heaven's will,
> What we might hope. (133–5)

DRYDEN AND POPE

Except for his odes (pp. 113–5), Dryden places central accents more simply and broadly than Marvell. In the *Heroic Stanzas* (1659), for example, the questions

> How shall I then begin, or where conclude
> To draw a fame so truly circular?
> For in a round what order can be showed,
> Where all the parts so equal perfect are?[3]

[1] L. 220: 'Whom thou hadst left beneath with mantle rent.' For 32 as the justly divisible number, see p. 39. The line pattern formed by the paragraph divisions is as follows: *6 / 6 / 32 / 4 /* **8** */ 10 /* **8** */ 12 / 12 / 18 /* **8** */ 6 / 28 / 16 / 40 / 6 / / 8 / 10 / 10 /* **8** */ 8 / 14 / 4 / 6 / 4 / 18 / 10 / 4 / 18 / 6 / 46 /* **8**. The 7 paragraphs of 8 lines each (bold face) symbolize the 7 strings of the lute (65 f., 'his sacred lute creates / The harmonious city of the seven gates'), just as the 4 pairs of equal paragraphs mime the 'most equal' senators who 'as pillars keep the work upright' (93 f., in one of the paragraphs concerned). The equal paragraphs *6 / 6, 12 / 12, 10 / 10* and *8 / 8* exhibit harmonic concords in their numerical proportions. Thus $6:12 = 1:2$, the octave (diapason); $6:10 = 3:5$, the major sixth; $6:8 = 3:4$, sesquitertian; $12:10 = 6:5$, the minor third; and $12:8 = 3:2$, sesquialter (fifth, diapente). For the inclusion of non-Pythagorean musical proportions in architectural theory from the sixteenth century onward, see Wittkower 133.

[2] *II Kings* ii 12.

[3] Ll. 17–20; *The Poems of John Dryden* ed. James Kinsley, 4 vols (Oxford 1958) i 7.

are obviously meant to lead one to the centre. There, the 3 middle stanzas duly treat Cromwell's majesty, the central Stanza xix containing an image of 'sovereign gold'. In *Astraea redux* (1660) the regime has changed, but the reader again strikes sovereign gold in the central line. Perhaps Dryden honours Charles above his predecessor by making the gold this time of a superior, philosopher's variety— 'gold that chemists make'.[1] More explicitly but less exactly, 'Restores the exiled to her crown again' is near the centre of *To My Honoured Friend Sir Robert Howard* (1660).[2] And in *Absalom and Achitophel* (1681), the centre line ambiguously describes the London mob as 'lofty to a lawful prince restored' (though afraid of an unlawful conqueror).[3]

Dryden's heaviest central accent falls in *Mac Flecknoe* (1682):

The hoary prince in majesty appeared,
High on a throne of his own labours reared.
At his right hand our young Ascanius sate
Rome's other hope, and pillar of the state.[4]

Both the enthronement and the shared sovereignty here imitate in burlesque Latinus' enthronement at the centre of the *Aeneid*.[5] The 'young Ascanius' Shadwell is to succeed Richard Flecknoe–Aeneas, just as the original Aeneas succeeded Latinus. Complicating this allusion, however, are others to the enthronement of Milton's Messiah— itself an imitation of Virgil's central enthronement—and to the anti-triumph of Satan and his 'perfect image' Sin.[6] And when Flecknoe leaves his drugget robe to Shadwell (the mantle falling 'to the young prophet's part, / With double portion of his father's art'[7]) those who recall *II Kings* ii 9–13, or Marvell's numerological treatment of the division of Elisha's robe, will enjoy yet another implication of the symmetrical structure.

With Pope comes a change to symmetry less precise spatially. His poetry's substance is often structurally balanced and its form may

[1] L. 162 of 323; ed. Kinsley i 20.
[2] L. 50 of 106; ed. Kinsley i 14. The last 4 lines, the prophecy, are printed as a distinct unit, and perhaps should be excluded from the count; in which case the crown is more exactly located.
[3] L. 516 of 1031; ed. Kinsley i 230.
[4] Ll. 106–9 of 217; ed. Kinsley i 267 f. My italicization of the central line.
[5] See p. 62 f.
[6] Discussed in Michael Wilding, 'Allusion and Innuendo in *Mac Flecknoe*', *EC* XIX (1969) 355–70.   [7] Ll. 216 f.; ed. Kinsley i 271.

give the impression of being equally architectural; but the symmetry usually proves inexact numerically. There are occasional exceptions. Thus, at the centre of the *Epistle to Dr Arbuthnot* (1734) we see the literary dictator Addison 'give his little senate laws / And sit attentive to his own applause'[1] on the throne of the central line. The epistle *To Mr Addison, Occasioned by His Dialogue on Medals* (1720) is probably another exception, of particular interest for its evidence that Pope knew something of the iconography of the triumph.[2] It reviews various triumphal forms in which ambition has tried to perpetuate her name; among them the medal, the most centrally organized form of all:[3]

> she now contracts her vast design,
> And all her triumphs shrink into a coin.
> A narrow orb each crowded conquest keeps,
> Beneath her palm here sad Judea weeps:
> Now scantier limits the proud arch confine. (23–7)

Appropriately, the central couplet presents a visual epitome of the triumph triumphed over by Addison: 'In one short view subjected to your eye / Gods, emp'rors, heroes, sages, beauties, lie.'[4] This couplet divides the other 32 equally into the familiar *16 / 16* pattern. In a poem so much concerned with Roman custom, it is natural to look also at the end, anciently the triumphator's processional place. Sure enough, the conclusion (63–72) honours Craggs as the 'other Pollio', and an earlier version, without this conclusion, ended at the lines 'Or in fair series laurelled bards be shown, / A Virgil theme, and here an Addison'.[5] Even in such instances, however, Pope's revision and alterations blur the symmetry and efface all impression of hard-edged construction.

The *Epistles to Several Persons* are more characteristic. Here again there seem to be two positions of eminence, central and final; or,

---

[1] Ll. 209 f. of 420; *The Poems of Alexander Pope* gen. ed. John Butt, 11 vols (1939–69) iv ed. J. Butt (corr. edn 1961) 111.

[2] On the circular structure of the content of *To Mr Addison*, see Howard Erskine-Hill, 'The Medal Against Time: A Study of Pope's epistle *To Mr Addison*', *JWI* xxviii (1965) 274–98.

[3] Ernst H. Kantorowicz traces the influence of coins in the revival of the French sun-rulership cult in 'Oriens Augusti—Lever du Roi'.

[4] Ll. 33 f.; *Poems*, vi ed. Norman Ault and John Butt (corr. edn 1964) 203. I omit from the count ll. 5–10, which were only added in edns from 1726.

[5] See *ibid.* 205 f.

alternatively, an evil dominating figure may occupy the centre while an ideal figure comes last. *To a Lady* (1735), for example, has great Atossa at the centre and Martha Blount at the end; *To Burlington* (1731), the falsely magnificent Timon at the centre and a vision of imperial works and worthy kings at the end. Such substantive dispositions encourage one to look for exact symmetry, especially in view of the spatial terms Pope used to describe the *Epistles* and their Aristotelian ethics.[1] But the formal structures turn out to be only roughly proportionate. Thus Bathurst the man of goodwill comes somewhat later than the centre of the epistle bearing his name, with the ideal Man of Ross later still. Near, but not at, the centre is the line "'Tis George and Liberty that crowns the cup'.[2] True, the centre itself coincides with a transition from the miserly Cotta to his extravagant son ('Not so his son', 197th out of 394 lines), and thence to the generous Bathurst: '(For what to shun will no great knowledge need, / But what to follow, is a task indeed.)' (201 f.). But the second half can scarcely be regarded as the exclusive domain of ideal figures. Bathurst knows 'that secret rare, between the extremes to move / Of mad good-nature, and of mean self-love' (227 f.) and perhaps for that reason occupies a position that in many readers' recollections will *seem* central. In spatial terms, however, this centrality is less precise than a Marvell or a Milton would have made it. From a numerological standpoint one must agree with Bateson's opinion that 'the logical contrasts and the symmetrical structure are much clearer in Spence's notes than they are in the *Epistles* themselves'.[3]

After Pope, the convention of central accent lapsed, for reasons to be discussed in the next chapter. It had been abandoned so completely by the end of the eighteenth century that when stanza forms regained popularity their function was no longer even understood in spatial

---

[1] E.g. 'The middle the point for virtue', Joseph Spence, *Observations* ed. J. M. Osborn, 2 vols (Oxford 1966) i 131 (1–7 May 1730); or Pope's remark that the significance of characters in *To Bathurst* lies in their positions and relations to the others ('To send you any of the particular verses [on the Man of Ross] will be much to the prejudice of the whole; which if it has any beauty, derives it from the manner in which it is *placed*, and the *contrast* (as the painters call it) in which it stands, with the pompous figures': Letter to Tonson Sr, 7 June 1732; *Correspondence* ed. George Sherburn, iii (Oxford 1956) 290).

[2] L. 205 out of 394 (1732 edn); *Poems*, iii Pt. 2 ed. F. W. Bateson (2nd edn 1961) 110. Note that *hecatombs* are mentioned in 1732 l. 201.

[3] *Ibid.* p. xxv.

terms. Several exceptions prove the rule. Gray, and to some extent Collins, occasionally exploited architectural possibilities in organizing stanzas: Fielding, and Sterne in *Tristram Shandy*, carried the old conventions over into new forms of prose fiction.[1] But in general not only had the significance of the spatial centre gone, but even the memory of its former significance.

[1] See p. 123 on the structure of Gray's *Elegy*. Fielding's numerology is discussed in Douglas Brooks, 'Symbolic Numbers in Fielding's *Joseph Andrews*', *Silent Poetry* ed. Alastair Fowler (1970) 234–60.

5. Styles of symmetry

In previous chapters we discussed similarities rather than differences between formal patterns. Differences of historical period were largely ignored: a synchronic descriptive method seemed the simplest way to a grammar of spatial conventions. The present chapter, however, makes a tentative essay at comparing and ordering the styles of various authors diachronically. Since we are treating structures with a spatial aspect, it has seemed appropriate to admit certain art historical terms and therefore to accept the obligation these carry to explore the connection between literary styles and the styles of visual art. In choosing this direction I am aware of the arguments, partly valid, against applying terms denoting art styles to literary forms. The terms *renaissance, mannerist* and *baroque*, for example, have varied widely in their connotation, and even in their application, from critic to critic. But as René Wellek pointed out in 'The Concept of Baroque in Literary Scholarship' this is no objection to their continued use. The terms have already proved themselves by provoking valuable controversy about the problems of delimiting periods and of clarifying interactions of different arts. The critic cannot expect static terms with permanent contents: he must be prepared, if he is to say anything about the relation of the sister arts, to make propositions about art styles that are themselves in process of continual redefinition. After all, every art historical—and literary historical—grouping, whether according to period or to style, necessarily involves falsification, since all are relatively simplistic abstractions from the confused and complex welter of the historical process. Yet we continue to make such groupings and to use such terms and to refine our understanding of them and through them.

The term mannerism is better, not worse, defined now than it was twenty years ago; even though it has come to have more uses. Most scholars would agree about at least some of the meanings of the term and on its application to some artists and authors. Moreover, it is possible to specify to some extent how one means to use such a term. Thus, I regard it as based partly on external style, partly on ideology, and therefore as delimited in its primary application, even if only loosely and indirectly, by chronological occurrence. It connotes a set of heterogeneous elements including both structural properties (such as formal motifs and stylistic habits) and internal characteristics (such as favourite moods and substantive preoccupations) expressive of ethos or of group psychology. In short, I concur with much of Wellek's position. However, I take *mannerism* to be now firmly enough established to replace *baroque* as a label for the early phase of that style. And I prefer Shearman's account of mannerist style, with his stress of complexity and finesse, to accounts such as Pevsner's that emphasize emotional disturbance or tension. (Thus, for example, the highly patterned rhetorical styles of the sixteenth century are to be regarded as mannerist, even when unaccompanied by signs of 'malaise, double vision, and tormented sensibility', and we are free to reject Wylie Sypher's difficult denial of the term to the conceited style of much Elizabethan literature.) I wish I could also have used Rudolf Wittkower's clarifications of *mannerism* and *baroque*, for which I have much admiration. But the tentative preliminary character of the present enquiry prevented this. Analogies with gross differences of style are as much as we are ready to cope with at this stage: finer distinctions such as those between different phases of mannerism are beyond us. For the commonest pitfall in this field is to attempt too much explanation before even descriptive adequacy has been achieved.

The only well grounded objection to the extension of art historical terms to literature is not a theoretical but a practical one: namely, that it has tended to proceed by somewhat vague yet arbitrary intuitions and unsupported analogies. The present approach may, I hope, go some way towards meeting this objection. For it draws analogies between aspects of literature and of visual art (particularly architecture) that are undeniably comparable and indeed commensurate: spatial proportion and symmetry. Of course there is far more to the analogy between the arts than this. And the danger of false analogies remains: it will not do to identify stanzaic poems with palazzo façades, stanzas with columns and stanza patterns with orders, merely because these casual liaisons tempt the fancy. But the structural approach, though limited, may yet arrive, if it is made with care, at firmer results than can be imagined from the heights of speculation commanded in fantasy by the analogist of ethos and unsubstantiated impression. At least it may avoid such diffuse abstractions as Deutschbein's 'inner form' and even such arbitrary assertions, sensitive but still unargued, as we find in Wylie Sypher's *Four Stages of Renaissance Style*. Changes in structural style are not the whole story of literature's relation to visual art: but they may provide a useful check on analogies of other sorts.

CLASSICAL RECESSED SYMMETRY

The Homeric epic already displays elaborate symmetry. As Cedric Whitman has shown, the structure of the *Iliad* depends throughout on the architectonic device of 'ring composition', that is, a return to things previously mentioned (or things resembling them) in reverse order.[1] The first and last books, for example, have a balanced pattern that in tabular form looks like this.[2]

a	Plague and funerals		
	b	Quarrel of allies, seizure of Briseis	Book i
		c Thetis with Achilles	
		d Thetis with Zeus	
		d Thetis with Zeus	Book xxiv
		c Thetis with Achilles	
	b	Reconciliation of enemies, restitution of Hector's body	
a	Funeral of Hector		

Such recessed symmetries, observed in Homer's work since ancient times,[3] are manifested by every structural element—not only by the

[1] Cedric H. Whitman, *Homer and the Heroic Tradition* (Cambridge, Mass. 1958) 253.   [2] *Ibid.* 259 f.

[3] *Ibid.* 254. The term *recessed symmetry* is L. Richardson's: see his *Poetical Theory in Republican Rome* (New Haven, Conn. 1944) 132.

episode structure within individual books, but even by the scheme of days of the overall action.[1]

The structural approach of *Homer and the Heroic Tradition* has been criticized by G. S. Kirk, *The Songs of Homer* (Cambridge 1962), who regards the circular patterns merely as inevitable logical developments of the story. But analysis of the famous and much-imitated epic catalogue of the Greek army (*Il.* ii 494–759) strongly confirms Whitman's theory. For the catalogue is another example of ring composition; and its exact numerical patterns can hardly be explained away as logical necessities. Here Whitman nods, for he treats the passage as an unstructured 'simple vision of the Achaean panorama' (262). Yet the detachments form the array *8 | Agamemnon's | 5 | Odysseus' | 5 | Achilles' | 8*, so that the wise Odysseus comes exactly at the point of balance, spatially as morally, between the quarrelling rivals.[2] Odysseus and Agamemnon are also linked in another pattern concealed in the catalogue. Its entries close with stock lines giving numbers of ships per detachment, and these numbers are separately ordered in a less obvious recessed symmetry *342 | Agamemnon to Odysseus | 342*. The latter array becomes meaningful when we recall that at the council Odysseus takes up Agamemnon's ancestral sceptre, an important symbol of power.[3]

Professor Whitman relates the structural style of the *Iliad* to the dominant decorative style in the visual art of its period: 'The principle of circularity, including concentricity, or framing by balanced similarity and antithesis, is one of the chief dynamic forces underlying the symmetry of Geometric vase design.'[4] From its smallest elements (such as the rhetorical device of *hysteron proteron*) to its largest (book structure) the symmetry of the *Iliad* is of its time. Indeed, the grouping of books according to the scheme *2 | 5 | 2 | 5 | 2 | 5 | 2*, omit-

[1] Whitman 257; see p. 129 below.
[2] 1 *Boeotians* | 2 *Minyans* | 3 *Phocians* | 4 *Locrians* | 5 *Abantes* | 6 *Athenians* | 7 *Aias' ships* | 8 *Diomedes' ships* | 9 *Mycenaeans: AGAMEMNON* | 10 *Lacedaemonians* | 11 *Nestor's ships* | 12 *Arcadians* | 13 *Elians* | 14 *Echinadians* | 15 *Ithacans: ODYSSEUS* | 16 *Aetolians* | 17 *Cretans* | 18 *Rhodians* | 19 *Symans* | 20 *Calydnians* | 21 *Myrmidons: ACHILLES* | 22 *Phylacians* | 23 *Pheraeans* | 24 *Meliboeans* | 25 *Oechalians* | 26 *Ormenians* | 27 *Argissans* | 28 *Enienes* | 29 *Magnetes*. The numbers of ships are: *50 | 30 | 40 | 40 | 40 | 50 | 12 | 80 | Agamemnon's 100 | 60 | 90 | 60 | 40 | 40 | Odysseus' 12 | 40 | 80 | 9 | 3 | 30 | 50 | 40 | 10 | 7 | 30 | 40 | 40 | 20 | 40*.
[3] Whitman 160 f.
[4] *Ibid.* 255; cf. 253 and Ch. v *passim*.

ting the problematic Book x, seems to have a specific analogue 'in the alternations of narrow and wide elements in Geometric ware'.[1] Yet these patterns may not have been purely decorative: in a suggestive passage (254) Professor Whitman notes that they depend on the fundamental categories of similarity and opposition that Plato was to embody in his cycles of Sameness and Difference.

In Latin poetry we may distinguish two main developments in structural style. The less common, already mentioned in an earlier chapter, was the appearance of centrally accented symmetry of an *a b C b a* type. Perhaps in reflection of social ceremonial forms, the centre occasionally took on a sovereign significance, as in the symbolic structural scheme of Virgil's *Eclogues*. This scheme, discovered for our time by Paul Maury, accepted and developed by Perret and Duckworth, and finally explained in literary-critical terms by Brooks Otis, is set out in tabular form below.[2]

i   Roman: loss and recovery of a homestead
   ii   Theocritean: erotic narrative of Corydon
      iii   Theocritean: Amoebean dialogue
         iv   Return of *Saturnia regna*
            v   Deification of Daphnis-Caesar
         vi   Passing of *Saturnia regna*
      vii   Theocritean: Amoebean dialogue
   viii   Theocritean: erotic narratives of Damon and Alphesiboeus
ix   Roman: recovery and loss of a homestead
         x   Gallus-Daphnis.

For full details and for discussion of the correspondences between paired eclogues the reader is referred to Otis. The point that concerns us here, and that Otis does not mention, is the central emphasis. Placing the eclogue devoted to the stellification of Daphnis-Caesar at the centre of the recessed pattern makes it triumphal in character. The scheme becomes one not merely of balance but of celebration of the deified Julius.

[1] *Ibid.* 284.
[2] Brooks Otis, *Virgil: A Study in Civilized Poetry* (Oxford 1964) 129; see also Paul Maury, 'Le secret de Virgile et l'architecture des Bucoliques', *Lettres d'Humanité* III (1944) 71–147; Jacques Perret, *Virgile l'homme et l'œuvre* (Paris 1952) 17–29, 111–120; and G. E. Duckworth, *AJP* LXXV (1954) 1–15. Cf. Otis's analysis (199) of a symmetrical passage in the *Georgics*, with 'the triumph of human song' as the central term.

Similarly with the structural scheme of the *Aeneid*, which is well analysed by Otis[1] as symmetrical about Book vii. The table below shows the main elements of the structure.

       i Juno: storm: peace
ii Defeat of the Trojans (Aeneas)
  iii Interim of wandering (Aeneas' uncertainty)
    iv Tragedy of Dido
     v Ship-burning (Aeneas): interlude of games: Nisus and Euryalus
      vi The future: show of heroes
       vii Peace: Juno: war
      viii The future: shield
     ix Ship-burning (Turnus): interlude of *Aristeiae*: Nisus and Euryalus
    x Tragedy of Pallas
  xi Interim of movement (Turnus' uncertainty)
xii Victory of the Trojans (Aeneas)

But we cannot fully understand this arrangement without reference to the significance of the central place. It is to answer the question *qui reges* that Virgil reinvokes the Muse at vii 37: it is to emphasize Latinus' sovereignty that he makes the throne of Latium and the poem's metrical centre coincide with the centre of the episodic structure.[2]

More characteristic of Latin poetry, however, was a second development of structural style. This tended towards a preference for recessed symmetries without a central accent, often without any central term at all. Among many examples from individual books of the *Aeneid* I choose the opening of Book i, as analysed by Otis (228). This analysis is shown in tabular form below (numbers refer to lines).

a Scheme of fate (1–7)
 b Juno's wrath (8–23)
  c The storm (34–123)

  c Calm (124–222)
 b Venus' perturbation (223–53)
a Jupiter's prophecy (254–96).

[1] 217 ff., 344 and 418.   [2] See p. 62 f.

Neptune's demonstration of sovereignty over the waves (124–56), though it might possibly be construed as a separate term, to give a centrally accented scheme of the type *a b c D c b a*, far more obviously and easily forms an antithesis to Aeolus' sovereignty over the winds (50–86). Even where symmetry was of the *a b c b a* type, the central term most often went unaccented. Kenneth Quinn, who finds tripartite arrangements in the episode structure of each entire book, treats *Aeneid* vi 9–263, for instance, as comprising an odd number of sections—*The sibyl A: at the temple of Apollo | Misenus A | Aeneas finds the golden bough | Misenus B | The sibyl B: at Avernus*—but we have no reason to regard the third section as symbolically central.[1]

In other genres, the same preference for unaccented symmetry obtained. Even Virgil's Fifth Eclogue, though it is itself the central term of an overall scheme of eclogues, exhibits an internal metrical symmetry of even-numbered terms. The line lengths of the speeches of its dialogue form the array

INTRODUCTION   *a*   *b*   *c*   *d*   *d*   *c*   *b*   *a*
3 / 4 / 1 / 1 /   3 / 3 / 4 / 25 / 8 / 3 / 25 / 4 / 3 / 3

And N. E. Collinge has described many similar patterns in the structure of Horace's *Odes*—generally of a looser, less numerically exact kind.[2]

Regularity and simplicity characterize classical recessed symmetry. Whether of an *a b b a* or unaccented *a b a* type, its iconographic function (indicating the place of honour) is less important than its co-ordinative function (linking similar or antithetic elements). Often it is thematically expressive, as in the book structure of *Aeneid*. But at other times it seems an exclusively formal device, communicating aesthetic qualities of balance and ordered variety.[3]

RENAISSANCE TRIUMPHAL STYLE

In late antiquity, the style of symmetry, if somewhat more conceited and metrically neater, remained essentially unchanged. Christian

---

[1] *Virgil's Aeneid: a Critical Description* (1968) 160 ff.
[2] N. E. Collinge, *The Structure of Horace's Odes* (1961).
[3] I have ignored a different approach to classical numerology, found in George E. Duckworth, *Structural Patterns and Proportions in Vergil's Aeneid: a Study in Mathematical Composition* (Ann Arbor, Mich. 1962). Duckworth's demonstration of golden sections seems to me methodologically unsound because of its use of approximation; though its aim is not necessarily mistaken.

literature, however, introduced different principles of composition, whereby numerical patterns had specific symbolic content, according to a system of pious associations with the numbers used. This method of number symbolism, which took its programme from patristic Biblical Poetics and most of its material from exegesis of the numbers (both substantive and formal, actual and supposed) in Holy Scripture, continued in use throughout the Middle Ages.[1] It embraced symmetry, since symmetry was Scriptural; but it invariably stressed the centre and endowed it with an implication of divine sovereignty. At the same time, knowledge of purely structural recessed symmetry survived in a coexistent secular tradition—perhaps thanks to intensive study of Virgil, as Michael Batts seems to suggest.[2] Thus in the Twelfth Aventiure of the *Nibelungenlied* there is symmetry of an only mildly accented *a b c b a* type:[3]

a   Introduction: decision to send invitation

   b   Rising action: messengers depart for Xanten

     c   Climax, delivery of message

   b   Falling action: return of messengers

a   Conclusion: report of news: preparation of welcome

Biblical number symbolism predominated over structural symmetry, however. The result was an intricate and esoteric style of composition, as a glance at the volume of criticism provoked by the numerology of a single medieval poem will show.[4]

Early renaissance symmetry usually belongs to an *a B a* type. The central accent is strongly pronounced, the broad lines of the structure

[1] On the exegetic tradition, see Maren-Sofie Røstvig, 'Structure as Prophecy'; on Biblical Poetics, Curtius, Index s.v. *Bible: Biblical Poetics.*

[2] Michael S. Batts, 'The Origins of Numerical Symbolism and Numerical Patterns in Medieval German Literature', *Traditio* xx (1964) 462–71.

[3] *Ibid.* 469. For other examples, see J. A. Huisman, *Neue Wege zur dichterischen und musikalischen Technik Walthers von der Vogelweide, mit einem Exkurs über die symmetrische Zahlenkomposition im Mittelalter* (Utrecht 1950) and C. A. Robson, 'The Technique of Symmetrical Composition in Medieval Narrative Poetry' in *Studies in Medieval French Presented to Alfred Ewert* (Oxford 1961). It is possible, however, that the numbers forming the pattern of Walther's *Marienleich* have a symbolic value.

[4] E.g. on *Pearl*, Coolidge Otis Chapman, 'Numerical Symbolism in Dante and *The Pearl*', *MLN* LIV (1939); Maren-Sofie Røstvig, 'Numerical Composition in *Pearl*: a Theory', *English Studies* XLVIII (1967); and P. M. Kean and Russell A. Peck, both in *N & Q* CCX (1965).

clearly evident. Thus, every reader of Chaucer's *Troilus* recognizes that the height of the protagonist's good fortune, if not the metrical location of this 'high place',[1] comes in the middle phase of both action and structure. Substantive symmetries coincide with formal, mutually reinforcing each other. Even when the symmetry is of an *a b b a* type, however, central emphasis can be managed, as in Petrarch's *Trionfo della Pudicizia*. We saw its characters form the replicated pattern *16 | | 8 | 8*, with the second half, like the whole, divided evenly. Nevertheless, Laura dominates the triumph from one of the central places of the large array, the other being occupied by the last of the 16 virtues, Castità. Here again one is struck by the reinforcement and clarity of structures. Numerical patterns simply render more emphatic what is obviously the Triumph of Laura's Chastity.

The elaborate symmetry of Dante's *Divina commedia* is more strongly accented still. In the central canto of the central book comes what Charles Singleton describes as the pivotal point of the action, Dante's 'conversion' towards the power he finds at the heart of the universe.[2] This metrically central canto contains the theologically central argument that love is the dynamic force moving both creator and creature. This argument overlaps symmetrically into the adjacent Cantos xvi and xviii: beginning and ending with free will (*libero arbitrio*), it extends just 25 *terzine* in each direction.[3] Moreover, the line totals of the centre 7 cantos form a symmetrical array of the type *a b b C b b a*:[4]

xiv	xv	xvi	xvii	xviii	xix	xx
151	145	145	139	145	145	151

[1] P. 65 above. The complaint of Anelida in Chaucer's *Anelida and Arcite* appears to have a modified form of recessed symmetry: *Proem* (9 lines) / *Strophe* ($4 \times 9 + 16 + 9$) / *Antistrophe* ($4 \times 9 + 16 + 9$) / *Conclusion* (9), with the last stanza of strophe and antistrophe distinguished by consistent internal rhyme. Repetition of the first line as the last further suggests ring composition. See *The Complete Works*, ed. F. N. Robinson (rev. edn 1957) 790.

[2] Charles S. Singleton, 'The Poet's Number at the Centre', *MLN* LXXX (1965) 7.

[3] *Ibid.* 1 f. Singleton explains the 25s by summing their digits ($2 + 5 = 7$); but a simpler explanation lies in the addition $25 + 25 = 50$; for 50 was the number of penitence and remission of sins (a symbolism based on the custom of the Jubilee Year: see Valeriano 465, Bongo 531 ff.).

[4] Singleton 4; cf. 6, where an explanation is again offered in terms of summation of digits: $1 + 5 + 1 = 7$, $1 + 4 + 5 = 10$ and the centre verse of xvii is the 70th. Though one dislikes such irrational manipulations they were practised in Dante's time and may be intended here.

The narrative action reinforces this pattern, since in the central Canto xvii Dante ascends to the Cornice of the Slothful, the fourth and central circle of the 7 of Purgatory proper. One notices the recurrence of the *3 / 1 / 3* motif of solar sovereignty, to be met yet again in the pageant of the Church in *Purgatorio* xxix.[1]

The 7 *liste* of the Pageant also belong to a numerological pattern. For they correspond to 7 stars grouped 4 and 3 that earlier symbolized the Cardinal and Theological Virtues. These 7 star-virtues come at *Purgatorio* viii 85–93, before the entry to Purgatory proper, so that they form, with the *liste* in the earthly paradise, a spatially symmetrical arrangement:

viii	ix	x–xxvii	xxviii	xxix
7 virtues as stars	Gate	7 cornices of Purgatory	Paradise	7 virtues as candles

The scheme is obviously dominated by number symbolisms.[2] On the other hand, one can discern a purely structural symmetry in the overall grouping of cantos in the *Purgatorio*, as set out in the table below.

CORNICES

CANTOS	i–vii	viii	ix	x–xiii	xiv–xx	xxi–xxvii	xxviii	xxix	xxx–xxxiii
CANTO-TOTALS	7	1	1	4	7	7	1	1	4
	7 star-virtues			Line-totals symmetrical about xvii			7 candle-virtues		

Although this grouping could be interpreted broadly in terms of the centrally accented tripartite array *13 / 7 / 13*, its finer structure displays a less symbolic symmetry of the form *a b b c A a b b c*. Such ambiguity of grouping, inherent in renaissance numerology from the beginning, was later to be taken up and featured by mannerist poets. In the *Divina commedia*, however, it remains a minor effect subordinated to the broad design.

---

[1] See pp. 36 f.
[2] E.g. 7 virtues, 7 Gifts of the Spirit, 7 sacraments, 7 beatitudes, 4 Cardinal Virtues, 4 evangelists, 4 beasts, etc. See further in *The Comedy of Dante Alighieri the Florentine: Cantica ii: Purgatory* tr. Dorothy L. Sayers (1955) 202 f.

The major effect is of mutually confirming, centrally accented symmetries expressing the cosmic sovereignty of love. Again and again Dante repeats the same pattern in different elements of the poem, substantive and formal. To all the instances already mentioned we might add others, such as a *3 / 1 / 3* arrangement of days in the chronological scheme (the action of Canto xvii falling on the central day, Easter Monday[1]). This is symmetry in the original, Vitruvian sense—'appropriate harmony arising out of the details': 'the correspondence of each detail to the form of the design as a whole'.[2] Everything reinforces the main, comparatively simple, design, which has little ambiguity or obscurity about it. Many-faceted as it is, the structure must have seemed crystal-clear and brilliantly emphatic to Dante's first readers.

MANNERIST ASYMMETRY, DIFFICULTY AND FINESSE

With the possible exception of some of Chaucer's, there are few good poems in English in a renaissance style. Sir Thomas Wyatt (1503–42) and Henry Howard, Earl of Surrey, though sometimes described as renaissance poets, already produce mannerist structures. Their manner of handling symmetry has a conceited sharpness or finesse that sets it off from the triumphal style of Dante and Petrarch.

Wyatt's 'My lute awake'[3] consists of 8 stanzas, each with a variable refrain line. But Stanzas i and viii have the same refrain 'My lute be still, for I have done', and many other resemblances between these stanzas—the address to the lute, verbal resonances ('And end that I have now begun': 'And ended is that we begun') and identical rhyme words—combine with this to suggest a circular return to the starting-point. The work completed being a song, one naturally thinks of this eight-stanza pattern as representing an octave, in which the first and last notes similarly correspond.[4] Moreover, since the eighth stanza-note by repeating the tonic begins a new octave, the array can be

---

[1] See below, p. 131.
[2] Vitruvius, *De archit.* I ii 4: 'Item symmetria est ex ipsius operis membris conveniens consensus ex partibusque separatis ad universae figurae speciem ratae partis responsus.'
[3] *Collected Poems of Sir Thomas Wyatt* ed. Kenneth Muir and Patricia Thomson (Liverpool 1969) No. 66, pp. 48–50.
[4] Cf. the similar pattern of Dryden's St Cecilia's Day Ode, discussed in Alastair Fowler and Douglas Brooks, 'The Structure of Dryden's *Song for St Cecilia's Day, 1687*', *EC* XVII (1967) 438 f.

construed as $7 + 1$. In the first group of 7 stanza-notes, Stanza iv is the central term and appropriately refers to a triumph. For the first time the lover's cruel mistress—'Proud of the spoil that thou hast got / Of simple hearts thorough love's shot'—is addressed in direct speech: the 'unkind' triumphantly occupies the central line.

With equal plausibility, however, one might construe the stanza-octave as $1 + 7$, in which case the central stanza would be v; with its prophecy of just vengeance, and the central line would enthrone the *Sol iustitiae*—'Think not alone under the sun / Unquit to cause thy lovers plain'. In fact, the song has two 'central' stanzas and a double system of structural symmetries. At first the imagery seems symmetrical about the lady's triumph: the hard marble of ii pairs with the cruel rocks of iii and the sun of v with the moon of vi to give an array of the form *a a B c c*. But the structure as a whole works against this shape of things, so that the lady's triumphal position becomes untenable. Thus, the 2 central stanzas iv and v have identical refrains, and the refrains of vi and vii are linked by their omission of any mention of the lute. Moreover, vi and vii also belong together substantively through their joint development of a flash-forward to the lady's remorse. The overall symmetry, in short, is of even-numbered terms, symbolizing the justice of equal division,[1] as shown in the table below.

	Content	Refrain type
i	Address to lute	a
ii	Stone	b
iii	Rocks	b′
iv	Lady's triumph	c
v	God's retribution	c
vi	Lady's remorse	d
vii	Lady's remorse	d′
viii	Address to lute	a

---

[1] For Justice as a Pythagorean epithet of 8, see Bongo 324 (its basis is the possibility of repeated equal division, as with 32). Wyatt's poem has other incidental number symbolisms: e.g. the avenging sun's location in St. v (for 5 as the number of justice and sovereignty, see Fowler 34 f., 206 f. with refs.) and l. 23 (the number of retribution for sin: Bongo 441), or the moon's location in l. 28 (days in a lunar month).

Once completed, the structural pattern implies that the retribution of the *Sol iustitiae* will exactly repay the unnatural lady's cruelty.

The most noticeable stylistic feature of this structure is its finesse. Wyatt almost completes one pattern (the expected symmetry centring on the lady's triumph), only to change it at the last moment into another: instead of simple emphatic symmetry about a single axis he contrives a subtler scheme of double, unequally important axes; until within the limits of a short lyric he succeeds in packing ambiguous complexities of stanza-grouping, of which I have mentioned only the most notable.[1]

Henry Howard, Earl of Surrey (1517–47), though often linked with Wyatt, really belongs to a younger generation with different poetic ideals. His verse is neoclassical; both in content and in form it draws inspiration from Virgil's more often than from Petrarch's. Emrys Jones's comment on the verbal style of the *Aeneid* translation—'The reader senses a continual striving after balance, parallelism, antithesis, symmetry and pleasurable asymmetry'[2]—applies with almost equal truth to Surrey's other poems. He sometimes carries symmetry into small-scale forms, such as patterns of syllabic distribution:[3]

When Windsor walls sustained my wearied arm

| I | 2 | I | 2 | I | 2 | I |

The very minuteness of this patterning (or perhaps it is the deliberate thoroughness) produces in the end an un-Virgilian impression, however. The extremity of stylistic effect seems more mannerist than neoclassical.

Surrey's epitaph on Wyatt, whose accented centre was noticed above (p. 70), seems to have a simple structure based on recessed symmetry. Several of the 9 full stanzas contain images matching those in corresponding stanzas on the other side of the sovereign centre. Thus Fortune appears only in iii and vii, and the smithy images (ii: hammers, anvil) correspond to the image of Nature's mould (viii). This structure is shown in the table overleaf.

---

[1] Omitting e.g. any mention of grouping by grammatical structure (4 stanzas, i–iii and viii, address the lute: 4 address the lady).

[2] *Poems* ed. Jones p. xvii.

[3] Cf. Jones's analysis of 'Behight by vow unto the chaste Minerve' (137) as 2/1/1/2/1/1/2 syllables.

i	ii	iii	iv	v	vi	vii	viii	ix
Intro-duction	Manufac-turing imagery	Fortune		King		Fortune	Manufac-turing imagery	Con-clu-sion
a	b		c	d		c	b	a

But Surrey finesses on this simple symmetry in several ways. First, he associates the 7 parts of Wyatt's mortal nature treated in the 7 central stanzas with 7 'heavenly gifts' (l. 2): namely, the 7 Gifts of the Holy Ghost.[1] Then he overlays this double scheme with a further pattern, whereby Stanzas i and ix surround the mortal 7 of Wyatt's 'simple soul' with the circular 9 of heaven ('Whose heavenly gifts increased by disdain': 'But to the heavens that simple soul is fled').[2] The jewel of the pure spirit finds its setting only in heaven, since earth fails to match it—'for our guilt, this jewel we have lost'. Finally, Surrey adds a concluding couplet that contrasts the fates of Wyatt's mortal and immortal parts. This coda brings the line total to 38, the number of years in Wyatt's life;[3] but it also introduces an asymmetry into the formal design.

In Elizabethan and later poetry, avoidance of simple symmetry became more pronounced. One manifestation of this trend was finesse of an expected central accent, a fashion exemplified in Shakespeare's

[1] On the Gifts of the Holy Spirit and the corresponding beatitudes and virtues, see Rosemond Tuve, *Allegorical Imagery* 442 and Index s.v. *Gifts of the Holy Spirit*. Some of the associations in Surrey's poem are more obvious than others, but the most probable arrangement is: St. ii *sapientia* ('wisdom'), iii *timor domini* ('grace assured'), iv *scientia* (literary art and genius), v *pietas* (associated virtue amitié: loyalty, 'courteous talk'), vi *consilium* ('judgement'), vii *intellectus* (blessed are the clean of heart: 'a heart, where dread was never so impressed / To hide the thought that might the truth advance'), viii *fortitudo* ('force').

[2] 'Th'other immortal, perfect, masculine...Nine was the circle set in heaven's place' (*Faerie Queen* II ix 22; see Fowler, Appendix i). On 7 as the number of man's imperfect mortal part, see *ibid.* especially 270, 272.

[3] Surrey made more prominent use of a similar symbolism in the epitaph on Clere (ed. Jones 32). Clere died in his 28th year 'Ere summers four times seven thou couldst fulfil', and Surrey arranged the proper names that give the poem its main effect accordingly. Thus, 7 place names (Norfolk, Lambeth, Cleremont, Kelsall, Laundersey, Bullen, Muttrell) trace the course and physical limits of Clere's earthly part—'Norfolk sprang thee, Lambeth holds thee dead'; but 4 personal names (Clere, Ormonde, Shelton, Surrey) denote the alliance, friendship and virtue that survive (for these meanings of 4, see Fowler 24–33 *passim*, 37, 168, 177, 190, 278, with refs.). Elegies using the duration of the deceased's life as a measure were common; e.g., both Diggs's and Daniel's elegies on Jonson (who died at the age of 64) are in 64 lines; see Herford, Simpson and Simpson xi 444 f., 491 f.

Venus and Adonis. Here the pace of the inverted sexual approach increases towards the metrical centre of the poem, until in the central hundredth stanza Venus at last finds herself close to the centre of Adonis' anatomical figure:[1] 'Now is she in the very lists of love, / Her champion mounted for the hot encounter' (595 f.). Adonis, however, though on the very saddle and throne of love, declines the expected triumph: 'He will not manage her, although he mount her' (598). This teasing stanza ('worse than Tantalus' is her annoy') loses much of its effect if the reader misses the numerological finesse. For the effect is exquisitely artificial: even the rhythm of sexual approach belongs to an elaborate pattern of temporal and cosmic numbers.[2] The detached presentation avoids any great heightening of tension; here as in so much mannerist art '*maniera* effects a sterilization of passion'.[3]

The instances in Marvell and Cowley discussed earlier (pp. 74–84) present similar features. A numerological centre surrounded by triumphal motifs arousing expectations of an appropriately dignified figure is occupied instead by an ambiguous or surprising central image —a conquered conqueror, a king's severed head, a falling Cromwell. Though Dryden inverts a central accent for burlesque effect as late as *Mac Flecknoe* (1682), he returns in doing so to an earlier style. Such finesse, whether in pursuit of sophisticated surprise, irony, or sheer complication, is a device typical of mannerism.

Complication of symmetry was carried to unequalled lengths by Spenser, who liked to superimpose multiple structural patterns in such a way that no single scheme could embrace his whole design. One may regard *Epithalamion* (1595) as the finest example of this intricate art.[4] It carries off a combination of doubled symmetrical schemes with an elaborate pattern of temporal number symbolism, yet gives so little impression of strain that the effort has at times gone entirely unnoticed. One could hardly imagine a more perfect accomplishment of the ideal of *difficoltà* overcome with ease, which Shearman (21 f.,

---

[1] For the pudenda as the centre of geometrical man, see the figures in Wittkower Pls. 2–4 and Fowler 261, 263.
[2] See Christopher Butler and Alastair Fowler, 'Time-Beguiling Sport: Number Symbolism in Shakespeare's *Venus and Adonis*' in *Shakespeare 1564–1964* ed. E. A. Bloom (Providence, R.I. 1964) 124–33.
[3] Shearman 64.
[4] Separately considered below, pp. 161–73.

53, etc.) identifies as a characteristic of mannerism in the visual arts.

Appreciation of Spenser's poem calls for familiarity with three types of symmetrical structure common in the epithalamic genre. One, a natural arrangement, dignifies the wedding ceremony at a central altar: the first half leads the bride to the church, the second brings her back and beds her. In the inset epithalamium in Drayton's Eighth Nymphall, for example, the central fourth of the 7 twelve-line stanzas finds Tita's marriage ceremony being solemnized by the arch-flamen of Elizium at an altar from which rise 'clouds from the burnt sacrifice'.[1] Phineas Fletcher's *Hymen at the Marriage* attempts a subtler version of the same scheme: the seventh of its 13 stanzas has the physical temple of the sacrament of marriage itself: 'Their bodies are but temples...Hymen come, these temples consecrate.'[2] A second type of arrangement dignifies Hymen, the pattern centring on an invocation to the god. Thus, the central stanza of Drayton's epithalamium exhorts 'Sing to Himen, Hymns divine', and the *Epithalame de M. de la Lorraine et Mme Claude* of Remy Belleau (*c.* 1527–77) includes a section with the stanzaic scheme 2 | *Venus* | 1 | *Hymen* | 1 | *Venus* | 2. The third type of arrangement, already noticed (p. 68), puts one or other or both of the principals in the central place of honour.

Epithalamion combines all these types. Most critics have agreed that it is symmetrical about the 2 central stanzas devoted to the wedding ceremony at the 'sacred altar' (xii, xiii); though Janet Spens[3] was content with the simpler stanzaic array 1 | 10 | 2 | 10 | 1, while Thomas Greene[4] sees a more elaborate pattern with the groups of 10 stanzas subdivided. Greene's convincing enough analysis may be summarized, in slightly modified form, as in the table set out below. Outwardly, this division into stanza groups is fully recessed, though the pattern remains unaccompanied by any symmetry in the content —except, perhaps, for a correspondence between the injunctions to

[1] Ed. Hebel iii 314.
[2] *The Poetical Works of Giles Fletcher and Phineas Fletcher* ed. F. S. Boas, 2 vols (Cambridge 1909) ii 224.
[3] Variorum Spenser *Minor Poems* ii 647.
[4] Thomas M. Greene, 'Spenser and the Epithalamic Convention', *Comparative Literature* IX (1957) 225 n., followed by Hallett Smith, 'The Use of Conventions in Spenser's Minor Poems' in *Form and Convention in the Poetry of Edmund Spenser*, ed. W. Nelson (1961) 141.

Muses and nymphs (ii–iv) and the prayers of xxi–xxiii. The incompleteness of the final stanza introduces a slight asymmetry, we note, unrecorded in the Table.

	Text	Number of stanzas
Invocation	i	1
Injunction to Muses and nymphs to attend the bride	ii–iv	3
Preparation of bride	v–viii	4
Procession and beauty of bride	ix–xi	3
Wedding ceremony	xii–xiii	2
Festival	xiv–xvi	3
Night	xvii–xx	4
Prayers to deities	xxi–xxiii	3
Envoy	xxiv	1

By far the most accomplished account of the symmetrical structure of the poem, however, is Max A. Wickert's 'Structure and Ceremony in Spenser's *Epithalamion*, in *ELH* xxxv (1968), which analyses the $1 / / 3 / 4 / 3 / / 2 / / 3 / 4 / 3 / / 1$ symmetry with a thoroughness and sensitivity of detail that I cannot hope to do justice to here. As Wickert is able to show, this stanzaic grouping is reinforced at the level of relatively small-scale metrical effects. Yet the particular quality of his approach is a concentration on the action of the poem, in which he convincingly demonstrates the same recessed symmetry as in the formal pattern: 'The setting for the outer triads is nature shadowed by the gods; both the tetrads take place in the confines of a chamber; and the dyad at the centre is flanked by two inner triads distinguished by the onlooking presence of urban society in some form' (140). Wickert presents a powerful argument for regarding the structure as a dynamic one: a ceremonial movement, processional and recessional, to and from the altar, as befits the poem's subject.

Upon this altar-centred stanzaic pattern, Spenser has superimposed another, if possible even more symmetrical. The latter, which combines the type dignifying the bride with the type dignifying Hymen, extends through the twelve-plus stanzas of the wedding day itself, that is, Stanzas v–xvii. Its completely recessed symmetry is formed by matching stanzas whose imagery or actual words echo one another in a simple and obvious way.[1] Stanza vii, for example, repeatedly refers to the 'joyful day' of the wedding and begs Phoebus 'let this day let this one day be mine'; and the matching Stanza xv similarly dwells on the word *day*: 'this day / This day...This day the sun is in his chiefest height...the longest day...day so long...all day.' The second scheme looks like this:

v Sunrise
  vi Venus
    vii 'This day'
      viii Hymen
        ix-x
          xi BRIDE CROWNED
        xii-xiii
      xiv Hymen
    xv 'This day'
  xvi Venus
xvii Sunset

Conceptualizing the relation between the schemes, one might say that in the brief time of the wedding day Spenser's bride, crowned with a garland 'like some maiden queen', occupies the place of honour, but that in the longer time of the whole poem, the religious significance of the marriage, centred on its sacramental mystery, appears.

One should stress, however, that multiplicity of structure was aesthetically self-justifying. The Elizabethan connoisseur would take pleasure in asymmetry in the placement of an inlaid symmetry, in complexity of overlapping groupings that eluded any single viewpoint and in effortless overcoming of difficulty. To keep two symmetrical patterns going simultaneously with an elaborate system of astronomical number symbolism was a demonstration of art, of precisely the kind most valued in the age of mannerism.[2] Thus Wickert goes

---

[1] The existence of this pattern helps to account for the alternative possibilities of stanza-pairings that have perplexed certain critics of Kent Hieatt's interpretation of *Epithalamion* who lack appreciation of mannerist complexity. On this question of matching stanzas see below, p. 166.

[2] See e.g. Shearman 46, 48; Nikolaus Pevsner, 'The Architecture of Mannerism', in *The Mint*, ed. Geoffrey Grigson (1946) 129. On mannerism in general, see

wrong to the extent that he suggests conflict between Hieatt's interpretation and his own: they are complementary—indeed, incomplete
—accounts of elements in a more complex pattern, of which yet
further elements are noticed below (pp. 164–73).

Donne's 'Nuptial Song' (1613) exhibits similar, if simpler, superimposition of structures. Considered earlier as an example of central
accent (pp. 71–3) because of the placing of the Church Triumphant in
Stanza vi, this epithalamium has also a recessed symmetry about the
wedding stanzas vi and vii. The pairings of stanzas are indicated in
most cases by the original stanza-titles, capitalized in the table below.

ii EQUALITY OF PERSONS: *unity of the new couple*

  iii RAISING OF THE BRIDEGROOM

    iv RAISING OF THE BRIDE

      v

        vi GOING TO THE CHAPEL

        vii THE BENEDICTION

      viii

    ix THE BRIDE'S GOING TO BED

  x THE BRIDEGROOM'S COMING

xi *Unifying effect of love*

Just as the refrain pattern left out the last stanza, so this leaves out
the first—a feature for which Donne's postponement of invocation of
the Muse to Stanza ii prepares us. Here again, apparent asymmetry
conceals partial and complex symmetry.

Donne's 'The Ecstasy' illustrates a different feature of the formal
style of the period: namely, variety of structural elements. It too has
been discussed as a triumphal poem, honouring the quintessential
unity of souls treated in the central block of 5 stanzas (p. 74). But its
symmetrical 7 / 5 / 7 stanzaic pattern is really made up of 2 asym-
metric groupings: *7 indirect speech* + *12 direct speech* and *12 forbearing
the body* + *7 discussing the body*. Now whereas the first of these groupings has a grammatical or formal basis, the basis of the second is logical or substantive. The structure of Sidney's 'O sweet woods the

Franzsepp Würtenberger, *Mannerism* tr. Michael Heron (New York, Chicago
and San Francisco 1963) and Daniel B. Rowland, *Mannerism—Style and Mood:
an Anatomy of Four Works in Three Art Forms* (New Haven, Conn. and London
1964). Specialist literature on the style is listed in the bibliographies in Würtenberger, in Shearman and in E. Battisti, *Rinascimento e Barocco* (1960).

delight of solitariness'[1] similarly mingles elements of different category, this time rhetorical and substantive. The first and third of its 3 fourteen-line stanzas both have accented central lines: i enthrones solitary contemplation ('Contemplation here holdeth his only seat'), iii an ideal partner wise enough not to spoil the solitariness of paradise ('Such goodness that in her simplicity triumphs'). Stanza ii, however, which reviews the social evils excluded from retirement, honours no sovereign image. Instead, this negative stanza displays a rhetorical symmetry whose most obvious basis is anaphora; / the initial words of the 10 middle lines form an *a b b b b | b b b b a* array. Though quieter and less emphatic than in Cowley's poem on a similar subject (pp. 74 f.), the symmetry here achieves effects no less interesting. Such variety in the means of division makes for a fluidity of movement that sometimes, as in the Donne example, looks forward to the baroque. On the other hand, it is not without renaissance antecedents. One recalls the variety of elements deployed in the *Divina commedia* (cantos, *terzina* totals, cornices, *liste*, days); though admittedly Dante's patterns were less economical and overdetermined than Donne's, more mutually confirmatory and harmonious.

We come closest to exact analogy with the visual arts when we consider the grouping of structural elements. As a representative example of literary mannerism, let us take Spenser's *The Faerie Queen* (1590, 1596). It may seem to some to have many late gothic features, but in reality these are instances of a selective assimilation of the earlier style that is now recognized as characteristic of mannerism.[2] The adventurousness of Spenser's structure, the dazzling fluency and the ease of its intricacies prompt comparison with Raphael's Palazzo Branconio dell'Aquila (1519–20). There are obvious dangers attendant on dealing with the structure of a literary work not only difficult but incomplete: we must avoid speculation and confine ourselves to obvious patterns formed by complete parts of the poem as it now stands. Fortunately we have the advantage of starting from an excellent structural analysis by Thomas Roche.[3] With Roche's account I am in substantial agreement, except that I do not believe,

---

[1] *The Poems of Sir Philip Sidney* ed. Ringler (Oxford 1962) 68 f.
[2] See e.g. Shearman 25. Elsewhere (141, 167) Shearman rightly discusses passages from Spenser as characteristically mannerist in their pursuit of variety and of stylistic artificiality.
[3] *The Kindly Flame* 199 ff.

as he seems to do (198 f.), that structure is mere subjective abstraction by the reader. The multiplicity of structural groupings possible in *The Faerie Queen*—no one of them wholly adequate—may have pushed Roche into this theoretical impasse. But multiplicity of pattern can just as well be construed as Spenser's deliberate intention; he may have meant to superimpose multiple schemes. Such, after all, was the nature of the art of his time, as exemplified for instance in Raphael's design. Even the limited extent of certain patterns Roche finds in the poem accords with the conscious ideals of mannerism— 'emphasis on the parts rather than the whole', as Shearman puts it (146).

The façade of Raphael's Palazzo dell'Aquila (Pl. 11), analysed in a brilliant article by Wolfgang Lotz[1] whose main argument Shearman accepts and develops (76 f.), manifested complexity of design both horizontally and vertically. Vertically, the half-columns of the *piano umile* surprisingly terminated in the niches of the *piano nobile* rather than in structural members: 'In the wall's own plastic pattern a concave form crowned a convex one, and in its structural pattern a negative was superimposed on a positive. The positive stress side-stepped to the half-columns of the window-tabernacles, and became weakened as it was divided and diminished in scale.'[2] In the upper floors, structural pattern increasingly gave way to decorative, unarticulated texturing. Horizontally, the composition showed an astonishing sophistication and finesse of grouping. The ground floor had 5 bays consisting of arched openings firmly defined by framing half-columns. The *piano nobile*, on the contrary, was framed by weak accents, since its terminal niches were hollowed only in relief. Shearman (77) interestingly compares it to a line of verse ('eleven units, alternating in value, began and ended with a weak beat like an hendecasyllabic verse'), though as we shall see the true analogy lies rather with larger compositional units. The *piano nobile* was thus arranged *a B a C a B a C a B a*—5 main terms, the window-tabernacles, spaced by 6 lesser terms. In the upper storey, however, since the panels dividing the windows were wider than the window-tabernacles themselves, a new rhythm emerged. The 11 units made themselves felt as 6 main terms

---

[1] 'Mannerism in Architecture: Changing Aspects' in *The Renaissance and Mannerism, Acts of the Twentieth International Congress of the History of Art (1961)* II (1963) 241.   [2] Shearman 76 f.

(the large panels) separated by 5 lesser terms (the small window-tabernacles). This is not to imply, however, any restlessness or tension between the alternative groupings; the transitions from floor to floor, particularly through the complex *piano nobile* and the fluid mezzanine zone, are handled too smoothly for that. One concludes, rather, that in the art of mannerist façades, as exemplified in such buildings as the Palazzo dell' Aquila and the Palazzo Spada (Pl. 12) at Rome, an intended pleasure lies in awareness of alternative patterns.

The Faerie Queen shows remarkably similar complexity and fluidity in the grouping of its major divisions and structural members. Most obvious is the projected disposition into the 'twelve books, fashioning xii moral virtues' of the title-page and the Letter to Raleigh, 6 of which survive in a complete form, divided each into 12 cantos.[1] These 6 books fall into 2 separately published groups of 3, one (I–III) presenting virtues of the individual life, the other (IV–VI) virtues of life in society (Roche 200). For the internal structural coherence of these parts I have argued elsewhere.[2] The 3 subjects of Part I, for example, unfold the Neoplatonic triad Veritas–Virtus–Amor, a sequence hinted at in such minor features as the encounters with the 3 sons of Aveugle. (Sansfoy is defeated in I and Sansloy in II, while for variety III disposes of true joy's enemies without introducing Sansjoy explicitly.[3]) Almost as readily, however, the 6 books form complementary pairs. The Legends of Holiness and of Temperance, jointly devoted to inner life, have a special mutual relation about whose existence even A. S. P. Woodhouse and T. M. Gang tacitly agree, while disputing its content.[4] Moreover, Books I and II not only follow closely parallel thematic courses, but are also connected by formal and numerological links.[5] In similar fashion, III and IV deal with complementary aspects

[1] This 12 × 12 plan, used on a smaller scale for the final poem in *The Shepherd's Calendar* (1579), is related to the 'square or quadrangle equilater' pattern of composition discussed by Puttenham (*Art of English Poesy* ed. Willcock and Walker 100 f.).

[2] *Spenser and the Numbers of Time*, Index s.v. *Triad*.

[3] See further *ibid*. 142–4.

[4] A. S. P. Woodhouse, 'Nature and Grace in *The Faerie Queen*', *ELH* XVI (1949); T. M. Gang, 'Nature and Grace in *The Faerie Queen*, the problem reviewed', *ELH* XXVI (1959).

[5] A. C. Hamilton, '"Like Race to Runne": The Parallel Structure of *The Faerie Queen*, Books I and II', *PMLA* LXXIII (1958), incorporated as Ch. iii in *The Structure of Allegory in 'The Faerie Queen'* (Oxford 1961); Fowler, Ch. ix, esp. 92.

of love, maintain narrative continuity (particularly through the stories of Amoret and Florimell) and, as critics agree, share a distinctly Ariostan treatment. And V and VI are again substantively complementary, opposing 'the claims of law and right...to society's courteous attention, lovingly offered...beyond the minimal demands of duty' (Roche 200).

The most interesting alternative grouping, however, and the one most in the manner of the Palazzo dell'Aquila façade, is that between six- and five-book division. For the existence of the former, one need not argue. It is a little less obvious that Parts I and II can also be regarded as comprising 5 structural units. But the slightest reflection about chronology leads the reader to perceive that whereas Books I, II, V and VI have actions lasting each a year, the actions of III and IV together occupy only a year. Consideration of the quests from Gloriana's court leads to a similar result (necessarily, since they take place yearly); there are only 5 quests, Red Cross's, Guyon's, Scudamour's, Artegall's and Calidore's. This list reminds us that Books III and IV also differ from the others in having patrons (as distinct from questing knights) not from Gloriana's court. Thus III is the Legend of Britomartis, who finishes the quest Scudamour begins, and IV is the Legend of Cambel and Triamond. Again, the same Books III and IV have the distinction of double patrons—Scudamour and Britomart, Cambel and Triamond—who form as it were a tetrad of concord. Moreover, the existing part of *The Faerie Queen* exhibits recessed symmetry about this double book III–IV dominated by the sovereign figure Britomart.[1] The matching Books II and V, for example, correspond in many ways, both formal and substantive: both deal with a cardinal virtue (II with Temperance, V with Justice), both have a 'core canto' in the ninth place (the Castle of Alma, the Court of Mercilla). Similarly, the matching Books I and VI have cores in the tenth canto (the House of Holiness, Mount Acidale), as shown in the table overleaf.

[1] This symmetry is in part noticed by Roche, who speaks of a 'mirror relationship' (200), between books in Parts I and II: cf. *ibid.* 202 f. discussing III–IV as a double book. On internal symmetry in IV, see H. C. Notcutt, '*The Faerie Queen* and its critics', *E & S* XII (1926), whose argument, however, is sometimes forced; on mid points in *The Faerie Queen* generally, see Fowler, Index s.v. *Mid point* and *Central position of sovereignty*. Michael Bayback, Paul Delany and A. Kent Hieatt, 'Placement "In the Middest" in *The Faerie Queen*,' *Silent Poetry* ed. Alastair Fowler (1970), corrects and develops this approach.

I   *Holiness: core canto x: quest achieved by Red Cross*

   II   *Temperance: cardinal virtue: core canto ix: quest achieved by Guyon*

     III–IV   *Chastity–Friendship: quest not achieved by*

       Scudamour, but by BRITOMART

    V   *Justice: cardinal virtue: core canto ix: quest achieved by Artegall*

VI   *Courtesy: core canto x: quest achieved by Calidore*

It should surprise no one that an incomplete poem of this period should be so fully organized. Mannerist artistic ideals demanded that each part, whatever the scale, should have its own individual interest. And, if we had the entire *Faerie Queen*, no doubt it would disclose yet more alternative structures embracing Parts I and II.

It would be misleading, nevertheless, to portray *The Faerie Queen* as having a severely formal structure. Throughout, sutures between book and book—achieved by such means as narrative links and over-laps—blur the external divisions so as to create the illusion of a single immensely complicated polyphonic texture. And the Faerie *mise-en-scène* unites all, like the verdure ground of a tapestry. Consequently the alternative formal groupings, far from being mutually exclusive, have their *raison d'être* in simultaneous coexistence. Spenser's aim is the elusive complexity of an art that by its *maniera* imitates the elusive-ness of life and the interrelatedness of virtues. Yet the poem's involvement of author and reader in effects of fictive distance, to-gether with the dynamism that carries its action through several cantos at a time, also repeatedly anticipates the style of the baroque. We remember how important Spenser's example was to Cowley, Dryden and Pope.

BAROQUE SYMMETRY: DRYDEN AND MILTON

The transition from mannerism's complex finesses to the perspicuity of the baroque style was already accomplished in the work of Abraham Cowley (1618–67). His playful use of central accent (pp. 75 f.) seems anything but esoteric: its gay effect would be lost if the wit needed study. Moreover, Cowley's symmetry is often of a pronounced, simple type, as in 'The Ecstasy'.[1] The *Pindaric Odes* (1656) signifi-cantly introduce the large units of composition characteristic of

---

[1] See pp. 76 f. above.

baroque structure. Divided often into irregular strophes in couplets, the odes exploit accords of metrical, rhetorical and logical elements, rather than symbolic architectonics. But they are far from being as unstructured as Carol Maddison's prosodic approach leads her to believe.[1] The Ode to 'The Muse',[2] for example, has 4 large strophes forming a line-total array *19 | 16 | 20 | 17*, in which inner and outer pairs add each to 36, the great quaternion.

To contemporaries of Dryden (1631–1700), his numerology would have been no less obvious than Cowley's. Ever intent on establishing a clear poetic tradition, Dryden preferred schemes whose precedents were familiar. Even in *Mac Flecknoe*, where the central accent is satirically inverted, unmistakable verbal allusions guide us to the structural precedents burlesqued, the enthronements in the *Aeneid* and *Paradise Lost* (p. 116). Dryden also preferred a relatively simple construction. Except in the St Cecilia's Day odes for the Musical Society, where he would naturally be on his mettle to produce elaborate formal devices, he aimed boldly at broad effects of structure. Consequently, the need for self-referring language went. Explicit reference to form, common in mannerist poems, became rare in baroque, though it never quite disappeared (in *Absalom and Achitophel* the phrase 'triple bond' draws attention to a triple rhyme).

Dryden's symmetries generally have pronounced central accents. A comprehensive pattern will embrace the whole poem: if there are multiple centres, these will contribute to a single dramatic movement. The *Ode to the Memory of Mistress Anne Killigrew* (1686), for all its apparent structural complexity, is no exception. Of the Ode's 10 unequal stanzas all the central 4 (and no others) are dignified with sovereign images: Stanza iv addresses God as the source of 'the heavenly gift of poesy'; v celebrates Mistress Killigrew's power as a poetess; vi tells how, not content with 'the spacious empire of the Nine'—which she ruled from the sovereign fifth place—she extended her sway to the 'next realm', painting (where again she was received 'in triumph', l. 105); and vii finds her painting the king and queen in their coronation majesty. This iconic placing of sovereign images among the Ode's stanzas is emphasized by the internal proportions of the stanzas themselves; for the line totals of the latter run

[1] *Apollo and the Nine* (1960) 384, 397.   [2] Ed. Waller 184–6.

STANZA	i	ii	iii	iv	v	vi	vii	viii	ix	x
LINES	22	16	17	15	17	39	22	16	13	18

The symmetry about God's Stanza iv, centring on the line total 15 (a number symbolic of approach to a throne) is extended by the device of subdividing a stanza.[1] Thus the long Stanza vi, which honours Mistress Killigrew's double triumph, is itself double: it consists of 2 notional parts, 16 and 22 lines, with between them a single line affirming that 'all bowed beneath her government'. In consequence the symmetry about the divine Stanza iv continues through 6 stanzas, as shown in tabular form:

Stanza	i	ii	iii	iv	v	vi			vii	viii	ix	x
Lines	22	16	17	15	17	16	(1)	22	22	16	13	18

Moreover, a subsidiary *b a a b* system honours the king and queen (at least as Mistress Killigrew painted them) in Stanzas vi–viii. And finally, in an independent pattern, the central line of the whole poem is l. 98, where Mistress Killigrew, having conquered painting, 'the whole fief, in right of poetry...claimed'.

The above might be the description of a mannerist structure—but only because I have ignored the dynamic movement from sovereign image to sovereign image, and the force unifying the whole into a single vision of human and divine creativity. From God as the source of poetic creation (iv), the Ode moves to heaven's vestal Mistress Killigrew, who is to atone, in the universe of art, for man's 'second Fall'. Her new creation, which transforms first the poetic and then the artistic world, triumphs through the central stanzas v and vi, imitating God's abundance in a variety equalled only 'when the peopled ark the whole creation bore' (l. 126). These stanzas not only

---

[1] On the symbolism of 15, see Bongo 409; also H. Neville Davies, 'The Structure of Shadwell's *A Song for St Cecilia's Day, 1690*', in *Silent Poetry* ed. Alastair Fowler (1970) p. 201–33, with many references. Since the present book was written, a numerological analysis of Dryden's *Ode* has been attempted independently by John T. Shawcross, in *Hartford Studies in Literature* i (1969). Shawcross notices some of the features mentioned above; but his interpretation of them in terms of arbitrarily assigned and apparently improvised number symbolisms seems to me methodologically unacceptable.

follow out the creative process from God through idea to image, but also extend divine sovereignty into the world. Thus even the political realm is changed by the dead woman's art: her portrait of the king 'called out the image of his heart' (130) and represented his soul at its best. Its power to idealize puts Mistress Killigrew's art in a mediating position between the seen and unseen worlds, between God and king ('Let this thy vestal, Heav'n, atone for all!'). And now the multiple centres are seen to be mutually reinforcing expressions of the same creative principle, the divine *tetractys*, a principle manifested alike in 4 central stanzas, 4 realms (universe, poetry, painting, kingdom), 4 persons honoured (God, Mistress Killigrew, king, queen). Just as the *tetractys* takes its source from the One who includes all, so the God invoked in Stanza iv returns in Stanza x (10 being a form of unity and of the *tetractys*) to close the Ode with his judgement.

A similar movement works in other of Dryden's odes,[1] giving the sense of a robust power stronger than Cowley's. It is the presence of this baroque force that makes Ruth Wallerstein's criticism of Dryden, brilliant though it is, beside the point.[2] Far from merely changing 'the pattern of the elegy into the form of the Pindaric Ode', he uses Pindar's triumphal forms to develop a new panegyric style. In this style, which is closer to the baroque than to the earlier styles Miss Wallerstein compares it with, a challenging yet harmonious and cursive movement is everything. Consequently, to extract a short passage from Dryden for comparison with a few lines from Donne unfairly shows the latter poet to best advantage, but not the former.

Milton's poetry has been characterized as baroque by many critics, usually on the basis of a general impression of the vigour and scope of its spatial range. In a chapter entitled 'Milton: the Baroque Artist', Miss Mahood speaks of the *Nativity Ode's* 'baroque amplitude of conception'[3] and draws attention to dramatic movements

---

[1] See Douglas Brooks and Alastair Fowler, 'The Structure of Dryden's *Song for St Cecilia's Day 1687*'.   [2] *Studies in Seventeenth-Century Poetic* 137–44.

[3] M. M. Mahood, *Poetry and Humanism* (1950) 175. The Ode's conceits, however, suggest mannerism of rhetorical style; its triple stanza centres mannerism of structure. The centre stanza of the Hymn itself is xiv, which anticipates the illusory return of the age of sovereign gold and replaces the darkness of hell with the light of 'peering day'. St. xvi, the centre of the whole Ode, however, brings the real and very different triumph of the 'bitter cross'. And in the intervening St. xv, Truth and Justice, rainbow-robed like glories, 'sit between,

through the space of the 'vortex-like' universe of *Paradise Lost*. Shearman, too, contrasts the same work's 'visions of more generous scope' with mannerism's jewel-like effects (146). Milton's early work, however, seems to me to have a strong element of mannerism, and I would even go so far as to trace some persistence of this style in his epics. In *Silent Poetry* I have described the style of *Lycidas* as mannerist, though on different grounds from those advanced by Wylie Sypher for a similar conclusion. Again, *L'Allegro* and *Il Penseroso* have far from obvious central accents. At the centre of the first, ll. 76 f., 'Towers, and battlements' perhaps enthrone some beauty, 'the cynosure' (Lesser Bear constellation) or focus 'of neighbouring eyes'; at the centre of the other, l. 88, the more serious Penseroso joins Hermes Trismegistus on a lonelier tower to 'outwatch the Bear', this time *Ursa maior*. So esoteric a correspondence, complicated as it is by the *canzone*-like preludes, seems more mannerist than baroque.

With *Paradise Lost* it is another matter: here structural analysis for the most part confirms the intuitive impression of baroque. The energetic and organic unity characteristic of the later style[1] can be demonstrated, as can qualities of movement, dramatic focus, massiveness and singleness of vision. For example, a strong upward movement through the Raphael episode (v–viii) leads to heaven and to Messiah's triumph, first in the angelic war and then in creation. At the centre of the poem's 10,550 lines[2] Messiah ascends his mobile 'sapphire throne', in an apocalyptic passage filled with powerful and enormous movement, which sweeps over heaven and down through chaos to the utmost depths of hell. Since the triumphal chariot is a mystically symbolic cosmic vehicle, the act of mounting it assumes sovereignty

/ Throned in celestial sheen'. At a fourth centre, that of the line count (122/3), is recalled the musical setting of 'the well-balanced world on hinges'.

[1] E.g. Shearman 149; Pevsner 125. On the baroque generally in the visual arts and in literature, see Germain Bazin, *The Baroque: Principles, Styles, Modes, Themes* (1968); Imbrie Buffum, *Studies in the Baroque from Montaigne to Rotrou* (1957); René Wellek, 'The Concept of Baroque in Literary Scholarship' in *Concepts of Criticism* ed. S. G. Nichols (New Haven and London 1963); and René Wellek and Austin Warren, *Theory of Literature* (New York 1956) 120 ff. I find Wylie Sypher, *Four Stages of Renaissance Style: Transformations in Art and Literature* (New York 1955) too impressionistic to be useful.

[2] In the first, 1667 edn: i.e. vi 762 in the 1674 edn, on which line-numbering is usually based. See further in the section 'Numerology' in *The Poems of John Milton* ed. Carey and Fowler 440–3, with refs. to Gunnar Qvarnström's pioneer work in this field.

over all the universe.[1] What more emphatic central image could be conceived? Moreover, the structural symmetry about this central accent is boldly apparent; a very few moments' reflection shows the fit reader its main terms,[2] which include those set out in the following table.

i–ii	iii	iv	vi	vii	ix	x	xi–xii
Conse-quences of angels' fall	Heavenly council: Satan enters world	First tempta-tion of man	Mes-siah's triumph	Mes-siah's creation	Second tempta-tion of man	Heavenly council: Satan leaves world	Conse-quences of man's fall
			RAPHAEL EPISODE				
a	*b*	*c*	*D*	*D*	*c*	*b*	*a*

True, there remain some mannerist complexities in the structure of *Paradise Lost*. One might instance the doubled centre; for, as we shall see (p. 132) Messiah's creation is the axis of a separate symmetry in the temporal scheme. Or consider the division of Books vii and x of the ten-book first edition (1667) to give the familiar 12 books of the 1674 second edition. This editorial device allows the simultaneous existence of two distinct schemes of books, both significant. Thus in the first edition the invocations (beginning 1667 i, iii, vii, viii) mark the inceptions of groups of 2, 4, 1 and 3 books, in allusion to the creative *tetractys*; just as the book total 10 denotes the *tetractys'* summed form. In the second edition, however, the invocations, now beginning Books i, iii, vii and ix, signalize the array *2 | 4 | | 2 | 4*, in allusion to the 1 : 2 proportion between rationality and concupiscence in Pythagorean theory.[3] Or, again, take the subsidiary patterns, such as the second half framed between the Mirror of Nature (vii–viii) and the Mirror of History (xi–xii). All such complications, however, are subordinated to a unifying vision that informs every part and element of the work. The patterns may be many, but they share a single import.

Milton's Christocentric vision controls not only patterns of structural members, but even the arrangement of smaller elements. On an intermediate scale, catalogues of places, far from being mere atmospheric fogs of exotic names, form elaborately patterned arrays

---

[1] See my notes to vi 749–59 in *The Poems* ed. Carey and Fowler.
[2] See further *ibid*. pp. 441 ff.
[3] For the arguments on which these analyses are based, see *ibid*. 442 f., 851 f.

symmetrical about images of divine sovereignty. Both the Asian and African lands reviewed in xi 388–407, for example, have as their centre Chersonese-Ophir, which was the source of Solomon's mystic gold of sovereignty, a type of Christ. The former catalogue may be construed:[1] *Cambalu and Samarchand | Paquin | Agra and Lahor | CHERSONESE | Ecbatan and Hispahan | Mosco | Bizance and Turchestan*, or *a b a B a b a*. In the same way, speeches form symmetrical arrays,[2] line lengths of speeches convey theological number symbolisms and the sun is 'centre to the world' at the centre of a 113-line paragraph.[3]

The same vision informs even the finer texture of the poem, in which no detail is too small to be moulded to the ideals of baroque plasticity. Thus, at ix 115–18 Satan condemns himself unwittingly by his implicit acknowledgement of God's sovereignty over the world he wishes to enjoy:

If I could joy in aught, sweet interchange
Of hill, and valley, rivers, woods and plains,
Now land, now sea, and shores with forest crowned,
Rocks, dens, and caves...

The landscape features here follow no random or casual sequence. Both line division and syntactical transition form the array *5 (hill, valley, rivers, woods, plains) | 4 (land, sea, shores, forest) | 3 (rocks, dens, caves)*, in allusion to the Pythagorean 3 / 4 / 5 triangle of virtue. Moreover, the first of these groups is ordered both syntactically, by *ands*, and semantically, by contrasts, into a pattern symmetrical about *rivers*, associated in this context with the virtuous rivers of Paradise. Finally, *forest crowned*, similarly associated with the forbidden tree of divine sovereignty, constitutes the central fourth term of the last 7, in accordance with the Biblical siting of the tree 'in the midst of the garden' (*Gen.* ii 9), a location that provoked much mystical exegesis.

In Milton's epic, literary baroque is at its most intelligible philosophically. It takes forms at once passionately Christocentric and reminiscent of the solar mysticism of the renaissance. We may not be fanciful, therefore, in trying to relate the changed style to the new

[1] For fuller detail, with an analysis of the catalogue of African names, see my notes to xi 388–95 and 396–407, *ibid.* pp. 1000 f.; cf. 438.
[2] See e.g. Gunnar Qvarnström, *The Enchanted Palace* (Stockholm 1967) 58; Røstvig, 'The Hidden Sense' 66 ff.
[3] See my note to viii 122 f., *The Poems* ed. Carey and Fowler 820.

cosmology; indeed, Milton himself seems to draw the same connection (as when Raphael asserts the sun's centrality with a central accent). From this point of view, the multiple ambiguous patterns of mannerism should perhaps be regarded as a poetic correlate of uncertainty between various complicated geoentric, heliocentric and geoheliocentric planetary systems. Eventually the success of the Copernican theory led to a single indubitable centre, more emphatic even than that of the Ptolemaic system in force during the early renaissance. Consequently, notions of the sun's sovereign position in the midst of the planets—'where the sun centres himself by right', as Giles Fletcher puts it—gained a new lease of life. Pythagorean and Neoplatonic solar theology enjoyed a revival, and that 'Orphic' solar mysticism whose broad conception of cosmic unity is well illustrated by Cartari's explanation that Apollo is protrayed *in mezzo delle Muse* because his light informs all man's intellectual activities: 'The place in the centre (*il luoco di mezzo*) is given to Apollo... also in the universe, because he diffuses his virtue through all things, which is why he is called the heart of heaven.'[1] In the baroque style, such ideas might be applied politically, as in the cult of the *Roi soleil*. Alternatively, there was Milton's more abstract return to the geometrical mysticism of Cusanus and Ficino. Their Hermetic doctrine of God as simultaneous centre and circumference of the universal circle, which profoundly influenced architectural design,[2] also underlies the strong emphasis on solar and divine centrality in *Paradise Lost*: 'as God in heaven / Is centre, yet extends to all' (ix 109).

From a structural point of view, then, the analogy between poetry and the visual arts, particularly architecture, has a definite content. In both arts, baroque style displays the increased emphasis on the centre that contemporary changes in cosmology and concentrations of political power might lead us to expect. Again, poetic structures, like architectural ones, tend to deploy massive forms; a preference for ambitious stanza patterns and long verse paragraphs corresponds to the use of gigantic orders and great masses of masonry. In architecture, one thinks of St Paul's and of Blenheim Palace (1705–24), in poetry of the Pindaric ode and of *Paradise Lost*.[3]

[1] *Imagini delli dei* 30. [2] Wittkower 28 ff.
[3] Examples of baroque recessed symmetry in the neoclassical drama of Corneille and Racine have been studied by Steinweg: see Qvarnström, *The Enchanted Palace* 79.

The modification of baroque that art history knows as rococo had also its analogue in poetic form. This development can be seen taking place in the revision of a single poem, Pope's *Rape of the Lock* (1712, 1714). For, of the two versions of the poem, only the first has a clearly distinct symmetrical structure.

The 1712 version exhibits recessed symmetry in both its cantos, but especially in Canto ii. There, an exceedingly elaborate circular construction in the Virgilian manner (set out in the table below) comprises no fewer than 17 units of paragraph length.

1 Belinda's rage and grief
  2 Thalestris: 'shall the ravisher display this hair?'
    3 Beau Plume appeals, rapping his snuff-box
      4 The Baron refuses to relinquish his spoils: he triumphs
       5 Belinda languishes weeping
        6 Belinda regrets succumbing to the court's lure
         7 'Jove had stopped the Baron's ears'
         8 War of six Homeric gods
          9–10 War of six ladies and beaux
        11 'Jove suspends his golden scales'
        12 Belinda subdues the Baron with snuff
       13 Belinda threatens the Baron: his plea
      14 The Baron ordered to restore the lock: the spoils lost
     15 Beaux' wits in snuff-boxes in the Lunar sphere
    16 The hair displayed stellified, to the *beau monde*
17 Appeal to Belinda: 'cease...to mourn'

The centres of the two cantos of 1714, by line count, bear an odd relation to each other. Central to Canto i is the famous couplet 'Here thou, great Anna! whom three realms obey, / Dost sometimes counsel take..and sometimes tea' (ll. 71–2 of 142): almost a sovereign image. But in the more troubled Canto ii, where the amazonian Thalestris holds the central place with her martial call 'to arms', the neighbouring couplet (ll. 94–5 of 192) finds a different Anna: 'Not half so fixed the Trojan could remain, / While Anna begged and Dido raged in vain.' Perhaps in this setting aside of Dido's sister Pope hints at the dire calamities that threaten the peaceful domestic nation unless Belinda and the Baron are reconciled.[1]

Turning to the familiar five-canto version with machinery, we find this regular symmetry abandoned or subdued. True, there are still traces of circular construction. In 1714 Canto i, for example, Ariel appears in the third paragraph and leaves with a warning in the third last; just as, in Canto iv, Umbriel figures in the paragraphs second from each end (2 symbolizing evil and the underworld). Moreover, the 16 paragraphs of iii divide $9+7$: the 'sacred nine' match the 9 tricks of ombre, the mutable 7 relate the loss of the lock.[2] By contrast, the 16 paragraphs of v are evenly divided $8+8$ by the balance of Jupiter the just distributor in the eighth (a number of justice). Again, a system of correspondences connects paragraphs of the first halves of iii (ombre) and v (war); among them the link between the Anna couplets, now at iii 7 f. and v 5 f.—places comparable to those of 1712, but less conspicuous. In partial compensation, the canto centres are lightly accented. Thus, the centres of i, ii, iv and v by line count have each a central image of light,[3] thereby confirming in unexpected fashion a theory of Rebecca Parkin's.[4] Although these images are far from prominent, they might lead an acute reader to pay special attention to the central couplet of iii and to Belinda's fatal loss, when her Queen of Hearts is defeated, of the light coquette's sanguine principle (iii 89 f.). In short, the 1714 version is at least as highly organized as the 1712; but its central accents seem more subdued, its recessed symmetries less consistent and less important, its structure altogether more fluid. In 1717 Pope could drop a couplet from ii and

[1] If the connection between great Anna and Dido's sister seems far-fetched, one should remember that the ancient Anna, deified as Anna Perenna the deceiver and softener of Mars, had been explicitly associated with an earlier Queen Anne in Ben Jonson's *Part of the King's Entertainment, in Passing to his Coronation* (1604) ed. Herford, Simpson and Simpson vii 101 f.

[2] iii 30. Ombre is first mentioned in a paragraph of 9 couplets. For other examples of division into $9+7$, see Fowler, Index s.v. *Heptad*.

[3] The centres correspond in recessed order: with 'His purple pinions opening to the sun, / He raised his azure wand, and thus begun' (ii 71 f.) cf. 'Spreads his black wings, and slowly mounts to day. / Sunk in Thalestris' arms the nymph he found' (iv 88 f.).

[4] See Rebecca Price Parkin, 'Mythopoeic Activity in the *Rape of the Lock*', *ELH* xxi (1954) 30–8.

insert Clarissa's speech of 30 lines in v without serious structural damage.

Smooth rather than energetic fluidity distinguishes Pope's later style from the baroque. It intimates a rococo elegance, in which exquisite details receive more attention than large structural patterns. Pope came to prefer the Horatian to the Virgilian style of construction: he was content, as we have seen (pp. 86 f.), to impart a general impression of approximate balance, so long as individual couplets told and a smooth fluency of style and tone was sustained. Hence the possibility, yet at the same time the formidable difficulty, of that continual revision in the interest of local effect which characterized his later work. Such a method of writing necessarily precluded exact symmetry, except as a compositional scaffolding to be abandoned once it had served its turn. In Pope's later poetry one often finds short passages in balance; hardly ever an exact numerological structure.

Many factors no doubt contributed to the major change in poetic taste that Pope's work at once reflected and assisted. Superficially, it might be seen as a change of fashion: the convention of central accent had become *vieux jeu*, so that Pope could fairly despise scribblers throned in the centre of their thin designs. But a deeper historian might look to larger-scale contemporary changes in aesthetic theory and sensibility— to the tendency, perhaps, towards a subjective or relativistic stance. In contemporary architecture, for example, Palladian conceptions of numerical proportion were modified and eventually abandoned.[1] Perrault denied 'that certain ratios were *a priori* beautiful', holding that correct proportions were agreeable only because familiar.

Although Pope's special interest in the visual arts should be kept in mind, we need not assume that he was intellectually conscious of movements of taste still largely Continental. Probably he neither rejected the doctrine of *ut architectura poesis* nor deliberately set himself to try for effects of subjective relativism. But he may well have sensed his public's preference for unesoteric forms. And perhaps he

---

[1] This movement is traced in some detail by Wittkower. See his section 'The Break-away from the Laws of Harmonic Proportion in Architecture', *Architectural Principles* 142–54. Wittkower (144 f.) regards Claude Perrault's *Ordonnance des cinq espèces de colonnes* (1683) as decisive: it 'advocates the relativity of our aesthetic judgement and, quite logically, maintains that musical consonances cannot be translated into visual proportions'.

himself felt more interest in tones, textures, imagery and melo-poeic effects than in structural aspects of form.

In this, many eighteenth-century poets followed him. Among the minority who did not was Gray, whose *Elegy Written in a Country Church-Yard* presents a fine example of late neoclassical structure.[1] Or possibly its style is more accurately described as retrospective mannerism, since it has a double central accent. In the fullest published version of 1751—the version preferred, for example, in the *Oxford Book of Eighteenth Century Verse*—there are 33 quatrains (the number of man's earthly sufferings?), the last 3 of which are set apart, belonging to, yet separate from, the poem itself, as 'The Epitaph'. The main elegy displays recessed symmetry of clearly defined sections. The outermost sections have 7 stanzas, the number of elegy: in the first the poet contemplates the church-yard, in the last his own death receives memorial from an uncouth swain, who introduces the Epitaph. These circumscribing sections frame a meditation in 16 stanzas (the number of virtue?), itself divided symmetrically by a central passage of 16 lines. The flanking sections are of 4 stanzas (the 4 of concord and virtue?): the first about the proximity of death and the danger of despising the forgotten proletariat ('Let not ambition mock...'), the second about memorials for the humble dead. The sections are set out in tabular form below.

7	4	8	4	7	(3)
The poet contemplates peasants' graves	Mock not!	The unhonoured poor	Memorials	The peasant contemplates the poet's grave	(Epitaph)

Even in this schematic analysis, Gray's structure becomes a little more intelligible, particularly the beautiful transposition of poet and swain. This identification is further reflected in the social implication of the central accents. At the centre of the poem proper come the lines 'Some Cromwell guiltless of his country's blood. / The applause of listening senates to command' (60 f.). Counting in the Epitaph, however, we find a central stanza telling how the crimes of the unhonoured

---

[1] The *Elegy* is Virgilian in its diction too: see e.g. Kenneth Quinn, *Virgil's Aeneid: a Critical Description* (1968) 261.

dead were circumscribed—'Forbad to wade through slaughter to a throne' (67). This point now goes unnoticed. But it would be interesting to know how much of the memorability and weight of this most familiar of poems is due to an unconscious feeling for its architectural shapeliness.[1]

The trend towards impressionistic or emergent form intensified in the Romantic poets' theory and practice. Their structural innovations brought about, indeed, what is perhaps the greatest transformation of poetic form known to literary history. For they not only continued to dispense with significant external divisions, as some of their eighteenth-century predecessors had done, but revived older divisions (stanza, canto, book) in a nominal manner that had the decisive effect of emptying them of any symbolic structural implication. The Romantics freely overrode metrical divisions, flowing on in obedience to internal and subjective, rather than to architectural and objective, dictates. Though there were occasional instances of numerical composition by Victorian and later poets (D. G. Rossetti, Dylan Thomas), it would be misleading to discuss these in the present context: they cannot be referred to any living tradition of structural iconography. Symmetries occurred, patterns were constructed; but they no longer had any conventional significance to the reader who beheld them.

[1] The original Eton MS is a holograph draft of a still longer version, with quite a different structure. In this version the throne stanza comes at the centre of a section of only 3 stanzas, flanked as in the printed version by four-stanza sections, but with differently distributed contents. However, we can be sure of the structural analysis, for it has Gray's own warrant: in the margin he marked both four-stanza sections—the first by numbering (or rather, renumbering), the second by a bracket. See the reprint in *Gray and Collins: Poetical Works* ed. A. L. Poole (1937) Appendix I, 183 f.

6. The unity of time

DRAMATIC UNITY: ITALIAN THEORISTS

The same preoccupation with time that has often been noticed in sixteenth- and seventeenth-century literature is obvious in the criticism of the period. Everyone knows that the unity of time was for some reason a major topic of renaissance literary theory, engaging the minds of all the best critics and some of the best writers. But most misunderstand the doctrine to such an extent as to dismiss it as arid pedantry, slavish neoclassicism, or abstract theorizing irrelevant (in England, at least) to the actual form of drama. The prescriptive approach puts us off and discourages enquiry.

On the occasions when modern scholars treat the unity of time seriously, they give the limelight to the problem of theatrical illusion.[1] Now it is true that the discrepancy between fictive time and acting time, forced by the improbability of compressing a complex action with reversals into a fictive duration contemporaneous with performance, troubled renaissance theorists. And the unity of time indeed became what Dr Johnson aptly described as a law 'enacted by despotic antiquity', irrelevant to the experience of modern audiences.[2] Nevertheless, we would be wrong to treat the doctrine exclusively in terms of theatrical illusion, even though it was discussed from that point of view in the renaissance itself because of the rhetorical mould

[1] See e.g. W. K. Wimsatt, Jr. and Cleanth Brooks, *Literary Criticism: A Short History* (1965) 191.   [2] Samuel Johnson, *Rambler* 156.

of criticism. For non-dramatic forms also had to obey a unity of time.

The doctrine becomes more intelligible if we relate it to a compositional method in which numerology based on temporal numbers was a common device. It has interest, then, both for its evidence of a theoretical debate about ideal numerological form and for its bearing on the structural organization of particular works. Classical inheritance as the unity was, it proved easily assimilable to renaissance conceptions of literary form, with which neither Aristotle nor Dr Johnson would have been in sympathy.

The unity of time is a prescription for constructing literary works according to a temporal modulus. And what else is this but temporal numerology? So regarded, the diurnal norm for a tragic action may seem less of an arbitrary external restriction and more of a formal pattern or model. Even the wording of the rule for tragic unity acquires new significance in relation to structural composition. For Aristotle's ὑπὸ μίαν περίοδον ἡλίου was rendered by renaissance Italian critics as 'within the space of one revolution of the sun' (*nello spacio di un giro di Sole*):[1] a significantly astronomical formulation emphasizing the unity and completeness of the spatial form. Moreover, the temporal modulus for a dramatic action was not so much a single day as a certain number of hours. Most often, critics took the controversial single day of Aristotelian tragedy, after Robortello, to mean an 'artificial day' of 12 unequal hours. Such was the interpretation adopted, for example, by Lovisini (1554), by Denores (1586) and—as the upper limit for a comic action—by Riccoboni (1579).[2] Alternatively, a modulus of 24 civil hours might be recommended.

As I mentioned, renaissance critics commonly discussed the temporal structure of drama in relation to performance time, for the reason that rhetorical conceptions dominated the language of criticism. Maggi's version of the unity of time (1550) is typical. He bases the doctrine on the audience's need for credible verisimilitude: 'to hear things done in the space of a month presented in two or at most three hours, the time a tragedy or comedy is acted in—the effect pro-

---

[1] Giason Denores, *Poetica* (1588) fol. 10v; see Bernard Weinberg, *History of Literary Criticism* ii 788. Cf. Lodovico Castelvetro, *Poetica d'Aristotele Vulgarizzata et Sposta* (Vienna 1570) 60, discussed Wimsatt and Brooks 160 n.

[2] See Weinberg, *History of Literary Criticism* i 318, 453 and 587. For the distinction between unequal and natural hours, see below p. 135 n. 5.

duced is one of absolute incredibility.'[1] Similarly Ingegneri (1598) emphasizes the necessity of maintaining an impression of truth, in the face of the many physical improbabilities of theatrical representation. 'The action', he says, 'which according to the masters of the art is allowed to embrace the space of a natural day—that is, of 24 hours —would be worthy of the highest praise if it could occur within the same time, and no more, in which it will be performed—that is, 4 or 5 hours.'[2] For Castelvetro (1576), restriction of the action to 12 hours is necessary for a different reason: the audience's limited powers of physical endurance.[3] Various though they may seem, these lines of argument took their start from the same rhetorical concern with audience reaction and led to the same close association of plot time with acting time.

Some critics identified or confused these two measures of time, as when Lottino says (c. 1566) that dramatic forms are restricted because they cannot contain 'more space of time than those few hours during which they must be presented to the people'.[4] Others limited both times separately, with an odd arbitrariness. Thus Rossi (1589)[5] calls for a spectacle of not more than 5 or 6 hours and an action of not more than 8 or 10. On the other hand, exact synchrony might be aimed at, and even achieved: a famous example in the next century is Racine's *Bérénice*, which has a plot time of about $2\frac{1}{2}$ hours.[6] But the critics of the *cinquecento* generally recognized the difficulties of attaining this ideal.

Short of complete synchrony, interruption of the action by act divisions might allow a dramatist to maintain notional verisimilitude. Piccolomini (1575), who holds that 3 or 4 hours of performance may represent a whole artificial day, even argues that 'division into acts is a device for adjusting the time of performance to the time of the action, with the intermissions accounting for the difference; in this

---

[1] *Cit.* Weinberg, *History of Literary Criticism* i 415.
[2] *Ibid.* ii 1091.
[3] *Poetica d'Aristotele* (Vienna 1570) 60: 'Il quale io no veggo che possa passare il giro del sole, siccome dice Aristotele, cioe ore dodici, conciosiacosache per le necessita del corpo, come e mangiare, bere, disporre i superflui pesi del ventre e della vesica, dormire e per altre necessita, non possa il popolo continuare oltre il predetto termine cosi fatta dirmora in teatro.' Cf. Weinberg, *History of Literary Criticism* i 69, 505.
[4] *Cit. ibid.* i 501.
[5] *Ibid.* ii 669.   [6] Wimsatt and Brooks 191.

way verisimilitude is saved'.[1] The interest of this passage lies in its implication that the unity of time has a bearing on structure and external division. For Piccolomini, act division serves the interest of preserving a temporal modulus—is, in fact, a kind of numerological device. Alternatively, act division might imitate fictive time in a less literal and more symbolic manner, as in Samuel Tuke's five-act *The Adventures of Five Hours* (1663).

EPIC UNITY

Numerological implications of the unity of time are clearer in the case of non-dramatic forms, where no problems of theatrical illusion complicate matters. Temporal limitations restricted other genres with almost equal stringency. Thus the time for a pastoral action was 'one hour or a little more';[2] for a heroic action, some critics allowed a month, others, more liberally, a year.[3] Pigna (1561) offers a typical justification of the larger measure in terms of rhetorical requirements: 'since a man may not...in one single day give an account of his greatness of soul, not less than a month is required to set forth the life of a great prince. This is not too long, since a composition made in this way is to be read, not to be listened to by a waiting spectator.'[4] Such considerations do nothing to explain the preference for a month, however, as against, say, 6 weeks. The choice of a complete temporal unit for the measure of an epic action is the kind of choice we call numerological. Significantly, critics related the measures of actions in different genres. Dryden with his heroic aspirations inevitably regarded the dramatic unity of time as modelled on epic practice: the dramatists'

measure and symmetry was owing to [Homer]. His one, entire, and great action was copied by them according to the proportions of the drama: if he finished his orb within the year, it sufficed to teach them, that their action being less, and being also less diversified with incidents, their orb, of consequence, must be circumscribed in a less compass, which they reduced, within the limits either of a natural or an artificial day.[5]

---

[1] *Cit.* Weinberg, *History of Literary Criticism* i 547.
[2] Denores, *cit.* Weinberg, *History of Literary Criticism* ii 1076.
[3] See Weinberg, *Critical Prefaces of the French Renaissance* (Evanston, Ill. 1950) 256; Ronsard allots a year, on the precedent of *Aen.* v 46–8. André Dacier, however, estimates the action of the *Aeneid* at 7 years (note to *Poetics* v 4).
[4] *Cit.* Weinberg, *History of Literary Criticism* i 470.
[5] 'The Dedication of the Aeneis', *Poems* ed. Kinsley iii 1005.

The actions of the great epics do not only form temporal patterns in the sense that their durations conform to a modulus, however. They form patterns also in their chronological distribution between external divisions (books, cantos) and internal divisions (episodes, events). The primal instance is the chronological structure of Homer's *Iliad*, analysed by Cedric Whitman according to the scheme of days set out below:[1]

It will be objected that the chronology of so long a work is far from easy to establish. Even supposing a structural pattern of this type to have been devised, what chance had it of being noticed? The answer is, A very good chance. We know that from the sixteenth to the eighteenth century, at least, careful readers counted the days of epic actions with astonishing thoroughness. Thus, in the Prefaces to the separate Books of his translation of this very epic, Pope continually directs attention to the calendar. Of Book i he writes: 'The time of two and twenty days is taken up in this book; nine during the plague, one in the council and quarrel of the princes and twelve for Jupiter's stay with the Aethiopians, at whose return Thetis prefers her petition.'[2] As Addison remarks, 'Those who have criticized on the *Odyssey*, the *Iliad* and *Aeneid*, have taken a great deal of pains to fix the number of months or days contained in the action of each of these poems.'[3]

[1] *Homer and the Homeric Tradition* 257.
[2] *Poems*, vii *Translations of Homer: The Iliad i–ix* ed. Maynard Mack (1967) 81. Pope, who omits the day of Chryses' appeal, follows a slightly different scheme from Whitman's; and in fact many different estimates of the poem's duration have been arrived at, from Dacier's 47 days (note to *Poetics* v 4) and Dryden's 48 days ('Discourse Concerning Satire', *Poems* ed. Kinsley ii 620) to Whitman's 54. But my point is that the mere reckoning days, whether it arrived at the right answer or not, might disclose some of the chronological pattern.
[3] *Spectator* 369 (ed. Bond iii 391); cf. *Spectator* 267 (ed. Bond ii 543 f.), *Tatler* 6, and René Le Bossu, *Traité du poème épique* (Paris 1675) ii 5, 18 and iii 12. My

Freedom from the blinkers of a naturalistic expectation allowed earlier readers to see chronology as pattern in a way that has since become difficult. We are blind to a whole set of formal patterns, so long as we assume that chronology must serve exclusively narrative requirements. Formerly, however, computation of the action was regarded as interesting and important in its own right. It might even determine the genre a work belonged to; in his *Sposizione* (*c.* 1570), Castelvetro denies Dante's poem the name of comedy on the ground that its action is not completed within a single revolution of the sun.[1] Judged by epic standards, however, the *Divina commedia* has remarkable unity of time: as Rinuccini noted, it relates a single journey by a single hero, completed in the brief time of 6 days.[2]

Anyone counting days of action[3] in the *Divina commedia* must notice that it is the seventh day that brings the poet to the earthly paradise and to the masque of the Church with its 7 *liste* divided by the griffin. As Vincent Foster Hopper remarks,

The 6 days consumed in traversing Hell and Purgatory suggests strongly the journey of humanity through the 6 earthly ages. The seventh is the Final Sabbath of the world, the age of the Final Resurrection, and accordingly the seventh day finds Dante in the Earthly Paradise. At noon of this day he rises to the Eternal Paradise, having ascended from the temporal to the spiritual world. In this same seventh day, he moves upwards through all the heavens.[4]

Hopper further suggests that at some unspecified point, but before the poet's visions in the eighth heaven of the redeemed, comes a transition to the 'eighth or Final Age of Redemption'. As Gunnar Qvarnström observes, however, this emerging of the cosmic week into eternity 'does not upset the established scheme of seven distinct epic days—it rather makes this scheme even clearer'.

attention has been drawn by Michael Wilding to Zachary Grey's note on *Hudibras* III iii 67, which I quote from the 1744 edn: 'I have before observed, that we may trace our heroes, morning and night: This particular is always essential in poetry, to avoid confusion, and disputes among the critics. How would they have calculated the number of days taken up in the *Iliad*, *Aeneid*, and *Paradise Lost*; if the poets had not been careful to lead them into the momentous discovery?' [1] Weinberg, *History of Literary Criticism* ii 829.
[2] *Cit. ibid.* ii 887. Cf. *ibid.* 983 (Caburacci on unity of time in Ariosto's epic).
[3] These are very distinctly marked, the passage of time being indicated throughout by astronomical *chronographiae*, some of them condensed, intricate and very carefully worked—such as the controversial *Purg.* ix 1–18.
[4] *Medieval Number Symbolism* 199; discussed Qvarnström, *Poetry and Numbers* 33.

What has not been noticed, at least in recent times, is that the 7 days of the *Divina commedia* are arranged, like the *liste*, in a symmetrical *3/1/3* pattern. Moreover, this pattern has a central accent. For the central day of the action, Easter Monday, is also the day when Dante reaches the fourth of the 7 cornices of Purgatory. And, as we have seen, this central cornice is the setting for the pivotal discourse on love that comes in *Purgatorio* xvii, the central canto of book and poem, the same canto that forms the axis of the numerological pattern of line totals.[1] These patterns are summed up in a unity of temporal structures that ensures the simultaneity of all the centres of the symmetrical arrays:

CANTOS OF THE WHOLE POEM[2]	$(1)+49+1+49$
CANTOS OF SYMMETRICAL LINE-TOTAL ARRAY	$3+1+3$
CORNICES OF PURGATORY	$3+1+3$
DAYS OF ACTION	$3+1+3$

The temporal duration of the *Divina commedia* shows its connection with the hexaemeric tradition. To the same tradition, in which most works were numerologically constructed, belongs *Paradise Lost*. Though Milton's chronology is unusually intricate and difficult to follow, early interest in the duration of the action can be documented. Addison discusses the matter in *Spectator* 369 and understandably gets the count wrong: he estimates the directly narrated terrestrial action at 10 days ('From Adam's first appearance in the Fourth Book, to his expulsion from Paradise in the Twelfth, the author reckons ten days'[3]), whereas modern opinion[4] puts it at 11. But at least Addison grasped, if only just, the principle of distinguishing direct from indirect narration. The question whether second-order time should be included in reckoning epic actions, which had been raised by Le Bossu,[5] was vital in the case of *Paradise Lost*, since its action, counting days of indirect narration, just exceeds the epic limit of one month. The overall action is 33 days, the part of it after the Fall carrying its duration beyond the 31 days of March (the prelapsarian month: see *Paradise Lost* x 329).

[1] See above, p. 97.
[2] Counting *Inf.* i as introductory, with Gmelin. See Qvarnström, *Poetry and Numbers* 32.　　　[3] *Spectator* 369; ed. Bond iii 391.
[4] See *The Poems of John Milton* ed. Carey and Fowler 443–6; Qvarnström, *Enchanted Palace* 88 f.
[5] See his discussion of the unity of time in the *Traité* (*cit.* p. 129 n. 3 above) on which Addison depends, while grasping its significance imperfectly.

A reader counting the days of *Paradise Lost* would be quite likely to notice that the ratio between direct and indirect narratives is 1 : 2, the octave proportion of harmony and well-ordered concupiscibility. And he could scarcely miss the allusion to the years of Christ's life in the day total 33, the same symbolic number that Dante used for the canto totals of books in the *Divina commedia*.[1] It would be natural for him, then, to look for chronological symmetry like that of Dante's week; which he would find in Milton's placement of the week of creation by Messiah (*Paradise Lost* vii) at the centre of the 33 days. Moreover, this week of creation itself has a central accent. Its fourth day, when Messiah creates the sun, is alone honoured with the description 'crowned': 'Glad evening and glad morn crowned the fourth day' (vii 386). The array has thus the strong central accent characteristic of baroque:[2]

DAYS $13 + 3 + 1 + 3 + 13$

$\underbrace{}$

Week of
creation

[1] For earlier treatments of this familiar number symbol, in Cassiodorus and others, see Curtius 496, Røstvig, 'The Hidden Sense' 8. More recently, Spenser had followed Dante in applying it numerologically, in *Ruins of Rome*.

[2] The chronology of *Paradise Lost* is worked out in detail in my Introduction, *The Poems of John Milton* ed. Carey and Fowler 443–6, and in notes referred to there.

7. Temporal numbers

A natural extension of the unity of time was to use temporal measures as moduli for the division of works into lines, stanzas, cantos, or other units. We have had a hint of this possibility already in act division in drama. But temporal numerology is distributed so widely in Elizabethan stanzaic poetry, and worked out with such fertility in the invention of new devices, that it must be far more than a mere application of misunderstood classical theory. We see one positive impulse behind it in the ready observance of decorum that shaped every formalized social activity of the age. A deeper motive, however, issued from contemporary understanding of creation itself as a process mystically accomplished according to a familiar temporal series. The world was made in the 6 days of a week; well might the poet, therefore, repeat the Psalmist's prayer: 'teach us to number our days, that we may apply our hearts unto wisdom' (*Ps.* xc 12).

Everyone was then familiar with the notion of designing monuments, buildings, religious images and processions numerically as models of time. Classical precedents were known or imagined. Thus, Valeriano on the circle of the year describes the golden circle in Simondius' tomb, 365 cubits in circumference 'singulis anni diebus in singulis cubitis exsculptis', and compares it to the image of the zodiac in the hall of the Palazzo della Ragione at Padua:[1] Sir William

[1] *Hieroglyphica* xxxix xi; p. 486.

Segar carefully notes that 365 young men followed 365 magi in Darius' triumphal procession, 'for the Persian year containeth even so many days':[1] and Sir Thomas Browne is enthusiastic about the possibilities for temporal number symbolism offered by the sacred groves of the ancients—

> Since they were so methodical in the constitutions of their temples, as to observe the due situation, aspect, manner, form, and order in architectonical relations, whether they were not as distinct in their groves and plantations about them, in form and *species* respectively unto their Deities, is not without probability of conjecture. And in their groves of the sun this [i.e. 5] was a fit number, by multiplication to denote the days of the year; and might hieroglyphically speak as much, as the mystical *Statua* of Janus[2] in the language of his fingers. And since they were so critical in the number of his horses, the strings of his harp, and rays about his head, denoting the orbs of heaven, the seasons and months of the year; witty idolatry would hardly be flat in other appropriations.[3]

Browne can take for granted, we notice, familiarity with the symbolism of the sun god's 4 horses (seasons), 12 rays (months) and 7 lyre strings (planets or spheres).[4]

The visual art of the Middle Ages and the early renaissance had indeed made temporal iconography exceedingly familiar. It is enough to mention the vast range of illuminated manuscripts, mural paintings and decorative sculptures with calendrical or astronomical subjects—the countless Labours of the Months,[5] the Zodiacs, the planetary series.[6] Many of the finest works of the period had programmes of this kind: one thinks of the Tempio Malatesta murals, of Cossa's Guardians of the Months in the Palazzo Schifanoia at Ferrara and of many fine Books of Hours. An extreme case (though by no means without parallel) is Peruzzi's ceiling for the Sala della Galatea in the Villa Farnesina at Rome, which sets out the state of the heavens on

---

[1] *Honour, military and civil* iii 24.
[2] Side-note: 'Which King Numa set up, with his fingers so disposed that they numerically denoted 365. Pliny.'   [3] *The Garden of Cyrus* i; ed. Keynes i 185.
[4] Cf. Virgil, *Aen.* xii 163 f: 'Twelve golden beams around his temples play, / To mark his lineage from the god of day' (tr. Dryden, *Aeneis* xii 247 f.). On numerical symbolism in the iconography of the sun, see L'Orange, esp. p. 9.
[5] Consult James Carson Webster, *The Labors of the Months in Antique and Mediaeval Art to the End of the Twelfth Century*, Princeton Monographs in Art and Archaeology xxi (Princeton, N.J. 1938) and É. Mâle, *The Gothic Image* tr. Dora Nussey (1961) 64–75.
[6] Many are discussed and illustrated in Jean Seznec, *The Survival of the Pagan Gods* tr. Barbara F. Sessions, Bollingen Series xxxviii (New York 1953).

1 December 1466—the geniture of Agostino Chigi.[1] And simpler examples were everywhere. Knole House had 365 rooms, 52 staircases and 7 courts; in Mansart's Marly Château 12 pavilions enveloped a central block symbolizing the sun. Processions, masques, pageants: shows of every kind represented Time and his parts.[2] To meet their designers' needs Cesare Ripa included elaborate iconographical programmes for the 12 months and the 4 seasons in his *Iconologia* (Rome 1593). Nothing speaks more eloquently of the passion for temporal schemes than the fact that although no firm iconographical tradition for representing the 24 hours existed, Ripa felt the need to invent a set of designs: 'One may often have occasion to portray the hours, and, though it would be possible to copy designs that have been described by many authors, I have preferred to describe them yet again, differently. For variety is a pleasure to the enthusiast.'[3] As late as Bach, patterns of temporal numbers were even used in music.[4]

The calendar is less well known now than when saints' days were observed and holidays scattered through the year.[5] But certain other schemes and numbers have remained in use, or can easily be recovered. Temporal numerology is often a simple matter of adjustment of line or stanza totals to such measures as 12 (months, or unequal hours), 24 (civil hours), 52 (weeks), 60 (minutes) and 365

---

[1] This example and others similar are discussed *ibid.* 76 ff.; see also F. Saxl, *La fede astrologica de Agostino Chigi* (Rome 1934).

[2] For ancient and Eastern buildings designed as cosmic models, see L'Orange 9 ff. Temporal figures in pageants were almost too common to list; but one is bound to mention at least Vasari's description of the ages of man and the ages of history in the triumph for Leo X (Life of Pontormo). For an English pageant of the 12 hours, see Withington i 234. A particularly splendid theatrical example is Jonson's Haddington masque, in which masquers 'under the characters of the twelve signs', placed within a gigantic gold and silver armillary sphere, symbolized the 'twelve sacred powers, / That are presiding at all nuptial hours' (ed. Herford, Simpson and Simpson vii 258).

[3] *Iconologia* (Rome 1603) 203.

[4] For Bach's use of the number 365, see Qvarnström, *Poetry and Numbers* 39.

[5] A bibliography is given in C. R. Cheney, *Handbook of Dates for Students of English History* (1961) pp. xi–xviii, to which add Jones's article in the Oxford *History of Technology* iii (Oxford 1957). R. L. Poole's 'The Beginning of the Year in the Middle Ages', *Proceedings of the British Academy* x (1921) is especially useful. The best account of the many different ways of reckoning hours, the most important kinds being civil or equal hours (like our own) and temporary or unequal hours (twelve-part divisions of the period of darkness or of light), will be found in G.-B. Riccioli, *Almagesti novi tomus primus*, 2 Pts (Bologna 1651) i 34–7. See further p. 60 and p. 165.

(days). Alternatively, astronomical measures might be used: 12 (signs); 23½ (degrees of the sun's maximum declination); 24 (sidereal hours); 30 (degrees per sign); 89, 90, 92 and 93 (days per season); 359 (degrees of the sun's daily motion); 360 (degrees of the sun's annual motion about the ecliptic, or apparent daily motion).

SIMPLE TEMPORAL NUMBER SYMBOLISMS: HEXAEMERIC AND COMPUTISTIC APPLICATIONS

There seem to be few ancient examples of temporal numerology, apart from simple computistic applications of temporal numbers by such late Latin poets as Claudian (whose shorter poems number 52) and Ausonius (*Eclogues* ix, x on the months, one 12 lines, the other 24 with 2 lines to each month). Important exceptions of lasting influence are Virgil's *Eclogues* i and ix, which consist each of exactly 12 speeches ('amor tantum mihi crescit in horas'), so that they follow in numerological terms as well as in content the ancient convention whereby pastoral poems ended with nightfall. This concluding *topos*, labelled by Curtius (90) 'We must stop because night is coming on', continued through medieval literature, to be reinterpreted spatially by Spenser and Milton. Both *Prothalamion* and *Lycidas* follow the convention, and both use the 180 measure of the degrees of the diurnal sun's half-circle: the former for its line total, the latter for its long-line total (180 – 1). We recall that Virgil's *Eclogue* ix was also a precedent for the name Lycidas.

In the Middle Ages, application of temporal numbers to literary form became somewhat commoner. A decisive influence was that of the hexaemeric writers, who organized their works in patterns corresponding to the 6 days of creation, or the 7 days of the divine week. Thus St Ambrose arranged his *Hexaemeron* in 6 books, St Gregory wrote 6 hymns *De dierum creatione* and St Augustine (who explained the 6 days of creation in terms of Neoplatonic number symbolism) divided his *De Genesi* into 12 books.[1]

In the fifteenth century Pico della Mirandola reinterpreted this hexaemeric tradition by the obscure light of cabalism and Neo-

---

[1] Basil the Great's influential *Homilies on the Hexaemeron* had a more complex arrangement in 9 divisions, designed to honour the creation of plants (including the tree in the midst of the garden) in the central section: *Morning 1 | Evening 1 | Morning 2 | Evening 2 | Day 3: Creation of Plants | Day 4 | Day 5 | Morning 6 | Evening 6.*

pythagoreanism. Pico's own account of creation, the *Heptaplus*, is divided into 7 books of 7 chapters each, an arrangement that follows, as his Preface explains, a precedent set by earlier works in the tradition. It is meant to be numerologically significant:

I have divided my whole exposition into 7 books or tractates, more in order to imitate Basil and Augustine than to revive the attention of the reader resting, as it were, at the frequent intermissions. Add to this that, since the 7 expositions are distributed through 7 books, and the 7 individual books are divided each into 7 chapters, all the parts correspond to the 7 days of creation. We have done this according to a most appropriate and harmonious design, so that just as the seventh day, according to Moses, is the Sabbath and a day of peace and rest, so each of our expositions always leads in its seventh chapter to Christ, who is the end of the Law and our Sabbath, our peace and rest, our happiness.[1]

—'As explicit a profession of numerological intent, in plain prose, as any sceptic could wish for. Among later Platonists, Pythagorean number symbolism came to be thought of as fundamental to the whole conception of a hexaemeron. Henry More was to remark that anyone seriously considering 'what small sense can be made by a philosopher of the six days' creation and God's resting on the seventh, without this key of the natures of numbers and figures, will be enforced to confess, that there is one supreme wisdom that has ever attended the Church and the Holy Scriptures, from end to end, which in the abstrusest mysteries thereof has been pleased to make use of a method of concealment which is numeral, or, if I may so speak, Cabbalistical'.[2]

Under the influence of Reformation and Counter-Reformation Biblical Poetics, the hexaemeric tradition in poetry itself revived and even flourished strongly.[3] A Christian Muse inspired Du Bartas's much translated and annotated *Semaines* (1578, 1603); Tasso's *Le sette giornate del mondo creato* (1592); Christofle de Gamon's *La semaine ou création du monde contre celle du Sieur du Bartas* (1609); Traherne's *Meditations on the Six Days of the Creation*, in which the 'Sixth Day' comprises 12 six-line stanzas;[4] and Sir Richard Blackmore's *Creation, a philosophical poem in seven books* (1712).

[1] *Opera omnia* i (Basel 1573) 10.
[2] *An Explanation of the Grand Mystery of Godliness* (1660) 197; *cit.* Røstvig, 'The Hidden Sense' 94.
[3] See Frank Egleston Robbins, *The Hexaemeral Literature* (Chicago 1912); Watson Kirkconnell, *The Celestial Cycle*; R. A. Sayce, *The French Biblical Epic in the Seventeenth Century* (Oxford 1955); Røstvig 'The Hidden Sense' 72 ff.
[4] *Centuries, Poems, and Thanksgivings* ed. Margoliouth ii (Oxford 1958) 192-9.

Moreover, the practice of dividing long works into parts corresponding to days extended beyond the six-day hexaemera proper. To this extended hexaemeric tradition belongs John Swan's *Speculum mundi, or, A Glass Representing the Face of the World* (1635) in 6 days' works and La Primaudaye's *L'académie française*, divided in the English translation of 1618 into no fewer than 43 'days' works'.[1] Du Bartas's 'incomplete' *Seconde semaine* really belongs in the same sub-hexaemeric category, since it is arranged as $4+4+4+5 = 17$ subsections. In this instance we have the author's own defence of the division: his 'Brief avertissement sur sa première et seconde semaine' (1584) argues that in

the language of the Holy Spirit...mystical days and prophetic weeks are not measured by the ordinary course of the sun, as they often embrace several years or centuries. But for a full answer, I refer any critics to the last chapter of the *De Civitate Dei* of St Augustine, from which I have taken the title, the argument, and the division of the present work.[2]

Sylvester more simply divides the 4 completed days of the Second Week into 4 parts each, giving an actual total of $4 \times 4 = 16$ parts and a projected perfect-number total for the whole scheme of $4 \times 7 = 28$ parts. There is some suggestion that these subdivisions correspond to the 4 times of day, in Sylvester's 1606 title *Posthumous Bartas. The forenoon of the fourth day of his second week.*

On the creative imagination these structural precedents appear to have had a strong effect—stronger, even, than that of the separate secular tradition represented by such works as Boccaccio's *Decameron* and Basile's *Pentameron*. It was a short step from hexaemera and en-

[1] On La Primaudaye, see Frances A. Yates, *The French Academies* 123 ff. Vol. i is in 18 days' works, each of 4 chapters, making 72 chapters in all; vol. ii in 13 days' works, all of 8 chapters except the last, of 4 chapters, making 100 in all; and vol. iii in 12 days' works, all of 8 chapters except the 11th (of 12 chapters), making 100 in all: $18 \times 4 = 72$; $12 \times 8 + 1 \times 4 = 100$; $10 \times 8 + 1 \times 12 + 1 \times 8 = 100$. Vol. iv is divided into $16 + 7$ chapters, the last of which is subdivided into 24 sections.

[2] Guillaume de Salluste Sieur du Bartas, *The Works* ed. Holmes *et al.* i (Chapel Hill, N.C. 1935) 219. Du Bartas refers to *De Civ. Dei* xxii 30, St Augustine's influential exposition of the number symbolism governing the ages of human history. The 6 past ages into which the redemptive history was divided could be compared to days: 'the first age, as it were the first day, is from Adam unto the flood...' St Augustine begins the seventeen-chapter second part of the *De Civ. Dei* with a preface referring to the division of his work into books (Pref. to Bk VI). Sylvester alters Du Bartas's scheme to 4×4 parts, by omitting the 'Histoire de Jonas' from Day 4.

cyclopaedic *summas* avowedly ordered by temporal or astronomical divisions, to poems with similar, but more implicit, numerical arrangements; from, say, the 12 books of Palingenius' *Zodiacus vitae*, consisting of encyclopaedic contents distributed associationally under the 12 signs, to Spenser's *Shepherd's Calendar* in 12 eclogues 'proportionable to the twelve months'.[1]

During the Middle Ages, temporal numerology was relatively uncommon. Astronomy and astrology might be prominent in the content of poetry; but few poems outside the hexaemeral tradition had structures organized according to temporal numbers. Theological number symbolism queened it over all other forms. With the renaissance, however, the situation changed fundamentally. (In this respect, too, the *Divina commedia* is best regarded as an early renaissance work.)

For temporal numerology now grew so abundant as to become a characteristic form. Indeed, though theological number symbolism was to last on into the seventeenth century alongside abstract Neopythagoreanism, the feature most obviously distinguishing renaissance from medieval numerology is a wider use of temporal numbers. Literary-critical theories of the unities, hexaemeric precedents and deep emotional and philosophical preoccupations with time all conspired to produce a remarkable efflorescence of lyric poetry with forms based on temporal numbers.

An early exemplar was Garcilaso de la Vega's posthumous *Eclogue* i (Barcelona 1543), which consists of 56 lines of introduction and 365 lines of dialogue, divided 182 + 183. And it would be easy to multiply English instances of similar computistic use of temporal and astronomical numbers; as when Cowley concludes a twenty-four-verse paragraph with the lines:

The smooth-paced hours of every day
Glided numerously away.
Like thy verse each hour did pass,
Sweet and short, like that it was.[2]

[1] Marcellus Palingenius, *The Zodiac of Life* tr. Barnabe Googe (New York 1947). On the distribution of matter in Palingenius according to association with the signs, see Rosemond Tuve in *JEGP* xxxiv (1935) 1–19, J. H. Walter in *MLR* xxxvi (1941) 37–58 and Fowler 26, 63 n.

[2] 'Elegy upon Anacreon'; ed. Waller 60. In the same category of simple computistic patterns falls Turberville's 'That Time conquereth all things' in 52 lines (ed. Chalmers ii 616).

Such trivial decorums, however, have pale charms at best. We confine ourselves to two instances with a little more finesse. Dryden ingeniously makes his *Britannia rediviva* 361, not 360, lines, in keeping with the compliment that the sun 'stretched the sphere / Beyond the limits of the lengthened year' to see the birth of the prince at the summer solstice (actually 10 June 1688).[1] Moreover, since the daily retrogression of the sun's sphere round the ecliptic is about 1°, the impossible extra degree beyond the annual 360 may be regarded as increasing the year by a day. Consequently the larger line total of 366, when we include the five-line epigraph heading the poem, is also appropriate since it can be construed as 365 + 1. We find a similar device in the elegy 'To the memory of Mr Oldham', which has 25 lines, but just 12 rhymes. Time the destroyer of Dryden's fellow poet is addressed in a self-referring triplet:

Thy generous fruits, though gathered ere their prime
Still showed a quickness; and maturing time
But mellows what we write to the dull sweets of rhyme.[2]

After the sufficient twelve-couplet measure of Oldham's day (encompassed by 'Fate and gloomy Night'), Time confers on the twin poet who survives only a needless mellowing, a superfluous rhyme.

MANNERIST COMPLICATION: 'THE AMOROUS ZODIAC'

An unusually sustained and conveniently explicit example of temporal numerology is 'The Amorous Zodiac', (Appendix 2, p. 208) included in the 1595 *Ovid's Banquet of Sense* and almost certainly attributable to Chapman.[3] Gilles Durant's original, *Le zodiac amoureux* (1587), must have seemed by comparison a flat *soufflé*. The French poem is an elaborate panegyrical *blason* in the form of a mechanical *catalogue raisonné* itemizing a mistress' beauties from head to foot. Its sole point lies in a conceit, whereby the traditional medical melothesia distributing the body's 12 parts among the 12 governing signs is combined with an erotic *blason* of 12 physical charms. (Both schemes

---

[1] Ed. Kinsley ii 541–51. The conceit is Virgilian: 'He shall extend his propagated sway, / Beyond the solar year' (Dryden, *Aeneis* vi 1084 f.).

[2] Ed. Kinsley i 389.

[3] In view of the implied promise at the end of the immediately preceding 'A Coronet for his Mistress Philosophy' to write another poem to the same mistress, there seems little reason to doubt Chapman's authorship of 'The Amorous Zodiac'. But see *The Poems* ed. Bartlett 434 f., where the claim of Richard Stapleton is considered.

happened to start with the head and finish with the feet.[1]) But the English imitator gives this sinking confection lift and point, not only by enriching its imagery but also by shaping its structure into far more complex numerological patterns. His passion for formal expression is almost fanatical: he must find a spatial correlate for every aspect of the action. The result is a *tour de force*, extreme even by the standards of its time, which would scarcely claim attention but for its evidential value to the present argument. For Chapman exaggerates a style itself exaggerated: in its effects of sterilized eroticism and of unnecessary formal difficulties overcome with ease, 'The Amorous Zodiac' is almost a *reductio ad absurdum* of mannerist love poetry.

Chapman's pursuit of the ideal of completely self-referring statement may be seen as a continuation of his search for ever more oblique and delicate verbal decorums, with which to continue the zodiacal sequence unexpectedly. Direct enumeration of signs ('The Twins' sign': 'Leo's month') is varied both by rhetorical means, as in the assimilation of the celestial to the human in Virgo the last northern sign ('And now to bid the boreal signs adieu / I come to give thy virgin-cheeks the view') and by iconographical allusion, as in the description of his mistress' brow as 'gilded', a hint at the golden horns of Taurus (April, ix). Finally, by a numerological variation, the miming of the sun's course extends into decorums of structure. In this 'truly-blessed variety' (xxx), Chapman displays his age's characteristic preference for formal complication. However, he also draws attention to some of his numerological decorums with a quite unusual verbal explicitness. Several passages, indeed, only make sense when taken as applying to the spatial structure.

[1] The usual zodiacal melothesia runs: Aries, head and face / Taurus, neck / Gemini, arms / Cancer, breast / Leo, heart / Virgo, bowels / Libra, reins / Scorpio, genitals / Sagittarius, thighs / Capricorn, knees / Aquarius, legs / Pisces, feet. The 'Amorous Zodiac' blason: Aries, head / Taurus, brow / Gemini, eyes / Cancer, nose / Leo, mouth and tongue / Virgo, cheeks / Libra, neck / Scorpio, breasts / Sagittarius, hand / Capricorn, genitals / Aquarius, thighs / Pisces, calves and feet. On zodiacal melothesias, see Harry Bober, 'The Zodiacal Miniature of the *Très Riches Heures* of the Duke of Berry—Its Sources and Meaning', *JWI* XI (1948) 1–34; Edmond Liénard, 'La mélothésie zodiacale dans l'antiquité', *Revue de l'université de Bruxelles* XXXIX (1934) 471–85. The *locus classicus* was Manilius, *Astron.* ii 453–65, but the system remained so familiar from its medical use that a satiric passage could be made to depend on knowledge of it as late as Dryden; see *The Hind and the Panther* iii 168, where the belly and 'all that Scorpio claims' is attributed to the Presbyterian wolf.

The initial proposal is to shine in the mistress' beauties: to frame like the sun an 'endless zodiac' and to 'furnish both the year and sky':

Keeping even way through every excellence,
I'll make in all, an equal residence
Of a new zodiac: a new Phoebus guising,
When (without altering the course of nature)
I'll make the seasons good, and every creature
Shall henceforth reckon day, from my first rising. (St. v)

The sun poet keeps his promise to reside 'equally' in the signs, since he devotes 2 stanzas to each. Transitions, distinct and explicit, never allow the reader to forget this—'My second month, and second house', 'Resigning that', etc. There are three exceptions to this rule of 2 stanzas per sign, but they soon prove it. Thus Chapman explains the delay for 3 stanzas in Gemini as due to the influence of those 'Twin-born fires' his mistress' eyes:

But now I fear, that throned in such a sign,
Playing with objects, pleasant and divine,
I should be moved to dwell there thirty days:
O no, I could not in so little space,
With joy admire enough their plenteous grace,
But ever live in sun-shine of their rays. (St. xii)

The wittiness of this tribute partly lies in its neat provision of a formal analogy to an aberration in the real sun's motion: namely, the slowing that occurs near the auge or apogee.[1] In view of this, we expect some justification of the single stanzas assigned to Aquarius and Pisces (xxvii, xxviii), and find it, in a compensating Envoy making up the requisite 2 stanzas (xxix, xxx). Consequently the overall array of stanzas is

5 (INTRODUCTION) + 23 (ZODIAC: $2 \times 12 + 1 - 2$) + 2 (ENVOY) = 30,

[1] As was well known at the time; not only from textbooks and almanacs, but also from poetry: see e.g. Du Bartas 366: the line that cuts the zodiac at the tropic sign Cancer 'Of the Sun's stops, it Colure hath to name, / Because his teem doth seem to trot more tame / On these cut points: for here he doth not ride / Flatling along, but up the sphere's steep side.' The fact that Durant and Chapman put the auge in Gemini rather than in Cancer (its sixteenth-century position) might suggest that they are here following an ancient source of information. In all the decorums described in the present paragraph Chapman follows Durant. But see Copernicus, *Commentariolus*, in *Three Copernican Treatises* tr. Edward Rosen (rev. edn, New York and London 1959) 62, where the auge is oddly said to lie opposite 'a point of the firmament about 10° west of the more brilliant of the two bright stars in the head of Gemini'.

and the sun's own sign, Leo, occupies the central place of honour, Stanzas xv–xvi.

It seems impossible that Chapman should be able to depart from the rule of 'equal residence' in the signs, and still keep his promise to 'make the seasons good'. How can he make the seasons of equal length, when the signs are not? Only by arranging for a separate seasonal pattern, independent of the zodiacal. Hence spring runs only from vi ('To open then the spring-time's golden gate') to the last mention of 'ver' in viii; autumn from xx ('my autumn I'll commence') to xxii (in the stanza following the poet abandons 'the rest of my autumnal race' for a side-trip off the ecliptic); and winter from xxvi ('wintry solstice', the regular astronomical commencement of winter) to xxviii ('here my latest season I will end'). A measure, in fact, of 3 stanzas per season. True, summer occupies 6 stanzas, beginning with the pun in xi ('The shock of our joined-fires the summer starting'); but this exception is again justified, in the description of the lady's lips as 'doubling like fervent Sirius, summer's fires' (xvi). The time of the sun's greatest power and the day's 'longest durance' is lengthened out in the seasonal, as in the zodiacal, pattern.

The third prediction in v, that 'every creature / Shall henceforth reckon day from my first rising', proves also to have a structural reference. For, besides grandiloquently assuming the role of *declarator temporis*, Chapman here instructs us to reckon day numerologically from the stanza at which he rises. Now the sun does not 'enlight the world' until vii, so that the poem's day is just $(30-6)$ or 24 stanza-hours, each of 60 metrical syllable-minutes.[1] This pattern fits in with that of the zodiac, just as the real sun's diurnal and annual courses bear an organic relation. (Daily retardations in the sun's course add up to form his annual journey round the ecliptic.) Thus, the measures of 24 stanzas per day and of 2 stanzas per sign—24 stanzas, theoretically, for the whole ecliptic circle—are consistent, and together allude to the spatial division of the heavens into 24 sidereal 'hours'. Moreover, the interaction of the two solar motions finds further structural expression in a simultaneous bisection of annual and diurnal patterns at the same point, between Stanzas xviii and xix. This represents the

[1] Counting the Envoy. It may be objected that the sun poet was already mentioned rising (though in the future tense) in v. But Chapman has provided for this objection: 24 stanzas from v take us to the end of the poem, *not* counting the Envoy.

autumnal equinoctial point, at which the sun enters Libra (the Balance) the first of the southern signs, and day and night are equal. At this point, therefore, light and darkness, the apparent and the hidden, come into equilibrium:

In balancing the darkness with the light,
It so might weigh, with scales of equal weight
Thy beauties seen with those do not appear.

Further reinforcing this scrupulous division—'Twice three months used, to run through twice three houses'—is a bisection of the *blason* items. For Chapman has contrived simultaneously to divide the charms of his mistress into 2 clearly defined groups of 6. First come the charms of the head, corresponding to the visible hemisphere but forming also a complete microcosmic 'circle': head, brow, eyes, nose, mouth and cheeks. Then follow the hidden charms of the body: neck, breasts, hand, genitals, thighs and feet. And the point of transition, as the poet is careful to announce, is again the equinoctial point:

To balance now thy more obscured graces
'Gainst them the circle of thy head enchases. (St. xix)

The doubly emphatic bisection of day and year even extends to the poem's line total, 180, the number of degrees in half the sun's daily or annual orbit.

Other passages also have structural correlates. The obscure parenthesis '(To give my moons their full in twelve months' spaces)', for example, becomes clear when we see its meaning mimed by the stanza pattern. For 28 days is the lunar month[1] and Stanza xxviii completes the zodiacal sequence of 12 months' spaces. Moreover, the addition of the Envoy, which regularizes the zodiac, brings the stanza total to 30, a number very close to that denoting the days in the synodic lunar period, or interval between full moons.

The most elegant decorum without doubt occurs in xxiii, where we expect the sign Sagittarius but meet with a diversion:

To sort from this most brave and pompous sign
(Leaving a little my ecliptic line
Less superstitious than the other sun)
The rest of my autumnal race I'll end
To see thy hand, (whence I the crown attend,)
Since in thy past parts I have slightly run.

[1] Not an orbital period, but the lunar month of popular and civil usage; see *OED* s.v. *Month* 3.

Here Chapman varies the sequence of signs by substituting for Sagittarius the extra-zodiacal constellation Corona meridionalis, 'the crown'. This departure had some authority in Hyginus, who lumps Corona together with Sagittarius in his description of the latter (*Poet. astron.* xxvi). But a more important consideration would be the thematic relevance of the constellation's circular form. The image of the starry circlet epitomizes the zodiac and unites it with the immediately preceding poem in Chapman's book, the 'Coronet for his Mistress Philosophy'. Now the Southern Crown—which during the sixteenth century lay in the sign Sagittarius, but off the ecliptic to the south[1]—could have been mentioned as an additional felicity without interrupting the zodiacal series, as Corona borealis was in xix.[2] Or it could have been substituted for Sagittarius silently, as Argo navis was, for Cancer.[3] But Chapman has chosen to draw attention on this occasion, and on this occasion alone, to his deviation from the ecliptic. It is significant that he should do so in Stanza xxiii; for the ecliptic plane is inclined to the equatorial at an angle of 23 degrees and a fraction, so that the word *ecliptic* receives sole mention in the stanza whose number measures, in whole degrees, its angle of inclination.[4] The same symbolism may inform the choice of 23 as the net total of the stanzas assigned to the sun's ecliptic path through the zodiac.

Chapman's ingenious poem conceals other decorums for the pleasure of the more curious enquirer. But we may rest content with distinguishing, in recapitulation, the three main types of device

[1] Overlapping in the sixteenth century, like the constellation Sagittarius, into the sign Capricorn.

[2] 'The circle of thy head'—again with thematic insistence on the circular form. The Northern Crown lay on the same meridian with the constellation Libra, overlapping the signs Libra and Scorpio.

[3] 'It is thy nose (stern to thy bark of love)' (xiv). In the sixteenth century the rudders and stern of Argo navis lay in the sign Cancer. The astronomical allusion is very precise, since Argo navis has no bow (Pl. 1).

[4] Cf. Herbert's very similar decorum in 'The Church-Porch', where the lines 'Entice the trusty sun, if that thou can, / From his ecliptic line' come in St. xxiii. Several articles have discussed the architectural symbolism of the structure of Herbert's *The Temple*, and one its temporal symbolism; none, however, has ventured beyond general impressions to explore the exact numerology that abounds throughout the work. On the temporal imagery, see Stanley Stewart, 'Time and *The Temple*', *SEL* vi (1966) 97–110; on the architectural symbolism George Watson, 'The Fabric of Herbert's *Temple*', *JWI* xxvi (1963) 354–8 and John D. Walker, 'The Architectonics of George Herbert's *The Temple*', *ELH* xxix (1962) 289–305.

exploited in it. First, ambiguity with one sense substantive and meta-phorical, the other spatial and literal. Secondly, seeming departure from a regular modulus (or abandonment of a scheme) that turns out on closer consideration to be a finesse in the interest of variety, stylishness, or mere obscurity. Finally, superimposition of patterns—here overlapping of zodiacal, seasonal, diurnal and anatomical stanza arrays. The result is a characteristic mannerist asymmetry, concealing a more complicated order. Even the Introduction (5 stanzas) and the Envoy (2 stanzas), when resolved into 30 lines and 12 lines, are seen to bear thematic proportions.

NEW YEAR POEMS

In Elizabethan times it was a common practice to present poems as New Year's gifts. Such poems often exhibit temporal numerology, as do others that have the New Year as their subject. Not all, however, have structures as simple as that of Sir Arthur Gorges's 'New Year's Gift to the King's Majesty' in 12 lines. Indeed, the patterns of New Year poems, though stereotyped, present enough initial difficulty to warrant separate treatment. Two classes of pattern may be distinguished, one based on the number 8, the other, more obscurely, on 84.

1 January, the Feast of the Circumcision, was the eighth day of Christmas. Arithmological authorities discussed the number symbolism of this interval (regeneration; transcending the 7 of the mortal body) so often that it became familiar knowledge.[1] Moreover, New Year's Day became associated with the number 8 because Christmas Day was sometimes reckoned the beginning of the year.[2] It does not surprise us, therefore, to find Ben Jonson's 'A New Year's Gift Sung to King Charles, 1635' introduced by a Prologue on the New Year in 8 lines.[3] Similarly, Herrick's 'The New-year's Gift, or Circumcision's Song, sung to the King in the Presence at White-Hall' and 'Another New-Year's Gift, or Song for the Circumcision' both have 5 solo parts and 3 choruses, and the second is further divided into 8 metrical sections.[4]

[1] For many references, see Hopper 114, Fowler 53 n. and Bongo 326 ff.
[2] See Cheney 3 f., and Poole.
[3] *Underwood* lxxix; ed. Herford, Simpson and Simpson viii 263.
[4] *The Poetical Works of Robert Herrick* ed. L. C. Martin (Oxford 1963) 365–7). 'Another New-Year's Gift' has also, however, a symmetrical pattern of line totals and choruses about the section containing the altar.

146

Another type of pattern is exemplified by Drayton's Ode 'To the New Year', in 14 six-line stanzas or 84 lines.[1] Taking a hint from the previous type, it is not difficult to guess that 84 measures the days from New Year's Day to Lady Day (25 March), the regular beginning of the civil year in Drayton's time. His words suggest as much:

Great Janus, I thy pleasure,
With all the Thespian treasure,
Do seriously pursue;
To th' passed year returning,
As though the old adjourning,
Yet bringing in the new. (ll. 7–12)

Drayton uses a similar form for the First Eclogue of *The Shepherd's Garland* (1593), again in 84 lines, and with an action certainly taking place in March: 'Now Phoebus from the equinoctial zone, / Had tasked his team unto the higher sphere.'[2]

Returning to Jonson's 'New Year's gift', we now see that its $8 + 69 = 77$ lines measure the days between 25 December, 1 January and 11 March: all of them days from which the year was sometimes reckoned as beginning. For on 11 March (the vernal equinox) the sun entered Aries to commence the astronomical year. Hence, although Jonson starts 'To day old Janus opens the new year, / And shuts the old', he is soon looking ahead (ll. 24–7) to spring.

[1] Ed. Hebel ii 350–2.
[2] *Ibid.* i 47. Chapman's 'Hymn to Hymen' in 84 lines, though not occasioned by any New Year event, wishes Princess Elizabeth 'all year's comforts' (ed. Bartlett 366, l. 33). Here, however, the pattern is complicated by others, notably a symbolism of hours' and 'minutes' time' $(60 + 24 = 84)$.

8. Epithalamia

Temporal numerology was particularly common in the epithalamic genre. In a sample of 50 Elizabethan epithalamia, 16 of the 33 organized numerically used temporal numbers.[1] Others were based on a non-temporal symbolism of 5 or 8. The latter numbers have such importance for the formal iconography of the genre, and receive such illuminating explanation from the poets themselves, that they claim our attention first.

Anciently, 5 was a nuptial number because of an abstract philosophical symbolism. According to Plutarch, the Pythagoreans called it 'Marriage' because the association or addition of the first male and the first female number produced it: $2+3 = 5$ (*De E apud Delph.* 388 C). Sir Thomas Browne has this notion in mind when he writes that 5 was 'the Conjugal number, which ancient numerists made out by two and three, the first parity and imparity, the active and passive digits, the material and formal principles in generative societies'.[2] He mentions also the 5 lights customary in Roman nuptial solemnities, here referring his reader to Plutarch, whose discussion of wedding ritual in the *Roman Problems* was authoritative in the renaissance.

---

[1] The sample was fairly taken from the present point of view, since it consisted of epithalamia in Robert H. Case's anthology *English Epithalamies* (Chicago and London 1896); though of course there is a bias to quality.

[2] *The Garden of Cyrus* v; ed. Keynes i 222.

Plutarch speculates at length about the possible number symbolisms underlying the 5 *cerei* or wax tapers. Perhaps, he suggests, the odd number symbolizes peaceful union, since it cannot be divided into equal parts:

Is it because in their use of several numbers the odd number was considered better and more perfect for various purposes and also better adapted to marriage? For the even number admits division and its equality of division suggests strife and opposition; the odd number, however, cannot be divided into equal parts at all, but whenever it is divided it always leaves behind a remainder of the same nature as itself. Now, of the odd numbers, 5 is above all the nuptial number; for 3 is the first odd number, and 2 is the first even number, and 5 is composed of the union of these two, as it were of male and female. (*Quaest. Rom.* 264 A)

Or perhaps the 5 encourages fertility, as the largest number of children that can come to light at a single birth (the light of the tapers being a symbol of birth). 'Or is it because they think that the nuptial pair has need of 5 deities: Zeus Teleios, Hera Teleia, Aphrodite, Peitho and finally Artemis, whom women in child-birth and travail are wont to invoke?' (264B).

These ideas were familiar to renaissance antiquarians writing on Roman marriage customs,[1] or prescribing topics for the epithalamium as a literary genre. Thus Scaliger in his chapter 'Epithalamion' in *Poetice* (1561), discussing rival theories about the number symbolism of the tapers, includes Plutarch's suggestion that *facularum numerum a numero deorum coniugalium*.[2] And the poets followed suit. In the inset 'Tale of Teras' in his continuation of *Hero and Leander*, for example, Chapman explains why Hymen's bride is preceded by 5 torch-bearers, in lines whose thought follows Plutarch's almost too closely for the good of the poetry:

> Next before her went
> Five lovely children decked with ornament
> Of her sweet colours, bearing torches by,
> For light was held a happy augury
> Of generation, whose efficient right
> Is nothing else but to produce to light.

[1] The renaissance authorities on ancient marriage customs are reviewed in D. J. Gordon's erudite article '*Hymenaei*: Ben Jonson's Masque of Union', *JWI* VIII (1945) 107–45; see especially 29 f., 140 ff.

[2] *Poetices libri septem* iii 101, p. 152B–C.

The odd disparent number they did choose,
To show the union married loves should use,
Since in two equal parts it will not sever,
But the midst holds one to rejoin it ever,
As common to both parts: men therefore deem
That equal number gods do not esteem,
Being authors of sweet peace and unity,
But pleasing to th'infernal empery,
Under whose ensigns wars and discords fight,
Since an even number you may disunite
In two parts equal, nought in middle left,
To reunite each part from other reft:
And five they hold in most especial prize,
Since 'tis the first odd number that doth rise
From the two foremost numbers' unity
That odd and even are; which are two, and three,
For one no number is... (v 317–39)

The ceremony comes, we notice, in the *Fifth* Sestiad.

The same number is applied to the ordering of a masque, in Jonson's *Hymenaei* (1606), given to celebrate the wedding of the Earl of Essex to Frances Howard, daughter of the Earl of Suffolk. The ritual of union before the altar of Iuno or Unio begins with the entry of 'five pages, attired in white, bearing five tapers of virgin wax', which a sidenote identifies as 'the *Quinque Cerei*, which Plutarch in his *Quaest. Roman.* mentions to be used in nuptials'.[1] Later, Reason explains that

> these five waxen lights,
Imply perfection in the rites;
For five the special number is,
Whence hallowed Union claims her bliss.
As being all the sum, that grows
From the united strengths, of those
Which male and female numbers we
Do style, and are first two, and three.
Which joined thus, you cannot sever
In equal parts, but one will ever
Remain as common; so we see
The binding force of Unity:
For which alone, the peaceful gods
In number, always, love the odds;
And even parts as much despise,
Since out of them all discords rise.[2]

[1] Ed. Herford, Simpson and Simpson vii 210.
[2] *Ibid.* 216. Jonson cites Plutarch again, and Martianus Capella, *De nupt. Philol.* vi.

Side-note references to Plutarch and Martianus Capella show that Jonson is well aware of the arithmological tradition in which he writes. So, almost certainly, is Herrick, when he introduces 'those tapers five, / That show the womb shall thrive' in his *Epithalamy to Sir Thomas Southwell*.[1]

When the symbolism was so consciously understood and so prominent in the iconography and imagery of epithalamia, it hardly surprises us to find it applied also to their formal organization. A common arrangement is a group of 5 poems or songs. Perhaps the finest example of this—again, significantly, from a masque—is the suite of 5 songs by Thomas Campion, Thomas Giles and Lupo, printed at the end of Campion's *Description of a Masque* for the nuptials of Lord and Lady Hay (1607). Here the number symbolism is worked out with unusual precision, since the first 2 songs, 'Now hath Flora robbed her bowers' and 'Move now with measured sound', are dyadic, being divided each into 2 equal stanzas (2×13, 2×8); whereas after the conjuration 'Join three by three, for so the night by triple spell decrees' follow 3 undivided unified songs.[2] Other suites of 5 epithalamia include Henry Peacham's *Nuptial Hymns*, Francis Beaumont's *Nuptial Songs* (both for the marriage of Princess Elizabeth and Frederick Prince Palatine on 14 February 1613) and Francis Quarles's nuptial songs in *Argalus and Parthenia* (1629). Individual epithalamia in 5 stanzas, such as the anonymous 'The Bride's Good Morrow',[3] are also common.

The nuptial significance of 8 seems at first more esoteric. Fortunately Jonson comes to our help: the printed version of *Hymenaei*, in which the dancers are grouped in 8s (a 'first masque, of eight men', humours and affections,[4] matching a second masque of 'eight

[1] Ll. 55 f.; ed. Martin 55.
[2] *English Madrigal Verse, 1588–1632*, ed. E. H. Fellowes, revised and enlarged F. W. Sternfeld and D. Greer, third edn (Oxford 1967) 363 ff.
[3] Case 25; *Roxburghe Ballads* i 62–4. Its stanzas being of 14 lines, this poem has a line total of 70, as have the songs in Thomas Campion's *Description of a Masque* (1614). Scaliger introduces the number 70 into his account of the ancient bridal cestus, which was tied with a knot called 'Herculean' *propterea quod heros ille foecundissimus ab antiquis creditus sit: quippe cui septuaginta liberi superstites fuissent* (153A, col. 1). Cf. Jonson, *Hymenaei*, ed. Herford, Simpson and Simpson VII 216 side-note: 'That was *Nodus Herculeanus*, which the husband, at night, untied in sign of good fortune, that he might be happy in propagation of issue, as Hercules was, who left seventy children.'
[4] For an identification of the 4 affections, see Gordon 110.

ladies' attendant on Juno) annotates the symbolism with great display of erudition. Juno was anciently 'governess of marriage',[1] and the 8 ladies represent her powers:

Eight of her noblest powers descend,
Which are enstyled her faculties,
That govern nuptial mysteries.

As a side-note explains, 'they were all eight called by particular surnames of Iuno, ascribed to her for some peculiar property in marriage'. The 8 powers are next catalogued by Reason, whom the notes (heavier, here, than the text) show to be chiefly dependent on Martianus Capella:

First Curis comes to deck the bride's fair tress.
Care of the ointments Unxia doth profess.
Iuga, her office to make one of twain:
Gamelia sees that they should so remain.
Fair Iterduca leads the bride her way;
And Domiduca home her steps doth stay;
Cinxia the maid, quit of her zone, defends;
Telia (for Hymen) perfects all, and ends.[2]

This even multiplicity of powers is strange, in view of the emphasis laid throughout *Hymenaei* on Juno's unity. Indeed, in the epigraph on her altar, as on many subsequent occasions, Jonson actually identifies Juno with union—'Iuno, whose great name, / Is Unio, in the anagram'.[3] As Professor Gordon's brilliant study of the masque has shown, its theme is throughout Union: the union of the integrated psyche, the union of the well-ordered state, the union of the wedded couple whose nuptials provided the occasion. The ideal celebrated is as much political and cosmic as personal.[4] Professor Gordon, to whom the reader may be referred for a full study of the symbolism of *Hymenaei*, rightly draws attention to Jonson's audacity. For the masque's implication is not only an equation of *unio* with *unitas* the divine monad, but even of Juno with the latter: 'It was a daring innovation of Jonson's to equate *Unitas* with Juno. He may have been led to it by reading in Macrobius that one combines the male and the

---

[1] Ed. Herford, Simpson and Simpson vii 217. Jonson cites Virgil, *Aen.* iv 59, 'Iunoni ante omnes, cui vincla iugalia curae' (Before all to Juno, guardian of wedlock bonds').

[2] Ed. Herford, Simpson and Simpson vii 219 f.

[3] *Ibid.* 217.   [4] See Gordon, especially 115 f., 125.

female; from this he may have reasoned that marriage too effects such a combination, and that so does Juno, who is the patroness of the marriage.'[1] We do not grasp the full extent of Jonson's audacity, however, unless we know that Juno more usually signified *duality*. Thus Bongo, discussing as it happens the symbolism of 8, can casually remark that that cube 'rests on the first motion and duality of number, which is Juno'.[2] The unity that Jonson celebrates is thus most emphatically a two-in-one. In the private sphere, he means the unity of Christian marriage, two in one flesh. But in the political sphere he alludes not only to James's marriage with his kingdom in 1603 but also to the union of crowns that was then achieved.

The association of 8 with Juno patroness of marriage had earlier been introduced in the wedding masque with which *As You Like It* harmoniously ends. As we might expect, Shakespeare's use of the number is more complex and less explicitly erudite. Still, he has Hymen announce:

Then is there mirth in heaven,
When earthly things made even
Atone together. (v iv 115–17)

and 'here's eight that must take hands'.[3] No doubt the number symbolism here implies ideas of harmony (the octave) and of justice. (Repeated stress on the key word *even* alludes to the equity of 8, as a number repeatedly divisible 'evenly' or without remainder.[4]) But when the wedding couples sing the play's fifth song, a 'wedlock hymn' beginning 'Wedding is great Juno's crown', we know that Shakespeare is also writing in the same tradition of epithalamic number symbolism with Jonson.

Numerological applications of the 8 of Juno and Hymen are common. *Hymenaei* itself culminates in an epithalamium in eight-line stanzas. At the original performance 'only one staff was sung', so that it was a simple eight-line song. Herrick's Harleian MS epithalamium, which follows the symbolism of Jonson's masque in many respects, introduces Juno and Domiduca in its eighth stanza; just as Phineas Fletcher's *Hymen at the Marriage of My Most Dear Cousins*

---

[1] *Ibid.* 115.   [2] Bongo 322.
[3] v iv 135; cf. *ibid.* 18, where Rosalind says 'I have promised to make all this matter even'.
[4] On *Iustitia* as the Pythagorean name for 8, see Bongo 323 f., deriving ultimately from Iamblichus, *Theologoumena arithmeticae*. Cf. p. 39 above.

invokes Hymen in its eighth stanza.[1] Thomas Heywood, who took over the whole stanzaic pattern of Jonson's *Hymenaei* epithalamium for one nuptial hymn, has another consisting of 8 eight-line stanzas, in *A Marriage Triumph* (1613) sigs. D4r–E2v, C1r–C2v. Donne's Lincoln's Inn 'Epithalamium', his epithalamium for the wedding of Princess Elizabeth and Frederick Prince Palatine, Sir Henry Goodere's for the same occasion and Christopher Brooke's in *England's Helicon* (1614) repeating Donne's metrical pattern: all these have 8 stanzas. Epithalamia in eight-line stanzas, such as Jonson's for Jerome Weston and Lady Frances Stuart, are also common. These, however, have less evidential value, since the eight-line stanza was too common a form for its choice to have necessarily involved a numerological decision.

TEMPORAL NUMEROLOGY

Just as Elizabethan poets used Roman wedding ritual and mythological number symbolisms, so they found classical precedent for connecting temporal numbers with epithalamia. Here the prescriptions for the genre in renaissance literary theory were decisive. Scaliger's learned anthropological account of the origins and social context of epithalamic motifs includes a detailed time-table of ancient nuptials, in which their three-day duration was emphasized.[2] And Puttenham distinguishes 3 parts or phases in the epithalamium, according to the times at which these were sung in the course of a single nuptial night. Thus, 'the first breach was sung at the first part of the night when the spouse and her husband were brought to their bed and at the very chamber door'.[3] This part was to be loud, to cover the cries of the virgin 'feeling the first forces of her stiff and rigorous young man'; its tenor was to congratulate the couple and their parents, and to sound the amorous onset. The second part was even more precisely timed ('about midnight or one of the clock'); it was to encourage a new assault in the interest of procreation. The third part, congratulatory and homiletic, was to be delivered 'in the morning when it was fair broad day', and when 'the bride must within few hours arise and apparel herself, no more as a virgin, but as a wife'.

[1] MS Harl. 6918, fols. 43v–7, ed. Martin 457; ed. Boas ii 224.
[2] *Poetice* iii 101; p. 151 A–B, col. 2.
[3] *The Art of English Poesy* i 26; ed. Willcock and Walker 51.

To the influence of theoretical prescriptions should be added the example of Catullus, whom both Scaliger and Puttenham singled out as a model. Catullus' epithalamia set a fashion for semi-narrative wedding lyrics reviewing the ceremonies of the nuptial day in chronological order.[1] Since the texts of his epithalamia (modern numbering lxi, lxii and lxiv) were incomplete, they ought never to have provided numerological models. But the 47 stanzas of lxi and the 59 lines of the inset song in lxiv may have seemed tantalizingly close to temporal measures. And another recommended classical model, Claudian's narrative epithalamium for Honorius and Maria, a poem very well known indeed in the sixteenth century, came as close. Its line total of 22 (Preface) $+ 341 = 363$ offered a precedent for the numerological device of measures falling just short of temporal constants (here $24 + 341 = 365$). Less doubtfully, St Ennodius, the sixth-century Bishop of Pavia, a poet obsessed with formal patterns, provided a model epithalamium constructed to exact temporal measures.[2] Its opening section, beginning with mentions of the year and set off by changes in metre, has the line-total array $24 + 4 + 24 = 52$.

The spatial imagination of the renaissance naturally interpreted prescriptions and examples such as these (whatever their original intention) in a numerological sense. It was almost inevitable that renaissance epithalamists should simulate the temporal pattern of the wedding day numerologically.

A Neolatin epithalamium of some importance for the history of numerology is the paraphrase from *The Song of Songs* included in Francesco Giorgio's *De harmonia mundi* (1525). This comprises a suite of 3 songs: an *epithalamium in sponsum* of 12 four-line stanzas, an *epithalamium in sponsam* of 15 couplets and a nuptial hymn *in connubium* of 20 lines. On the strength of a temporal interpretation of the first stanza total, Professor Røstvig ('The Hidden Sense' 36) suggests that 'this fine...numerical composition in epithalamic verse may well have prompted the intricate structure of Spenser's *Epithalamion*'. Giorgio's songs have a special interest in view of their setting in one of the most significant arithmological treatises of the renaissance, though their numerology, for the most part non-temporal, can

---

[1] On the classical models of the renaissance epithalamium, see J. A. S. McPeek, *Catullus in Strange and Distant Britain* (Cambridge, Mass. 1939).
[2] *Carm.* i 4, ed. Vogel ccclxxxviii.

hardly have provided Spenser with a model. Nevertheless, it is right to think in terms of Neolatin influences, since epithalamia were at first commoner in Latin than in the vernacular. The genre was pre-eminently learned and classical.

By the seventeenth century, however, temporal patterns were widely distributed in vernacular epithalamic poetry, both French and English. The commonest pattern is a simple diurnal one miming the twenty-four-hour period of the wedding day by a line or stanza total of 24. Thus Quarles has a nuptial carol in 4 six-line stanzas, of which the first 3 end with the refrain:

Let Juno's hourly blessing send ye
As much joy as can attend ye![1]

Familiar examples of the commonest variants of the pattern may be seen in the epithalamium for Solomon and Sheba in *The Divine Weeks* (6 four-line stanzas)[2] and in the wedding song in *Amboyna* (3 eight-line stanzas).[3] Dryden's song follows out the astronomical course of the 24 nuptial hours:

The day is come, I see it rise,
Betwixt the bride's and bridegroom's eyes,
That golden day they wished so long,
Love picked it out amidst the throng;
He destined to himself this sun. (ll. 1–5)

The sun rises in the first line, and just before the poem's centre:

The day you wished arrived at last,
You wish as much that it were past,
One minute more and night will hide. (ll. 9–11)

If we think of 12 diurnal line-hours and 12 nocturnal, the bride's retirement suitably falls in the first hour of night. Day begins 'betwixt the bride's and bridegroom's eyes'; the poem ends circularly when the bride 'despairing shuts her eyes' after a display of all the defeated reluctance that excited a Restoration lover. On a larger scale,

---

[1] *Argalus and Parthenia* (1629) 111 f. Cf. the wedding song opening *The Two Noble Kinsmen*, again 6 four-line stanzas.

[2] II iv 2, 'The Magnificence', Sylvester 579 f., exactly reproducing the numero-logical pattern of his original, 'La magnificence' ll. 963–86. The last line in the French alludes to the diurnal symbolism: 'A ton ombre je veux coucher et jour et nuit.'

[3] Ed. Kinsley i 152 f. Cf. also Dowland's *A Pilgrim's Solace* (1612)xx, 'Welcome, black night, Hymen's fair day!', in 2 twelve-line stanzas (Fellowes 498 f.).

Jonson's Epithalamium for Jerome Weston and Lady Frances Stuart, like Spenser's for his own wedding, traces the course of an often-apostrophized sun through 24 stanza-hours.[1]

In another common pattern, a measure of 12 imitates the 12 temporary or unequal hours—usually the *nocturnal* hours. Thus, the Second Song in Beaumont and Fletcher's *The Maid's Tragedy*, beginning (significantly with a Spenserian echo) 'Hold back thy hours, dark night, till we have done', is in 12 lines. The hours referred to must be temporary hours, since it is only at the equinoxes, when weddings were seldom celebrated, that the natural hours of darkness number 12. Dowland's twelve-line 'Cease, cease these false sports, haste away!' similarly limits itself to the hours of darkness:

Hymen, O Hymen, bless this night,
That Love's dark works may come to light.[2]

The line total of Dekker's light-filled bridal song in *Patient Grissil*, however, may allude to the 12 hours of day,[3] while the 'soft hours' of Ford's twelve-line bridal song in *The Broken Heart* are nondescript and blurred by a reference to the year.[4]

The 12 divisions of the year are more clearly mimed, together with the 12 temporary hours of the nuptial night, in Thomas Carew's 'Hymeneal Song on the Nuptials of the lady Ann Wentworth, and the Lord Lovelace' (1638, printed 1642). For the 12 stanzas that trace the stages of a wedding night during which the bride replaces the sun and shines 'in glory all the night' do not all have the same metrical pattern. Every third stanza has a longer final line than that of the preceding 2 others. Thus the 12 stanzas are distributed between 4 groups of 3, as much like the months between the seasons as the temporary hours between the night-watches. The last season-watch of the 4 may perhaps serve to exemplify the pattern:

---

[1] *Underwood* lxxv; ed. Herford, Simpson and Simpson viii 252–8. The 24 hours might also be mimed by ordinal placing, as in the Cowley example mentioned above (p. 139). Thus, in Sir John Beaumont's Epithalamium for George Villiers, then Marquis of Buckingham, the only mention of 'days' is in the twenty-fourth line: 'Time, add thou many days, nay ages to their age' (Case 94; *The Poems of Sir John Beaumont*, ed. A. B. Grosart (1869) 150–2.
[2] *A Pilgrim's Solace* xxi; Fellowes 499. For mythological representations of the Hours as 12 in number, see p. 60n.   [3] v ii 89–100; ed. Bowers i 283.
[4] III iv 70–81; ed. B. Morris (1965) 53. Cf. also Crashaw's B.M. MS Harl. 6917 Epithalamium 'Come virgin tapers of pure wax', ed. L. C. Martin (Oxford 1927) 406 ff.

x

They know no night, nor glaring moon,
Measure no hours of sun or moon,
Nor mark time's restless glass:

xi

Their kisses measure as they flow,
Minutes, and their embraces show
The hours as they pass.

xii

Their motions, the year's circle make,
And we from their conjunctions take
Rules to make Love an almanac.[1]

In view of the astrological reference, it is possible that the 3 lines of the stanza also symbolize the 3 faces into which each sign of the zodiac was divided.[2] Other epithalamia with annual patterns include Donne's nuptial *Eclogue. 1613. December 26*[3] and the anonymous Epithalamium 'On Dr Corbet's Marriage' in *Wit Restored* (1658), both in 52 couplet-weeks. In the former poem, seasonal imagery abounds.

Lines or stanzas are sometimes shared exactly between day and night, even in epithalamia without any other temporal measure. Donne bisects his 'Epithalamion made at Lincoln's Inn' in this way: the first 4 stanzas end with the refrain 'To day put on perfection, and a woman's name', but the second 4 with the changed refrain 'To night put(s) on perfection, and a woman's name'. And Christopher Brooke's epithalamium in *England's Helicon* (1614) has a very similar arrangement of 4 diurnal followed by 4 nocturnal stanzas, signposted by marginal notes—'Sunrising'; 'Sunset'.[4] If equal division

[1] *Poems* ed. R. Dunlap (Oxford 1957) 115.
[2] Epithalamia in 12 × 3 lines were not uncommon. Cf. e.g. Carew's other epithalamium, 'Such should this day be, so the sun should hide' for Thomas Killigrew and Cecilia Crofts, ed. Dunlap 79 f. Discussing Le Fevre's French version of Giorgio's first nuptial song, Professor Røstvig, 'The Hidden Sense' 34 f., suggests that its 36 lines 'may be taken to reflect the 36 Decans or spiritual forces of Hermetic astronomy; there are 3 of them for each month or sign of the zodiac, so that each Decan, by representing 10 days, is connected with the number of the Deity'. Since none of the epithalamia discussed makes any allusion to the *decani*, however, it seems unnecessary to invoke esoteric Hermetic doctrine. The 3 faces of the signs, on the other hand, were regularly used in astrological calculations, and division of the zodiac into 36 parts would therefore have been immediately intelligible.
[3] *Poetical Works* ed. H. J. C. Grierson i (Oxford 1912) 131–5.
[4] *England's Helicon 1600, 1614* ed. Hyder E. Rollins, 2 vols (Cambridge, Mass. 1935) i 212–5.

occurred only in poems with a temporal modulus such as the nuptial song in *Amboyna*, it could be satisfactorily explained as imitating the division of the day into equal numbers of diurnal and nocturnal temporal hours. Since it is also found in poems without temporal numerology, however, another symbolism must be involved. The even division suggests a more abstract conception, perhaps of just balance between day and night, light and dark, masculine and feminine. But these polarities are contained within the poem's unity, just as the *unitas* of the monad contains both masculine and feminine, odd and even numbers.

A similar symbolism may underlie division in the more complex ratio 1 : 2, which is surprisingly common. Denoting as it does the octave proportion, this ratio would be the obvious spatial correlate to a sentiment of harmonious concord. Moreover, there was an appropriate psychological implication. According to Pico, the diapason was the proportion between the rational and concupiscible faculties in a well-ordered soul.[1] These considerations made the ratio particularly suitable for nuptial songs.

The simplest case is exemplified by Dekker's *Patient Grissil* song, whose 2 stanzas, of very unequal length in spite of their identical refrains, consist of 8 and 4 lines. In the nuptial song opening *The Two Noble Kinsmen*, the proportion is worked out metrically. Not only are there 16 long lines and 8 short, but the line lengths maintain the same ratio. Just as each stanza has 4 long lines and 2 short, so each long line has 4 stresses and each short line 2 :

The crow, the slanderous cuckoo, nor
The boding raven, nor chough hoar,
Nor chattering pie,
May on our bridehouse perch or sing,
Or with them any discord bring,
But from it fly!

In Dowland's *A Pilgrim's Solace* (1612), more intricately, a twenty-four-line epithalamium, divided into 2 stanzas each consisting of 8 lines and a four-line refrain, is followed by another epithalamium in 12 lines, itself patterned, metrically or by distribution between

[1] See my discussion of the 'goodly diapase' into which the proportions of the House of Alma are 'compacted' (*FQ* II ix 22) in *Spenser and the Numbers of Time* 281 n., citing Pico i 79.

voices, as $2+4+4+2$.[1] A favourite arrangement is to have Introduction and Envoy in $2:1$ harmony. Thus Richard Brathwait's inset epithalamium in *A Strappado for the Devil* (1615) 74–77 has $12+50+6$ lines, set off by paragraphing, and the nuptial songs in Beaumont and Fletcher's *The Maid's Tragedy* (16, 12 and 8 lines) form a sequence in the proportion $4:3:2$.

The same diapason proportion might be observed between the equal hours of day and of night. An early example is the twenty-four-stanza 'Epithalame au Seigneur Scevole' by the Pléiade poet Remy Belleau (1527–77). Belleau makes the sun set after 16 stanzas, to give $2:1$ proportion between the hours of light and of dark.[2] This poem would seem the likeliest model, if one were required, for the numerology of Spenser's *Epithalamion*, whose 24 stanzas are divided $16+8$ by a refrain change at the point of transition from day to night. But in the invention of such patterns polygenesis seems probable: a popular time for weddings was June, when in temperate latitudes the hours of light exceed the hours of darkness approximately in the ratio $2:1$. Donne's eight-stanza 'Epithalamion Made at Lincoln's Inn' combines the external $1:1$ division by refrain change with a subtler internal division. The sun does not set in the fourth stanza, the last one with the 'day' refrain variant; not until the end of the fifth stanza is it said to have 'run the world's half frame'. Thus the poem has 5 stanzas of diurnal action. Moreover, at the mid point of its last stanza the next day's light is already invoked ('O light / Of heaven, tomorrow, rise thou hot, and early') so that it has only $2\frac{1}{2}$ stanzas of night, not 3 $(5+2\frac{1}{2}+\frac{1}{2} = 8)$. By this means Donne contrives a concealed harmony whereby the light and darkness parts of the wedding day are in the proportion $2:1$.

Another way to temporal decorum was through imitation of the date of the wedding. Often this case is trivial, as with Donne's choice of a fourteen-line stanza for his 1613 Valentine Epithalamium for Frederick Prince Palatine and Princess Elizabeth.[3] But sometimes a

---

[1] Songs xx and xxi; Fellowes 498 f.

[2] *Les oeuvres poetiques*, 2 tom. (Paris 1585) i 272 ff. It is significant that Belleau's 'Journées de la bergerie' include eclogues based on *The Song of Songs*.

[3] Ed. Grierson i 135 ff. As we saw (p. 71), Donne mimed the date in another epithalamium in the same year—that for the wedding of the Earl of Somerset and Lady Frances Howard on 26 December. Its first 5 stanzas imitate the 5 days that intervene before the issuing forth of the sun for a new year at the beginning of the sixth stanza.

device based on date has unexpected structural value. For the same royal wedding Donne's friend Sir Henry Goodere wrote an epithalamium whose imitation of the date is so organic as to be essential to any full appreciation. Goodere's poem is in 8 eleven-line stanzas, each ending with a refrain line.[1] Its refrains vary through 4 forms—'This night, for which this month doth give away two days' (r_1), 'This night, which to this month doth recompense two days' (r_2), 'This night, which to this month supplies her two lost days' (r_3) and 'This night, for which this year may spare a month of days' (r_4)—disposed $r_1 r_1 r_2 r_2 r_3 r_3 r_4 r_4$: an arrangement suggesting a doubled pattern. The imagery, which plays paradoxically with opposed motifs of division and unity, contains a similar implication. For the Muse is to show how to divide Love from Majesty, but the poem's sheets are to unite the couple like the bed sheets between which they lie 'like two half-spheres', 'But grow a body perfectly, / As half-spheres make a globe by being met'.[2]

Since Goodere's epithalamium stresses the motif of pairing both formally and substantively, it would be reasonable to consider its line total of 88 as 2×44. St Valentine's Day (14 February) is the forty-fifth of the year, however, not the forty-fourth, so that the poem seems 2 line-days short of an appropriate total. But does not its refrain draw attention to precisely this fact? The 'two lost days' of the third refrain are primarily, of course, the 2 days by which February falls short even of thirty-day months. But we may regard them secondarily as the 2 'missing' line-days needed to make up the total of 2×45. It is hard to imagine any other interpretation that saves the refrain from utter vapidity, or explains how a poet in his senses came to give it such prominence.

SPENSER'S 'EPITHALAMION'

None of the above examples, except the original *Zodiac amoureux* and Belleau's 'Epithalame au S. Scevole', precedes Spenser's *Epithalamion* (1595). Indeed, Spenser may have been the first to introduce complex temporal numerology into English poetry. Certainly *Epithalamion*

---

[1] Case 51–3, from B.M. Add. MS 25707 fol. 37v. On the 1613 festivities, see C. K. Adams, Introd. to Catalogue of the National Portrait Gallery Exhibition *The Winter Queen. Elizabeth Queen of Bohemia and her Family* (1963).

[2] The reference, as with much imagery of hemispheres in epithalamia and love poetry generally, is to Plato, *Symposium* 189 E–191 D.

set an influential example, as the persistent Spenserian echoes ringing through later epithalamia show. For that reason, and because it was the first post-medieval poem to attract numerological interpretation in our own time, it calls for extended consideration.

Epithalamion consists of 24 stanzas, or 23 stanzas and an Envoy. The stanzas have each 14 or 15 pentameters, together with a concluding hexameter refrain. These 'long' lines are in most cases divided into 4 groups by interposition of 3 shorter lines. Stanzas xv and xxiii, however, have only 2 short lines apiece and consequently 3 groups of long lines each. And the Envoy has 6 pentameters, divided by a single short line. In all, therefore, the poem contains 365 long lines, divided into 92 groups by 68 short lines.

A. Kent Hieatt's *Short Time's Endless Monument* (1960) challenged the orthodox view of *Epithalamion* by arguing that the poem's spatial disposition mimes astronomical events of the day it celebrates. Hieatt saw that the 24 stanzas represent the nuptial day's 24 hours, the 'fair hours... begot / In Jove's sweet paradise, of Day and Night', on whom Spenser calls to adorn his bride. The first 16 stanzas all have positive variants of the changing refrain ('The woods shall to me answer and my echo ring', etc.), whereas the remaining 8 have negative variants ('The woods no more shall answer, nor your echo ring', etc.), the division coming when 'day is done' (l. 298). This arrangement expresses, in a way now familiar to us, the proportion between the times of light and of darkness during the month of June, including the year's longest day, St Barnaby's Day, the day of the poet's wedding. More precisely, nightfall comes after 16 and a fraction stanzas, since the phrase 'now night is come' falls in Stanza xvii, at the end of the first group of long lines. If the short lines mark quarter hours, there are $16\frac{1}{4}$ stanza-hours of light—exactly the length ascribed to the solstitial day, for the nearest latitude to S. Ireland, in contemporary handbooks.[1]

[1] For documentation, see Hieatt 11. A difficulty not dealt with by Hieatt is that 13 June, not 11 June (the St Barnaby's Day of the poem and Spenser's wedding) was given as the solstice in popular calendrical works—e.g. Prayer Books and Shepherd's Calendars—which tended to repeat old and inaccurate estimates. But more professional tables gave the solstice as 11 or 11/12 June. Commonest were calculations based on the Alfonsine Tables, which put the summer solstice near midnight on 11/12 June: e.g. William Bourne's *A regiment for the sea* (1574) ed. E. G. R. Taylor for the Hakluyt Society (1961), giving an 11 June date. Spenser's statement that St Barnaby's Day was the longest in the year thus

Besides the diurnal, *Epithalamion* has an annual pattern. For its 365 long lines represent the 365 days of the sun's yearly journey round the ecliptic through the 24 sidereal hours or divisions of the celestial sphere. Again there is a more exact decorum. The 23 full stanzas have 359 long lines, that is, the true number of degrees in the sun's daily orbit, so that from one point of view they complete the poem's and the sun's course. The Envoy, commenting as it were from outside on the song's defective prematurity, then refers to the solar sphere's imperfect daily motion (359°), compared with that of the starry sphere (360°). In the longer view, however, the Envoy is part of the poem, the count of long lines 365 and the 1° daily shortcoming of the sun's orbit cumulatively 'recompensed' by his 365-day annual retardation round the full ecliptic circle.[1]

Hieatt also described a more organic structural system, whereby imagery in each stanza matches imagery in a corresponding stanza 12 stanza-hours later. Thus the comparison of the bride to Phoebe in ix is answered by the appearance of the moon as Cynthia in xxi, the song shouted to Hymen in viii by Silence's true night-watches in xx. Stanza xii calls for adornment of the church, to receive the bride with 'honour due' as she enters on 'endless matrimony': Stanza xxiv adjures the song itself, in compensation for 'many ornaments' with which the bride should 'duly' have been decked, to be 'short time's endless monument'. And in a similar way, Hieatt maintained, imagery in xiii, xiv, xv, . . . , xxiv echoes imagery in i, ii, iii, . . . , xii. From this pairing of stanzas, he concluded that the hours kept by the poem's measure are not civil hours, but sidereal hours or twenty-four-part divisions of the celestial sphere.[2] Now, opposite sidereal hours correspond to each other in a definite sense. The ratio between the durations of day and night at any date is the inverse of the ratio 6 months later, when the sun is in the sidereal hour exactly opposite. Such hours may well be called hours 'which do the seasons of the year allot'.[3]

This is not the kind of simple poetic structure and non-significant prosody that modern renaissance scholarship had become accustomed

shows that he was working on the basis of astronomical information above the most popular level.   [1] Hieatt 42 ff.

[2] *Ibid.* 16–30, further developed in the same author's 'The Daughters of Horus: Order in the Stanzas of *Epithalamion*' in W. Nelson (ed.), *Form and Convention in the Poetry of Edmund Spenser* (New York and London 1961) 103–21.

[3] *Epithalamion*, l. 100; see Hieatt 38.

to. I have hardly touched on *Epithalamion's* intricate verbal ambiguities, which a sensitive reader will hear as witty allusions to the formal symbolism;[1] yet already it is plain that Hieatt was discussing formal patterns more complex than any previously recognized in an Elizabethan poem. They amounted, if allowed existence, to a whole system of unsuspected meaning. Perhaps it was inevitable, therefore, that several reviewers of *Short Time's Endless Monument* should have agreed with Enid Welsford in finding its thesis 'not a convincing one'.[2]

As we have seen, *Epithalamion* shares with many other wedding poems some of the main features of its temporal numerology. This does not mean, however, that Hieatt's whole theory about its structure is 'proved'. Conservative scholars are too much inclined to accept or reject numerological analyses *in toto*. They ask 'Is this theory sane?' instead of 'Which of these statements are true, which partly true and which false?'

That *Epithalamion* mimes the solstitial proportions of light and dark in its refrain change and placing of nightfall seems amply confirmed by the existence, not only of many analogues in epithalamic poetry, but also of the miniaturized imitation in Cowley's 'The Long Life'.[3] Still, this result is not without difficulties. For the *action* unfortunately does not begin with sunrise. In Stanza ii Spenser commissions the Muses to wake his bride 'early before the world's light giving lamp / His golden beam upon the hills doth spread'; not until v has dawn broken, so that 'Phoebus gins to show his glorious head'. Hence the action of the opening stanzas takes place during the period of darkness, not the period of light. Nor will it do to argue that though the sun has not yet risen in i–iv it may already be giving some light; in the renaissance there was nothing vague about the duration of the period of light, which was reckoned from sunrise to sunset precisely.[4] In one sense, then, Hieatt (19) is wrong in saying that the first 4 stanzas belong to day. Even if the action of these stanzas takes place

[1] These, together with minor decorums of position, are sensitively treated in *Short Time's Endless Monument*. See e.g. p. 70, on the placing of the phrase 'this day' at an appropriate date in the year of long lines—a point discussed, with additional suggestions, in my review in *RES* n.s. XII (1961) 417–19.

[2] *Ren. News* XIV (1961) 277. In her more recent *Spenser: Fowre Hymnes: Epithalamion* (Oxford 1967), Miss Welsford accepts much of Hieatt's thesis.

[3] See above, p. 14 f.

[4] Astronomers even specified what stages of sunrise and sunset should form the *termini*; see e.g. Riccioli, 'De crepusculis', i 37 f.

just before sunrise (night's 'damp' is already dispersed in ii) and even if night may fairly be said to fall after 16¼ formal stanza-hours of the poem's wedding day, there is yet a plain sense in which Stanzas i–iv do not belong to the hours of light. Their action obstinately falls within the period of darkness. We conclude, therefore, that while the refrain change and proportionate division of stanzas at nightfall are meaningful, these configurations exist independently of the nuptial day's other events. Night falls 16 stanza-hours after the beginning of the poem but not 16 stanzas after sunrise.

A distinct pattern, however, governs the spatial distribution of the action of the nuptial day. It we assign stanzas to day or to night simply according to the events they relate, we obtain the following array:

i ii iii iv	v vi vii viii ix x xi xii xiii xiv xv xvi
NIGHT	DAY

xvii xviii xix xx xxi xxii xxiii xxiv
NIGHT

in which nocturnal stanzas are divided by the interposed wedding day into 2 groups of 4 and 8, the same 1 : 2 octave proportion that we observed in several other epithalamia. Moreover, the content of 12 stanzas belongs to the period of day, the content of the remaining 12 to the period of night. Such an array can only represent the division of day and night into the unequal or temporary hours, 12 diurnal and 12 nocturnal.[1] Hieatt (41) considers the possibility that Spenser meant temporary hours, only to reject it on two grounds: that it doesn't lead to any explanation of the stanza pairing and that 'more than one division of his marriage day seems superfluous'. But the latter objection has little force in face of Chapman's intricately overlapping divisions in 'The Amorous Zodiac' of the same year. We may even

[1] The alternative possibility, imitation of equal division of the 24 civil hours between day and night at the equinoxes, can almost certainly be ruled out, since Spenser is celebrating a solstitial day. It might be argued that the poem mimes both solstitial and equinoctial days, reckoning the summer season from solstice to autumnal equinox; but this explanation seems over-subtle. A popular account of the artificial, temporary, unequal, or planetary hours was available in *The Calendar of Shepherds*; see e.g. the 1618 edn, sig. O 1v–2r, working an example for December (with day 8 equal hours, night 16 hours) and describing the situation in June as exactly contrary. For fuller and more scholarly treatment, consult Riccioli i 36. See also above, pp. 60 n. and 135 n.

say that multiplicity and ambiguity of articulation typified mannerist poetic structure.

As for Hieatt's former objection, it will not prevail once day is reckoned from Stanza v: given this, the stanza pairing is accounted for very well. Indeed, if we give the unequal diurnal and nocturnal hours their ordinal numbers—

NIGHT					DAY										
i	ii	iii	iv		v	vi	vii	viii	ix	x	xi	xii	xiii	xiv	xv	xvi
9	10	11	12		1	2	3	4	5	6	7	8	9	10	11	12

NIGHT							
xvii	xviii	xix	xx	xxi	xxii	xxiii	xxiv
1	2	3	4	5	6	7	8

—we discover why firmer correspondences exist between the particular stanzas forming the clearest pairs. Thus v (the first diurnal stanza-hour) naturally corresponds with xvii (the first nocturnal stanza-hour), vi (second diurnal) with xviii (second nocturnal) and so on. In fact, recourse to temporary hours enables us to integrate action with stanza structure. It also removes a blemish in Hieatt's theory: namely, the weakness of correspondences between i–iv and xiii–xvi. For, though the pairs of temporary hours represented by these stanzas belong to the same date or civil day, they do not belong to the same cycle of 24 temporary hours, since such astrological days were reckoned from sunrise. Consequently i mimes the ninth nocturnal hour of the eve of the wedding day, whereas xiii mimes the ninth diurnal hour of the wedding day itself. This being so, the very tenuousness of pairing between i–iv and xiii–xvi that Hieatt admits as a defect[1] is exactly what we should expect. When, however, we come to v and xvii, the first diurnal and nocturnal hours of the *same* day, we also come to the first clear correspondence: waking of the bride, matched by bedding of the bride. Stanzas v–xii form unambiguous pairs with xvii–xxiv.

Another part of Hieatt's theory needing modification is his account of the short lines. Because on the whole these are spaced out evenly, 3 to a stanza, he thought it reasonable to treat them as indicators of quarter hours: a plausible explanation that neatly accommodates the

[1] *Short Time's Endless Monument* 19.

placement of nightfall after the first quarter of xvii. But he runs into difficulties in xv and xxiii, stanzas with 2, not 3, short lines and therefore 3, not 4, 'quarters'. Counting the Envoy's, there are 68 instead of an expected 72 short lines.[1] Hieatt explains these irregularities in terms of the symbolic value of the number 68, which he takes to be the total of 4 (seasons) + 12 (months) + 52 (weeks). However, such an explanation is no explanation in the absence of precedent or authority for the arithmetical manipulation.[2] And unfortunately this particular manipulation seems to have no historical basis.

Nor has the number 68 any other symbolism in the arithmological literature. We conclude that the number of short lines has no significance, and that their numerological *raison d'être* lies solely in their function as markers. Since they divide the stanzas into groups of long lines, we have no interest in the short-line total, but only in the total of long-line groups: 92.[3] And since there is no reason, either, why the quarter hours should number 92 rather than 96, it follows that the short lines mark something else besides quarter hours.

This something would have been familiar to many Elizabethans as the number of days in the summer quarter of the year: that is, between the summer solstice and the autumnal equinox. Anyone who knew the rudiments of the Ptolemaic system knew the days in each quarter of the year, since these figures were used to calculate the auge or apogee (point of greatest distance) of the sun. If one imagines a cross superimposed eccentrically on the circle of the sun's annual orbit, the points where the cross cuts the circumference represent the solstices and equinoctial points, the unequal segments of arc represent the days in each quarter year, and the auge lies on the axis of symmetry. Now Ptolemy,[4] still cited by Copernicus (*De revol.* iii 16), gives the days in the summer quarter—solstice to autumnal equinox —as 92 full days.[5] Significantly, when we treat the stanza-parts or

[1] 72 or 3 × 24 short lines would give 96 or 24 × 4 quarter-stanza-hours.
[2] Other manipulations are easily invented that yield the same desired result. Thus 24 (hours) + 2 (day and night) + 30 (days in a solar month) + 12 (months) = 68. Or 24 (hours) + 4 (seasons) + 28 (days in a lunar month) + 12 (months) = 68.
[3] I.e. 21 × 4 (regular stanzas) + 2 × 3 (irregular stanzas) + 2 (Envoy) = 92.
[4] *Almagestum* III ii and iv; so also Pliny *Nat. hist.* XVIII xv. For a list of estimates by other astronomers, see Riccioli i 142. I am much indebted in this paragraph to Dr John North of the Museum of the History of Science at Oxford.
[5] See further below, p. 181 n.

piedi marked by the short lines as corresponding to the days of the season during which Spenser celebrated his wedding, we increase our appreciation of the irregular Stanza xv. Hieatt (67 f.) remarks that at the point in this stanza where a short line is expected Spenser puts instead the long line 'To choose the longest day in all the year'. Now in Hieatt's theory short lines do not mark days, so that the irregularity is apt only in that it occurs in a stanza mentioning the length of St Barnaby's Day. If, however, the short lines mark stanza parts symbolizing days of summer, the decorum becomes more exact: the stanza referring substantively to the longest day of summer is also the stanza with the longest *piede*-day (8 lines).

There remains the question of the Envoy. Why should *Epithalamion*—unlike, say, *Prothalamion*—have an incomplete final stanza? The prosodist offers a metrical explanation: in so far as *Epithalamion* is a *canzone*, the Envoy is its *tornata*. And Hieatt offers an explanation in terms of the long-line totals 359 and 365: if 365 long lines have to be distributed among 24 stanzas divided into *piedi* regularly enough to suggest quarters, and if 359 of them have to constitute a completed whole, then a final Envoy of half-stanza length is almost inevitable. Reasonable as these explanations seem, however, they do not tell the whole story. We may also enquire into the poem's proportions in a simpler way, by regarding it as $23\frac{1}{2}$ stanzas and asking what $23\frac{1}{2}$ meant to an Elizabethan. This number of course was very well known indeed as the degrees of inclination of the ecliptic (and hence of the sun's maximum declination) and was applied numerologically in this sense by other poets.[1] Moreover, declination of the sun is referred to in *Epithalamion* xv: 'This day the sun is in his chiefest height...From whence declining daily *by degrees.*' Altogether, it seems equally reasonable to interpret the poem's $23\frac{1}{2}$ stanzas as representing the $23\frac{1}{2}°$ of the sun's midsummer declination.

This embarrassing wealth of interpretations presents a problem characteristic of the style of numerology adopted by Spenser and some of his contemporaries. As with mannerist visual art, we often find it hard to decide which pattern is primary, which secondary; perhaps

[1] See above, p. 145 n. Maximum declination was discussed in many popular contemporary handbooks. See e.g. Blundevil, *Exercises* ii (1594), *cit. OED*, s.v. *Declination*, from the 1636 edn: 'The greatest declination which is 23 degrees, 28''; and Sacrobosco, *De sphaera* ii, Lynn Thorndike (ed.), *The 'Sphere' of Sacrobosco and its Commentators* (Chicago 1949) 90, 126.

because the question is inappropriate and the distinction alien to the style. If Spenser thought of the distinction at all (which will seem doubtful to many), he must have chosen to avoid making it. So far as we can judge by results, he preferred the esoteric to the obvious form, the elusive and ambiguous and inexhaustible to the certain and dramatic. The effect is artificial, yet hardly untrue to nature. (In the real world, for example, we would find it similarly difficult to decide whether change in the sun's declination causes or is caused by its annual retardation about the ecliptic.) Besides all the temporal patterns, *Epithalamion* has also a centralized array mentioned in a previous chapter, and itself belongs to a larger calendrical array taking in the *Amoretti* together with which it first appeared.[1] The overall spatial impression of inlaid, overlapping structures and ambiguously grouped units is dazzlingly brilliant. Erskine observed that each stanza, seeming inspired by a separate image, 'is a song in itself, and the complete poem is a series rather than an organic whole'.[2] Anyone who has examined the spatial arrangement of the stanzas, however, knows that they are far more highly organized than this judgement allows. Transposing stanzas would do more damage to *Epithalamion* than to many Romantic poems.

Knowledge of the formal structure has a profound effect on our interpretation of the poem's meaning and import. First, the spatial patterns heighten our sense of the nuptial occasion. They were devised specially for 11 June 1594, to commemorate that celebrated date for posterity, so that *Epithalamion* is a monument to the 'short time' of a single day. Secondly, the annual astronomical patterns relate Spenser's marriage to a larger background, as part of a long-term cosmic renewal of life and of time. As Hieatt has ably shown, they encourage us to pay more attention than we otherwise might to images that have a temporal symbolism, or that adumbrate the cosmic generative process.

Resonance between structure and imagery is particularly clear with the motif of the garland. This motif recurs throughout *Epithalamion*: the poet asks the Muses to wear garlands (i), the bride resembles Phoebe crowned with a green garland (ix), church pillars are to be decked with trim garlands (xii) and the bridegroom shouts in triumph

[1] See pp. 103–6, 181 f.
[2] Variorum *Minor Poems* ii 655.

'Crown ye God Bacchus with a coronal / And Hymen also crown with wreaths of vine' (xiv). Most striking of all, the nymphs of Mulla, themselves bedecked with gay garlands, are told to bring

Another gay garland
For my fair love of lilies and of roses,
Bound truelove wise with a blue silk riband.
And let them make great store of bridal posies,
And let them eke bring store of other flowers
To deck the bridal bowers. (iii)

To dismiss such floral imagery as trivial prettiness would be a mistake. Garlanding befits the day celebrated (it was the custom to decorate churches with flowers and garlands on St Barnaby's Day[1]); but it has also a deeper meaning. The garlands of *Epithalamion* represent the seasonal rounds of flowers woven through the year by the Horae:[2] they symbolize the circle of time itself:[3] and they are presented to the bride as garlands of verses. Their form is the 'endless' form of the poem Spenser is decking his love with (xxiv): circular in the return of its refrain line, in the ringing echoes of its hours, in all its cyclic temporal patterns. An ornament for the bride, yet a monument (record, chronicle) made to last without end through the short historical time of the created world.

It is characteristic of Spenser's lyric precision that he should gather all these suggestions together in an exact spatial representation. Not only are the 24 hours expressed spatially, as we have seen, but also the classical Horae. We might expect as much from vi, where the poet invokes the Graces together with the Hours 'which do the seasons of the year allot'. The Horae, who attended Venus as welcome marriage guests, also presided in the earlier classical period over the stages of natural growth; later, the seasons themselves (numbering either 3 or 4) were called Horae. Now Spenser gives the Graces or Charites, close companions of the Horae, very particular injunctions:

And ye three handmaids of the Cyprian queen,
The which do still adorn her beauty's pride,
Help to adorn my beautifulest bride:

[1] Hieatt 20.
[2] Ovid, *Fasti* v 217–20, where Flora tells how 'the Hours assemble, clad in dappled weeds, and cull my gifts in light baskets. Straightway the Graces draw near, and twine garlands and wreaths to bind their heavenly hair.' See below, p. 181.   [3] On which see Valeriano 486.

And as ye her array, still throw between
Some graces to be seen,
And as ye use to Venus, to her sing. (vi)

And they are obeyed to the letter in the poem's formal arrangement. For explicit mentions of graces occur 'thrown between' the 12 diurnal stanza-hours according to the following pattern:[1]

v	vi	vii	viii	ix	x	xi	xii	xiii	xiv	xv	xvi
1	2	3	4	5	6	7	8	9	10	11	12
	G				G				G		

If we regard the 12 diurnal stanzas as forming a continuous circle, the graces are evenly spaced out and simulate the seasonal division of the year's 12 months as 3×4. Alternatively, we may imagine a linear array of the form $s\,G\,s\,s\,/\,s\,G\,s\,s\,/\,s\,G\,s\,s$ (where s indicates an ordinary stanza). The $1:2$ octave proportion between stanzas preceding and following the 'grace' stanzas has been encountered elsewhere (p. 159); but it is particularly appropriate here in view of the iconographical tradition whereby the Graces themselves were arranged in a $1+2$ physical array, one facing and two turned away from the observer.[2]

Invocations of Hymen are distributed in a similarly regular manner, to imitate the timing of songs at actual weddings. Thus Spenser contrives to introduce yet another division of time (as shown in the table overleaf).

Regular location of the first 3 mentions of Hymen at six-hour intervals leads us to expect the next in xx. But there we get 'still silence' instead, together with an assurance that silence will keep 'true night watches'. This passage, opaque to any but a numerological view, accounts for the absence of Hymen from xx and draws attention to the 'true' placing of his invocation in xxii. The delay has a twofold explanation. Stanza xviii enjoins the youths (who sang 'io Hymen' in

---

[1] St. vi, see last quotation in text; x, 'Adorned with beauty's grace'; xiv, 'And let the Graces dance unto the rest'. The main invocation of the Graces in vi is itself a number symbolism, giving content to Iamblichus' idea of Venus' association with the generative hexad by unfolding her, as it were, into 3 Horae + 3 Charites.

[2] See Edgar Wind, *Pagan Mysteries in the Renaissance* (1967) 44, 46 and 26–35 *passim*. Cf. *FQ* VI x 24, describing the Graces: 'And eke themselves so in their dance they bore, / That two of them still froward seemed to be, / But one still towards showed her self afore.'

STANZA	HOUR	TEXT
i	5	
ii	6	Hymen is awake,
iii	1	
iv	2	
v	3	
vi	4	
vii	5	
viii	6	Hymen io Hymen, Hymen they do shout,
ix	1	
x	2	
xi	3	
xii	4	
xiii	5	
xiv	6	Hymen also crown with wreaths of vine,
xv	1	
xvi	2	
xvii	3	
xviii	4	
xix	5	
xx	6	——
xxi	1	
xxii	2	and thou Hymen free,
xxiii	3	
xxiv	4	

viii) to be silent and xx invokes silence again, so that 2 silent stanzas as it were may be left out of account, to make the invocation 2 stanzas late. Alternatively, we may consider the placing of the last Hymen invocation as self-justifying, since it comes near the end of the sixth nocturnal hour, that is, at midnight, when tradition called for an epithalamic hymn to be sung.[1] Hence the poem truly keeps night-watches in distinct ways that correspond to the alternative division of the night into 3 or 4 parts. Silence in the fourth nocturnal stanza-hour (xx) 'keeps' or marks a true night-watch of the three-part, four-hour kind, whereas the invocation of Hymen at midnight marks the commoner four-part division of the night.

By its re-enlivening of the poem's language and symbolism, Hieatt's theory has radically altered our approach to *Epithalamion*. Nor is this change likely to be reversed. On the contrary, the modifications of the theory suggested above would have the effect of

[1] See Puttenham, *loc. cit.* p. 154 above.

heightening its stress on the theme of mutability. For we are now to see the poem's broadest movement as a dark–light–dark sequence: the time of light with its triumphant celebration of life forms but a brief interval between enveloping darknesses. Yet this will not seem too sombre an interpretation, if the implication of the song's dark frame is understood. The long-expected yet calm night of joy can be welcomed (l. 315) as bringing the consummation of the wedding day and initiating the generative process, which, while it shortens life, also renews it. Moreover, the formal correlate in the proportion between the poem's nocturnal parts—the first 4 and last 8 stanzas—is propitious. Like the stanzas divided by the Graces they form a 1:2 octave ratio, implying that night completes life harmoniously. And even the dreadful 'darkness' (l. 412) of the greater night that closes the 'short time' of mortal day is not final: a Christian altar stands at the poem's centre, so that new life conceived may inherit 'heavenly tabernacles' (xxiii).

9. Sonnet sequences

The most subtle and conceited of all numerological patterns are those in the sonnet sequences of the late sixteenth century. In our initial approach we should regard every Elizabethan sonnet sequence as a long poem in fourteen-line stanzas,[1] potentially as well organized as any other stanzaic poem of its period. For the authors of many sequences of love sonnets mannered their eroticism with a cool deliberation, arranging individual sonnets—themselves often ardently passionate yet highly structured—in intricate symmetrical patterns or according to relatively *recherché* number symbolisms. Modern ignorance of this is due partly to bad editorial scholarship, partly to the Romantic habit of ripping sonnets out of their original settings in order to make them individual emotional effusions or chapters in autobiographical narratives. For the songs, anacreontic verses and epithalamia that accompanied several sonnet sequences in the earliest

---

[1] As indeed, the titles of many sequences suggest, by referring to the sonnets as quatorzains: e.g. 'divers quatorzains' (Constable 1594): 'Amours in quatorzains' (Drayton 1594). The example of the Pléiade probably had a strong influence on the organization of Elizabethan sonnet sequences; see V.-L. Saulnier, *Scève: le prince de la renaissance Lyonnaise* (1948) 133 f. But sonnets had been mingled with other forms (*canzoni*, madrigals, etc.) to make structural patterns, based on temporal number symbolism, ever since Petrarch the great anticipator. In this connection it is interesting that Weinberg (ii 781) should take Francesco Patrizi to task for treating Petrarch's *Canzoniere* as a single poem in his *Deca dogmatica universale* (1587; MS Pal. 421).

editions contributed to overall structural schemes unintelligible without them. However, the formal patterns of the sequences may also be obscure for the simpler reason that their authors designed them to give this effect. The esoteric, never out of fashion, was like everything else carried to an extreme in mannerist art and literature.

In 1598 the Countess of Pembroke brought out an edition of her brother's works, including a corrected version of *Astrophil and Stella* with 11 lyrics intimately related to the sequence in theme, narrative content and spatial relation. Here is the arrangement of the songs (roman numerals) and sonnets (arabic), which internal evidence shows to be in accordance with Sidney's own intention:

I	II	III	IV	V–IX	X	XI
1–63	64–72	73–83	84–85	86	87–92	93–104	105–108

As Mr Adrian Benjamin has shown, the sonnet total of 108 contains a number symbolism of an exceedingly esoteric character, paying the most delicate possible compliment to Lady Penelope Rich's virtue.[1] The intimate secret it conceals is an affirmation of her faithfulness, for the number 108 alludes to the game played by the suitors of another Penelope, Homer's. The main features of that game, anciently described by Athenaeus and Eustathius, are summarized by Sir Thomas Browne, who tells how the 'prodigal paramours disposed their men, when they played at Penelope. For being themselves an hundred and eight, they set fifty four stones on either side, and one in the middle, which they called *Penelope*, which he that hit was master of the game.'[2] Thus the absence of a 109th or Penelope sonnet-stone from Sidney's sequence confesses Astrophil's failure as a lover. Similar allusions are made in the overall stanza total of the songs and in the line total of iambic songs, both 108. Esoteric as this number symbolism may seem, we have evidence that certain contemporaries of Sidney's understood it. Among elegies to him, that in Spenser's *Astrophil* is 2 × 108 lines, the *Lay of Clorinda* 108. And Alexander Craige's *Amorous Songs, Sonnets and*

---

[1] 'A Note on the Structure of *Astrophil and Stella*', forthcoming in *RES*.
[2] Ed. Keynes i 188. Browne cites Eustathius' commentary on *Odyssey* i 130, in turn dependent on Athenaeus. Benjamin traces many verbal allusions in *Astrophil and Stella* to bowls, the Elizabethan game most nearly akin to the Penelope game.

Elegies (1606), some addressed to Penelope Rich, similarly number 108.[1]

An outstanding feature of the distribution of Sidney's songs and sonnets is the movement from a long unbroken sequence of 63 sonnets to a broken sequence of 45 interrupted by songs. This pattern is repeated in the arrangement of the lyrics themselves, since they too comprise a long unbroken sequence (Songs V–IX), with others interspersed among the sonnets singly. Moreover, the stanzas of the unbroken block of songs number 63, those of the remaining songs, necessarily, 45.

The meaning of this arrangement, typically mannerist in its compensated asymmetrical symmetry, is to some extent obvious enough. 63 was used as the sonnet total of a complete sequence both by Henry Constable, for his 1592 *Diana*,[2] and by Michael Drayton, for his *Idea. In sixty three sonnets* (1619).[3] The number symbolism, explicitly announced in the first case[4] and easily inferred in the second, depended on the significance of 63 as the chief climacteric age, a critical stage of development for body and soul alike.[5] Now by Sonnet lxiii *Astrophil and Stella* has certainly reached a critical phase of heightened intensity, marked in the form by interposition of lyrics, in the narrative by Astrophil's outbreaks of passion, by his dishonourable suggestion of Song VIII and by his consequent loss of Stella. Hence the stanza totals of the songs symbolically follow the course of Astrophil's tragic failure:

I	II	III	IV	V–IX	X	XI
		28		63		17

The number 28, a 'perfect' number, signified virtue: 63 denoted a life crisis: and 17 was a familiar Pythagorean number symbolic of

---

[1] See Benjamin, who notices references in the elegies to stones in human form. The traditional association of stones with grief and melancholy makes one hesitate to attach special significance to these images, but they are unusually frequent and undeniably apt to the present context.

[2] Later *Augmented with divers quatorzains of honorable and learned personages. Divided into viii decads* (title of 1594 edn).

[3] Ed. Hebel ii 309–42. Drayton's *Idea's Mirror. Amours in quatorzains* (1594) (ed. Hebel i 96–124) is also organized numerologically, consisting of $1 + 51 = 52$ sonnets and containing references to the sun's course (e.g. xlvii, xxv, etc.).

[4] See the Preface, quoted pp. 2 f. above.

[5] Censorinus, *De die nat.* 14, *cit.* Fowler 269. Drayton makes his intention very nearly explicit by listing, opposite Sonnet xii in *Idea*, 9 faculties of the soul. As the prefatory sonnet states, 'My verse is the true image of my mind'.

misfortune and discord.[1] As for the number of whole songs, 11, it signified both transgression and grief.[2]

On the other hand, the exact distribution of sonnets in the 1598 *Astrophil and Stella* at first appears random. Yet if we consider the totals of sonnets intervening between songs

I	II	III	IV	V–IX	X	XI
63	9	11	2	1	6	12	4
63		22		1		22

we find a symmetry about Sonnet lxxxvi, the sonnet concerned with a 'change of looks' in Stella the 'sweet judge', who thus occupies a central seat of judgement in the formal structure in the midst of numbers signifying chastity (22, 22). Governing the overall arrangement of the sonnets, Benjamin finds symmetry of a different kind: a systematic correspondence between sonnets of the first 54 and the second. Both Sonnet xxii and the corresponding twenty-second sonnet of the second half, lxxvi, compare Stella to the burning sun at its zenith, and both introduce an image of heavenly twins ('fair Twins' golden place': 'her shining twins do move / Their rays'). Sonnet lv, which before the tragic ending promised to be the Penelope stone, brings a new invocation of the Muses and a resolve 'on her name incessantly to cry'.[3]

The symmetries formed by the metrical array of the songs naturally receive more elaboration. They are arranged like this:

SONG	I	II	III	IV	V	VI	VII	VIII	IX	X	XI
LINES PER STANZA	4	4	6	6	6	6	6	4	5	6	5
STANZA TOTAL	9	7	3	9	15	9	3	26	10	8	9
LINE TOTAL	36	28	18	54	90	54	18	104	50	48	45
			a	*b*	**C**	*b*	*a*				

[1] 28 is perfect since it equals the sum of its aliquot parts: i.e. $1+2+4+7+14 = 28$. It was virtuous because it hit the mean, neither exceeding nor falling short of the aliquot parts: see Bongo 464 ff. On 17, see *ibid.* 416 and above p. 52 n.

[2] Bongo 377 ff., 383.

[3] For the reversal of the order of Sonnets lv and lvi, and the separation of the songs from the sonnets in the unauthorized edition of 1591, see *The Poems of Sir Philip Sidney* ed. Ringler 542. As will be readily understood, the presence of the various symmetries discussed in the present section counts heavily against the validity of reordering the units of the 1598 array. In particular, we can

The stanza or line totals of the group of 5 consecutive lyrics in six-line stanzas, III–VII, clearly exhibit recessed symmetry. (Is it coincidental that odd and even pairs of these line totals form the Penelope game number: $18+90 = 108$, $54+54 = 108$?) Moreover, this symmetry extends still further, if the exceptionally long VIII can be regarded as more than one unit. For this division we have some verbal warrant, since the lyric concludes with the statement 'my song is broken'. Referring primarily, of course, to Astrophil's grief, this statement secondarily alludes to Song VIII's being broken off just before the twenty-seventh stanza needed for a line total of 108. (Unbroken, VIII would have brought the Songs' stanza total to 109, hitting the Penelope stone and making Astrophil 'master of the game'.[1]) But the statement that Song VIII is broken also invites us to consider it as divided. Its organic division, we find, is into 3 parts: it opens with a seven-stanza narrative section, continues with 9 stanzas of passionate direct speech by Astrophil and concludes with 10 stanzas (shared between narrative and direct speech) of Stella's refusal. Thus the symmetrical pattern centred on Song V is really sustained from I up to and including parts of VIII, as shown in the table below.

SONG	I	II	III	IV	V	VI	VII	VIII	VIII
LINES PER STANZA	4	4	6	6	6	6	6	4	4
STANZA TOTAL	9	7	3	9	15	9	3	7	9
	a	b	c	a	D	a	c	b	a

The ennoblement of Song V at the centre of so elaborate an array befits a triumphal lyric, or at least one specially decisive. But Sidney at once fulfils and finesses this decorum: his Fifth Song, coming immediately after the 'change of looks' of the focal Sonnet lxxxvi,

almost certainly rule out rearrangement of the songs among the sonnets, such as Ann Romayne Howe (*SP* LXI (1964) 164–7) and A. C. Hamilton (*ELH* XXXVI (1969) 68) attempt. This sort of rearrangement would now have to be based on the difficult speculative assumption that Sidney's arrangement of the songs was narrative, and that his sister decided to rearrange this structurally random sequence in an elaborate numerological pattern.

[1] It may be relevant that the line total of the songs is 545 or 5×109. For Browne states that the Penelope game has a resemblance to 'the game of pentalithimus, or casting up five stones to catch them on the back of the hand', and throughout *Astrophil and Stella* patterns of 5 can be observed (an unbroken block of 5 songs, a group of 5 consecutive symmetrical songs, etc.).

celebrates Stella's triumph as a cruel and unjust tyrant (ll. 56 ff.). And its central stanza admits the sovereignty of her name ('thou rich in all joys') only to revile her as five times thief for refusing to requite his love. The Song is indeed decisive, marking as it does the sour culmination of Astrophil's praise of Stella and his turn from hope to despair, defiance and disrespect.

Song V is not, however, the only structural centre: two others[1] share this honour. The central stanza of all the songs comes in VII, midmost of the 13 song parts that result from dividing VIII. Song VII, unlike V, is a lyric of pure 'firm love', demanding no requital but celebrating Stella as an angelic 'image of the skies'. Astrophil reaches this tragically brief triumph of pure wonder at Stella's beauty by way of the inner harmony ('sacred tunes') treated in the intervening Song VI. There, music is associated in competition with Stella's beauty, and reason asked to adjudicate the crown:

Then reason, princess high,
Whose throne is in the mind,
Which music can in sky
And hidden beauties find,
Say whether thou wilt crown,
With limitless reknown.

This Sixth Song has also a formal claim to a sovereign position, being the central lyric of the 11 and containing the central *line* of the whole array. Moreover, it occupies the centre of an overlap between the continuous group of 5 songs (V–IX, S in the accompanying Table) and the symmetrical group of 5 consecutive songs in six-line stanzas (**6** in the Table).

The same overlap of the 3 centre songs can be distinguished in the prosodic pattern formed by the distribution of iambic (I) and trochaic metres (T):

I	II	III	IV	**V**	**VI**	**VII**	VIII	IX	X	XI
x	x	x	x	**S**	**S**	**S**	**S**	**S**	x	x
x	x	**6**	**6**	**6**	**6**	**6**	x	x	x	x
I	*T*	*I*	*T*	*I*	*I*	*I*	*T*	*T*	*T*	*T*

Generally the iambic songs express praise, the trochaic songs desire or complaint; the only exception being V, whose substitution of unexpected dispraise has been discussed. In I–IV, the two moods

---

[1] Distinguished metrically from the rest, in that they admit no feminine rhymes.

alternate, whereas the overlap songs are all iambic and those of the last phase (VIII–XI) all trochaic complaints. Finally, the number of framing songs (x) before and after the overlapping blocks of 5 bear in both cases the harmonious octave proportion 2:1 and 1:2 (4 before and 2 after, 2 before and 4 after).

From the standpoint of formal style, two distinctive features of *Astrophil and Stella* strike one immediately; proving subsequently to be aspects of the same feature. First, the ingenious complexity of the formal structure, whose broad lines only have been sketched above.[1] Secondly, the asymmetrical or partially symmetrical character of its multiple patterns. No one song or sonnet is the sole centre of the work. Here the analogy with mannerist architectural façades or landscape gardening designs seems illuminating. Shearman remarks of mannerist gardens that 'nothing predominates, and there is no dramatic focus...The successive, cumulative impression is more important' (125). Or again, in more general vein: 'The emphasis on the parts rather than the whole in so many Mannerist works is... positive and functionally expressive of a desired quality' (146). We glimpse, behind such analogies, a principle underlying formal design of every kind in this style. Perhaps the analysis of poetic structures such as those of *Astrophil and Stella* may even have a bearing on art historical disputes about the nature of mannerism. What we have seen of related multiple axes of symmetry at least confirms the view of mannerism as complex, intricate and undynamic (Shearman 22, 123, etc.), rather than Pevsner's view of it as restless and unbalanced, unharmonious and tense.[2] In poetic form, individual mannerist asymmetries generally contribute to a complex symmetry, which remains completely, if obscurely, harmonious.

SPENSER'S 'AMORETTI'

In the same way, Spenser's *Amoretti* should be considered in conjunction with *Epithalamion* and the 4 anacreontics that join with them

---

[1] I have said little about decorums of number symbolism, which probably govern much of the distribution of material. Thus the sovereign Song V has 15 stanzas, because 15 was the number of approach to a throne; see H. Neville Davies, 'The Structure of Shadwell's *A Song for St Ceilia's Day, 1690*', in *Silent Poetry* ed. Alastair Fowler (1970) 205–18, for other instances of the symbolic use of this number.

[2] Nikolaus Pevsner, 'The Architecture of Mannerism' in *The Mint* ed. Geoffrey Grigson (1946).

to form a single composite, yet integral, work of great complexity. Temporal and other numerology in the structure of *Epithalamion* has been analysed above. But this is only part of a larger and more complex structure sustaining the whole printed work *Amoretti and Epithalamion* (1595).

Many have noticed that two *Amoretti* sonnets, xxxv and lxxxiii, are identical. This correspondence falls into place to form one element of a symmetrical array, if we treat the composite *Amoretti and Epithalamion* as a unity:

		Amoretti			Ana-creontics	Epi-thalamion
i–xxxiv	xxxv	xxxvi–lxxxii	lxxxiii	lxxxiv–lxxxix	i–iv	i–xxiv
34	I	47	I	6	4	24
34	I	47	I		34	
a	*b*	*c*	*b*		*a*	

The centre term of this array, *Amoretti* lix, has an appropriate subject, the maintenance of a mean and steady course: 'Thrice happy she, that...like a steady ship...keeps her course aright'; her assurance, independent of both friends and foes 'neither to one her self nor other bends'. Such is the happy lover's mistress, who rests assured at the still centre of the poem written in her honour.

Temporal number symbolism determines Spenser's particular choice of sonnet and anacreontic totals. For the whole work can be construed as 89 (sonnets) + 4 (anacreontics) = 93, or 89 (days of winter) + 4 = 93 (days of spring).[1] As we have seen, the *piedi* of *Epithalamion* itself similarly correspond to the days of summer. Hence the *Amoretti* and anacreontics represent numerologically the 2 seasons

---

[1] Almost all the authorities cited by Riccioli (i 142), including the Alfonsine tables, Copernicus and Tycho, agree in estimating the winter quarter (solstice to vernal equinox) as 89 full days, the spring quarter (equinox to summer solstice, 11 June, St Barnaby's Day) as 93 days (Copernicus estimates 92 days 23 hours 32 minutes for 1500). Ptolemy, however, gives different figures (spring quarter 94 full days). This presents a difficulty, since if Spenser used more recent and accurate authorities for the winter and spring figures, one would expect him to do the same with the summer quarter in *Epithalamion* (see p. 167 above). But most of the recent authorities cited by Riccioli give 93 days for the summer quarter, not 92. It is possible that Spenser means us to save appearances

preceding Spenser's wedding, whereas *Epithalamion* represents both the wedding day itself and the season to which it belongs. But in such a mannerist work this is not, of course, the whole story. Each sonnet can also be subdivided, like the stanzas of *Epithalamion*, into 4 parts (3 quatrains + 1 couplet), while the anacreontics between them muster 9 clearly marked subdivisions; so that the whole array is also a year and a day: $89 \times 4 + 9 = 365$.

The foregoing discussion prompts the idea that *Amoretti* may have a calendrical structure like that of *Epithalamion*. And this proves to be the case, as Alexander Dunlop shows in two perceptive articles.[1] The central 47 *Amoretti* alone—Sonnets xxii–lxviii—correspond to the days in the Lenten season of 1594, that is, from Ash Wednesday (13 February) to Easter Day (31 March). Not every sonnet, naturally, has a content announcing its date; Spenser has more on hand than an almanac. But there are enough indications to ensure the objectivity of the pattern Dunlop describes. The Easter sonnet, for example, begins:

Most glorious lord of life, that on this day,
Didst make thy triumph over death and sin:
and having harrowed hell, didst bring away
captivity thence captive us to win:
This joyous day...

Considering the style of the formal structure, particularly the way in which calendrical and symmetrical patterns are superimposed, we again notice multiple axes of symmetry. For Dunlop's Lenten calendrical pattern does not occupy the same 47 sonnets that formed the centre of the larger symmetrical array discussed above (p. 181). Confined to the *Amoretti*, his scheme is $21 + 47 + 21 = 89$. Once more, a number symbolism sets the limits of this scheme: 22, the number of the sonnet beginning the Lenten section, symbolized Temperance.

by regarding the 24 stanza-hours of *Epithalamion* as supplying the missing day—'let this one day be mine'. Alternatively, further research may disclose which astronomical authority Spenser was following. For the present, I am content to advance the explanation set out in the text as a working hypothesis. As Thomas Roche has pointed out to me, there is another instance of inset calendrical patterning in Barnabe Barnes's *Parthenophil and Parthenophe. Sonnets, madrigals elegies and odes* (1593). Here Barnes or his printer makes the device explicit by marginal notes: astrological symbols are printed above appropriate sonnets in a zodiac of 12 (Pl. 3).

[1] 'Calendar Symbolism in the "Amoretti"', *N & Q* CCXIV (1969) 24–6; 'The Unity of Spenser's *Amoretti*' in *Silent Poetry* ed. Alastair Fowler (1970) 153–69.

It is hardly to be expected that the sonnet sequence of a poet so intellectually brilliant as Shakespeare should lack the structural art and finesse valued in his age. And in fact his sequence abounds with the intricate formal devices requisite to its genre. Of all Elizabethan sequences, indeed, with the exception of that of Spenser, his rival, Shakespeare's is the most complex formally. Yet to understand the main lines of its structure, we have only to keep in mind the same two features observed in other sequences: first, that poems published with sonnets belong to the structural pattern; second, that words may refer literally to their own arrangement, providing a self-referring commentary on the form. By attending to these features, Shakespeare's *Sonnets*, together with 'The Lover's Complaint' printed with them in the first quarto edition of 1609, are easily seen to exhibit an elaborate structural symmetry.

This has interesting critical implications. But the textual implications are if possible still more far-reaching, since a majority of scholars have believed the 1609 *Sonnets* to be disordered, so that trying to rearrange them in a better order (that is, an order more intelligible as a biographical sequence) is a useful activity. One almost feels sorry to break up a game that has given harmless amusement to so many—among them Sir Sidney Lee, Denys Bray, H. C. Beeching, Brents Stirling and J. Dover Wilson.[1] As we shall see, however, the rules of that game are based on false assumptions. The spatial arrangement of Shakespeare's sequence in fact leaves little room for permutations: its form asserts a design far too positive for us to be free to change it at will. Every scholar rearranging the sonnets has in effect committed the biographical fallacy—or else the textual fallacy of explaining difficulties away as failures of transmission.

The text of the 1609 quarto comprises 154 correctly numbered sonnets, together with a poem in 47 seven-line stanzas, 'The Lover's Complaint'. Not all the sonnets are metrically similar: Peter Alexander's statement that Shakespeare differs from most other sonneteers of his time in not mixing sonnets with poems of other forms

---

[1] *The Sonnets* ed. J. Dover Wilson (Cambridge 1966) pp. xxvii ff.; Brents Stirling, 'Sonnets 127–154' in *Shakespeare 1564–1964* ed. E. A. Bloom (Providence, R.I. 1964) 134–53, developed in *The Shakespeare Sonnet Order: Poems and Groups* (Berkeley and Los Angeles 1968).

needs qualification. Besides 'The Lover's Complaint', any accurate description of the sequence must take account of 3 metrically irregular sonnets, that is, 3 sonnets not pentameter quatorzains. These are: xcix (a fifteen-line stanza), cxxvi (a twelve-line stanza in couplets) and cxlv (tetrameters). The attention previously given to these sonnets typifies the biographically fallacious approach of the textual critics. Sonnet cxxvi, which fitted the substantive division into 'W.H.' and 'dark lady' sonnet groups, they treated as a 'coda' to the former; whereas they did not regard cxlv as a structural division at all, and either ignored or explained away xcix as a 'rough draft'. Beeching[1] actually speculated that the first line of xcix was an 'afterthought', Shakespeare 'intending afterwards to reduce' the sonnet to 14 lines; in spite of the self-referring hint in the truly extrametrical l. 5, 'In my love's veins thou hast *too grossly* dyed'. The first step in any structural analysis must be to examine the pattern formed by the irregular sonnets.

Recalling the second of the features mentioned at the outset, we may be inclined to regard a passage in cxxxvi, which has never received a satisfactory interpretation, as self-referring:

In things of great receipt with ease we prove,
Among a number one is reckoned none.
Then in the number let me pass untold,
Though in thy store's account I one must be,
For nothing hold me...

In their primary sense these words refer to the speaker; but they seem pedestrian, overelaborate and obscure, unless they have some further point. This I find in a secondary reference to the sonnet itself. It is to be excluded from, yet at the same time included in, the reckoning. Now if we count cxxxvi out, the sonnet total becomes 153, one of the best known of all symbolic numbers.[2] It may well be, therefore, that the structural pattern of the irregular sonnets constitutes arrangement in a sequence of $153 + 1$.

The number 153 was famous as the total catch of fish in *John* xxi 11,

---

[1] Followed by Dover Wilson (206).

[2] See Sir Edwyn C. Hoskyns, *The Fourth Gospel* ed. F. N. Davey (1947) 553–6, reviewing the interpretations of Origen, Cyril of Alexandria, Ammonius, Severus and especially St Augustine, as transmitted through various catenas or Biblical commentaries. One might add that Raban Maur gives the number of fish caught as 154 instead of 153 (Migne v 494); but this may be only a copyist's error.

fulfilling the prophecy of *Ezekiel* xlvii and the parable of *Matthew* xiii 47 f. ('the kingdom of heaven is like unto a net, that was cast into the sea, and gathered of every kind: Which, when it was full, they... gathered the good into vessels, but cast the bad away'). It had attracted many interpretations from the Church Fathers and from arithmologists, the dominant theme being symbolism of the Elect. By Shakespeare's time, most commentators understood the distinctive mathematical feature of 153 to reside in its triangularity.[1] As the sum of the first 17 natural numbers, when set out in Pythagorean fashion it forms an equilateral triangle with a base of 17 (as shown in the diagram below).

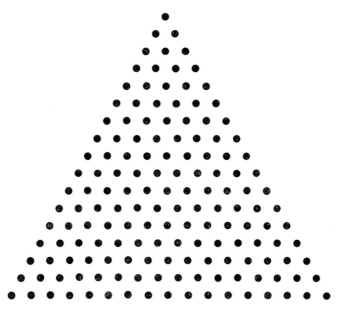

The series of triangular numbers was a common topic of arithmology, partly because several familiar symbolic numbers belonged to it, including the perfect numbers 6 and 28, the expanded form of the *tetractys* 10, the 'great quaternion' 36 and the number of complete life 120.[2] The first 17 terms of the series, with their bases, are:

[1] Bongo 594. The authority most often cited is St Augustine. On the Augustinian arithmological tradition, see Maren-Sofie Røstvig, 'Structure as Prophecy: The Influence of Biblical Exegesis upon Theories of Literary Structure', esp. 41–55.

[2] Perfect numbers are numbers that equal the sum of their aliquot parts (e.g. $1+2+3 = 6$); 10 is a form of the *tetractys* since $1+2+3+4 = 10$; the great quaternion had many interesting properties, but got its name from being the

TRIANGULAR NUMBER	1, 3, 6, 10, 15, 21, 28, 36, 45, 55, 66, 78, 91, 105, 120, 136, 153
BASE	1, 2, 3, 4, 5, 6, 7, 8, 9, 10, 11, 12, 13, 14, 15, 16, 17

These terms constitute successively greater triangular portions of the 153 triangle, which contains them all.

We can now discern the structural pattern governing the arrangement of Shakespeare's irregular stanzas. They are so located in the sequence that each is denoted by a triangular number within the greater triangle 153. Thus the octosyllabic cxlv begins a culminating ten-sonnet triangle cxlv–cliv, the twelve-line cxxvi begins a twenty-eight-sonnet triangle[1] and the fifteen-line cxix begins a fifty-five-sonnet triangle.[2] Moreover, two of these triangular numbers had great arithmological significance, 10 as the principle of divine creativity itself, 28 as a symbol of moral perfection.[3]

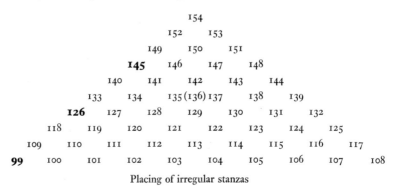

                          154
                    152   153
                149   150   151
          145   146   147   148
          140   141   142   143   144
      133   134   135 (136) 137   138   139
  126 127   128   129   130   131   132
118   119   120   121   122   123   124   125
109   110   111   112   113   114   115   116   117
99 100   101   102   103   104   105   106   107   108

Placing of irregular stanzas

Shakespeare mentions the triangular shape in Sonnet cxxiii:

No! Time, thou shalt not boast that I do change,
Thy pyramids built up with newer might
To me are nothing novel, nothing strange,
They are but dressings of a former sight...

sum of the first 4 odd and even numbers. All the numbers mentioned were treated as triangular: see e.g. Bongo 198, 262, 269, 357, 496 and 582 f.

[1] Sonnets cxxvi–cliv; omitting cxxxvi, as explained above.

[2] Sonnets xcix–cliv; omitting cxxxvi, as explained above. Other triangles are formed by substantive divisions in the sequence: Sonnets i–xvii e.g., which most critics regard as a distinct section, introduce a 136-sonnet triangular group xviii–cliv (omitting cxxxvi, as explained above). It may be worth mentioning that the dedication of the sequence is designed typographically in the form of triangles.

[3] Bongo 356 ff., 464, 472 f. The base of the remaining triangular number 55, that is, 10, had also great symbolic value.

In its primary sense, this passage refers to the obelisks excavated in Rome and re-erected (1585–90) by Pope Sixtus V;[1] but it also glances at the form of the sequence itself, for *pyramid* and *triangle* were often synonyms. Puttenham, discussing the 'taper called pyramis' as a shape for poetry, defines it as 'the longest and sharpest triangle that is...The Latins in use of architecture call him *obeliscus*, it holdeth the altitude of 6 ordinary triangles'.[2] Self-referring ambiguity again occurs in cxxv, a stanza difficult to interpret satisfactorily, unless it applies in part to the sequence's external form:

Were it aught to me I bore the canopy,
With my extern thee outward honouring,
Or laid great basis for eternity,
Which proves more short than waste or ruining?

The very next stanza is the 'short' cxxvi, beginning the base of the pyramid of 28. We conclude that the 'basis for eternity' described as more short than waste is in one sense Sonnet cxxvi itself, the sonnet on Love defying Time.[3] Time, which figures very prominently in earlier sonnets,[4] is never mentioned in the sequence after cxxvi. Moreover, from a numerological point of view, 28 is suitable to eternity, as a number symbolizing the perfect bliss in heaven towards which saints yearn.[5]

To the objection that the last sonnets seem less edifying in their content, one would feel tempted to reply, in the case of a lesser poet, that ironic contrast between substance and form is a familiar feature of mannerist style. However, even in their substance Stanzas cxxvi–cliv sometimes reflect a consciousness of eternal bliss lost through

[1] Leslie Hotson, *Mr W. H.* (1964) 85–92; rightly accepted by Dover Wilson (236).
[2] *The Art of English Poesy* ed. Willcock and Walker 95 f. Cf. Sir Thomas Browne, *The Garden of Cyrus* in *Works* ed. Keynes i 214: 'triangles or pyramids'. See further in Hotson 85 f.
[3] The ambiguity of the 1609 spelling 'bases' does nothing to weaken this point, for the plural would refer to all the stanzas up to cxxv, which are in a sense pedestal for the pyramid cxxvi–cliv. Grammatical considerations do not decide between the possibilities, for *Which* in l. 4 might apply to the whole preceding action, rather than to *basis*, and in any case plurals ending in -*s* are not unknown in Shakespeare (see E. A. Abbott, *A Shakespearian Grammar* (1875) Sect. 333, 'Third Person Plural in -*s*'). Since cxxvi is from one point of view short in respect of its final couplet, it is interesting that Drayton should compare the final couplet of a stanza to an architectural base (p. 19 above).
[4] Shakespeare explicitly refers to Time on more than 70 occasions in Sonnets i–cxxvi, and implicitly on many others.
[5] Bongo 472 f.

lesser desire, an awareness of 'the expense of spirit in a waste of shame' (cxxix) and a conscience-stricken sense of the need for the 'poor soul the centre of my sinful earth' to 'buy terms divine' (cxlvi). Imagery of heaven, hell, good angels and fiends abounds.

The pyramidal numbers imply, most obviously, that Shakespeare designed the sequence to function as a monument. 'Of all figures the firmest',[1] the pyramid seemed the monumental form *par excellence*, embodying the ancient ideal of poetry as memorial—*exegi monumentum aere perennius*.[2] Cowley thought nothing was more necessary 'than verse to virtue', which

> when it dies, with comely pride
> Embalms it, and erects a pyramid
> That never will decay.[3]

The pyramid was especially appropriate for elegies and epitaphs. Milton's epitaph 'On Shakespeare' (which conceivably alludes to the form of the dead poet's *Sonnets*) takes this for granted when it ostensibly denies the need for memorial in Shakespeare's case: 'What needs my Shakespeare...that his hallowed relics should be hid / Under a star-ypointing pyramid?'[4] Elegies using the pyramidal numbers, particularly 28 and 120, were common.[5] Thus the monu-

---

[1] Sir William Temple, *Works* i (1731) 105.

[2] Horace, *Odes* III xxx 1.

[3] Ed. Waller 182; cf. *ibid*. 243: 'Lo, this great work, a temple to thy praise, / On polished pillars of strong verse I raise.' Poetry might even announce itself as pyramidal on the title-page, as in John Vicars, *God in the mount. A panegyric pyramides, erected to the everlasting high honour of England's God* (1642).

[4] Ed. Carey and Fowler 123.

[5] Surrey's epitaph on Clere uses 28 substantively (ed. Jones 32: 'Ere summers four times seven thou couldst fulfill': 4 personal and 7 place names mentioned), and we find 28-line totals in Cowley's elegy 'On the Death of Sir Henry Wootton', in 3 elegies to Edward King (*Iusta* xiii, xix: *Obsequies* iii) by R. C., Michael Honeywood and Anon., and in the concluding section of Spenser's *Ruins of Time* (discussed by Røstvig, 'The Hidden Sense' 88; self-referred to in ll. 407 f., 'In vain do earthly princes then, in vain / Seek with pyramides, to heaven aspired'). No less than 5 of Milton's shorter lyrics have 28 lines (Røstvig, 'The Hidden Sense' 52), and so has Jonson's 'To the Lord Treasurer' (ed. Herford, Simpson and Simpson viii 260 f.), with ll. 25 ff. self-referring: 'though I cannot as an architect / In glorious piles, or pyramids erect / Unto your honour: I can tune in song / Aloud; and (happily) it may last as long'. 120 symbolized the term of worthy life, partly because it was the altitude in cubits of the Temple, partly because it was the age of man before the Flood (Bongo 586 ff.): 'his days shall be an hundred and twenty years' (*Gen.* vi 3). In consequence, the number was frequently used as a line total, both of epithalamia and of elegies: e.g. Jonson, *Hymenaei* (ed. Herford, Simpson and Simpson

mental form of Shakespeare's sequence literally fulfils the ever-renewed promise to immortalize his beloved's name: 'Not marble, nor the gilded monument, / Of princes shall outlive this powerful rhyme' (lv); 'Speaking of your fame' (lxxx); 'Your name from hence immortal life shall have....Your monument shall be my gentle verse' (lxxxi); 'And thou in this shalt find thy monument' (cvii); 'Even as when first I hallowed thy fair name' (cviii).

More deeply considered, the arithmological properties of Shakespeare's chosen pyramid may have a specific bearing on the structure of the *Sonnets*. Bongo's chapter on 153, while recording explanations by Gregory, Severus and others, follows in the main the dominant Augustinian tradition. It explains 17 as the union of 10 (the Decalogue) with 7 (Gifts of the Holy Ghost), and infers that the triangle rising on 17 as base, 153, denotes believers risen in Christ and endowed with the Spirit.[1] Pursuing an alternative line of speculation, Bongo further notes that 3 (a symbol of the Trinity) $\times$ 17 = 51, a number not devoid of mystery, since it symbolizes the 50 natural years of the Hebrew Jubilee Year of reconciliation and rest, together with the One of true rest.[2] Finally, $3 \times 51 = 153$, and 'all agree' that 153 'pertains to the resurrection of eternal life'.[3] This Trinitarian interpretation of 153 agrees with a conception of the pyramid found

vii 225 ff.); Thomas Heywood, 'Nuptial Song' (Case 44); Henry Peacham, Epicedium 'Stay royal body' in *The Period of Mourning* (1613); Henry King 'In immaturum obitum', *Iusta* xvi and 'No, death!', *Obsequies* i (120 lines + concluding couplet epitaph) and J. Beaumont, 'When first this news', *Obsequies* ii. See also Qvarnström, *Poetry and Numbers* 71 on 120 as a stanza total in Benlowes; and cf. Marvell, *First Anniversary* 119–120: 'If gracious heaven to my life give length, / Leisure to time, and to my weakness strength.' The line total of Henry King's 'The Exequy' is also 120; but here the meaning is complicated by others. A total of 60 couplets is appropriate for a poem full of temporal symbols and imagery ('How lazily time creeps about...so I compute the weary hours...so many years / As day tells hours...each minute is a short degree / And every hour a step towards thee' etc.). And there is a further division, as in *Lycidas*, into 11 paragraphs, a number symbolizing mourning and the termination of mourning (Bongo 383).

[1] Bongo 594: 'Cum itaque legis denario per septenarium Spiritus sanctus accedit, fiunt decem et septem, quae in trigonum resurgentia, conficiunt numerum 153 qui potest occurrere ad Ecclesiae sanctitatem, quae per Christum facta est.' For a numerological application of the idea of 17 as the base of 153 by Benlowes, see Qvarnström, *Poetry and Numbers* 82.

[2] Bongo 594 f.: 'sed vera requies in unitate est.' St Augustine makes a slightly different 3-part division ($153 = 3 \times 50 + 3$), though the interpretation of individual numbers is closely similar.

[3] Bongo 593.

in symbological authors, who take the triangular faces to represent the three-fold creative principle.[1] The above doctrines offer both substantive and formal suggestions to the interpreter of Shakespeare's pyramidal sequence.

Substantively, he will be inclined to pay more attention to the religious language that differentiates the *Sonnets* of Shakespeare from most secular sonnets of his time, and perhaps to develop C. S. Lewis's view that 'the greatest of the sonnets are written from a region in which love abandons all claims and flows into charity. . . . This transference of the whole self into another self without the demand for a return [has] hardly a precedent in profane literature.'[2]

Formally, he will look for a three-part division of the sequence corresponding to the traditional threefold division of the number 153. A further encouragment of this division is the poet's thrice-repeated affirmation of a Neoplatonic trinity in his beloved: 'Fair, kind, and true, is all my argument. . . Which three till now, never kept seat in one' (cv). Again the irregular stanzas provide a signpost. For, if we leave them out of the reckoning, the regular sonnets number 151 (or 150, omitting cxxxvi as before), that is, the number of psalms in the *Book of Common Prayer* (or *Vulgate* version, respectively). Now, a threefold division of the *Psalms* was traditional. Bongo's discussion of 150 begins with this as a familiar idea: he takes the manipulation $150 = 3 \times 50$ to mean that the form of the *Psalms* symbolizes the Trinity. Thus a numerological approach unexpectedly confirms Hotson's theory that the contents of several of Shakespeare's sonnets correspond to those of psalms bearing the sane numbers in the *Book of Common Prayer*. Though I do not regard every correlation Hotson proposes as convincing, the broad lines of his hypothesis seem

[1] J. E. Cirlot, *A Dictionary of Symbols* tr. J. Sage (1962) 255, citing Nicholas of Cusa. (The pyramid as a whole also presents 3 aspects, in its base, faces and mystic apex.) Valeriano 754 summarizes a different notion, still perpetuated in Athanasius Kircher: namely, that the pyramid represents geometrically the creative influence of a zodiacal sign; the base being in heaven, the point at earth's centre. Interest in the esoteric meanings of pyramids and the hieroglyphs inscribed on their faces persisted well into the seventeenth century, as witness Kircher's *Obeliscus pamphilus* (Rome 1650).

[2] *English Literature in the Sixteenth Century* (Oxford 1954) 505. The comparison of the sequence to Chapman's 'The Amorous Zodiac' implied (though denied) in Shakespeare's Sonnet xxi points in the same direction: Chapman's poem is fitly juxtaposed with 'A Coronet for his Mistress Philosophy', since it treats human love with cosmic imagery (though not in a way Shakespeare approved).

sound.[1] However, the connections between psalms and sonnets are more definite and more structural than he suggests. They rest, not on casual transference of associations, but on a deliberate and meaningful structural scheme. The entire set of regular sonnets corresponds numerically to the entire set of psalms; though substantive correlations could only be communicated in the case of familiar psalms. Hotson's conclusion that Shakespeare numbered all the sonnets himself is not yet proved, but we may fairly infer that he must have numbered a great many of them.

Besides the meanings already discussed, the pyramid also had a temporal symbolism: paradoxically it stood both for time and for immortality. Its temporal significance sprang only in part from the antiquity of the Egyptian pyramids. More familiarly, the pyramid was used in actual practice as a means of measuring time: in a tall obelisk form it could function as the vertical gnomon of a horizontal sundial.[2] Indeed, the very obelisks referred to in Sonnet cxxiii—the Roman obelisks—were used in this way, so that their description as *Time's* pyramids and as his 'registers'[3] is most exact. These

[1] *Mr W. H.* 269–81. The list of echoes of the penitential psalms at 281 n. is to my mind conclusive.

[2] On the obelisk by St John Lateran as a gnomon, and on Rheticus' use of the Roman obelisks for a variety of astronomical purposes, see T. Przypkowski, 'Les plus grands cadrans solaires modernes en Europe', *Berichtsbuch des VI Internationalen Kongresses für Chronometrie, München, 19–23 Juni 1959* (Stuttgart 1961) 889–900, with references. Even if Shakespeare knew nothing of the horological application of these particular obelisks, he must have been familiar with the general notion of pyramidal gnomons, at a time when the theory and construction of dials of all kinds neared the height of their sophistication and many technical works on dialing were available both in learned and in vernacular languages. But there is no need to go further than an author whom Shakespeare certainly read: Pliny. Pliny discusses the horological application of the Egyptian obelisk brought to Rome by Augustus and set up in the Campus Martius (*Hist. nat.* XXXVI xv 72): as he explains, it had a small sphere on the pinnacle (like that of the Lateran obelisk) to give definition to the shadow, from whose length was calculated the variation of the day in terms of equinoctial hours, graduated rods being let into the pavement to assist the measurement. This obelisk was rediscovered, with its markings, in 1463; see M. Bandini, *Dell' obelisco di Cesare Augusto* (Rome 1750); also W. Richardson, *The Book of Sun-dials* (1889) 11; Bern Dibner, *Moving the Obelisks*, Bundy Libr. No. 6 (Norwalk, Conn. 1952), citing many early works on the Roman obelisks, including Petrus Angelius Bargaeius, *Commentarius de obelisco* (Rome 1586), I. Hieronymus Catena, *De magno obelisco circensi* (Rome 1587), and Michael Mercati, *Degli Obelischi di Roma* (Rome 1589). Time carries an Egyptian obelisk in an allegorical sketch by Bernini; see Panofsky, *Studies in Iconology* 82 and Fig. 58b.

[3] Probably the obsolete *OED* sb.², = 'keeper of a register'; though *OED* sb.¹ I 7 b = 'index' is possible.

considerations, taken together with an extraordinarily high frequency of references to time measurement, lead us to expect that Shakespeare's sequence contains further structures based on temporal numerology, and that in a formal as well as in a substantive sense the *Sonnets* constitute an important phase in Shakespeare's poetic meditation on time.[1]

Our expectation of temporal numerology is quickly confirmed by incidental decorums, such as the location of the phrase 'our minutes hasten to their end' in Sonnet lx.[2] At first, Sonnet lii, with its reference to 'the long year', seems to fall into the same trivial category. But then we notice that a further year of 52 stanza-weeks would bring us to civ, a sonnet entirely devoted to meditation on the 'process of the seasons' and to reckoning years passed away since the poet first saw his beloved. It seems as if the sequence as a whole may be ordered according to a modulus of 52 stanzas per year, so that a division into 3 year-parts (i–lii, liii–civ, cv–cliv) constitutes yet another threefold arrangement.

However, in that case we should expect the third part to contain 52 stanza-weeks, like its predecessors. Instead, it contains only 49, if we omit cxxxvi as before. True, there is an argument for including cxxxvi on the strength of its self-referring hint that it should be included in one reckoning ('in the number let me pass untold, / Though in thy store's account I one must be'). But this still leaves us 2 short of the expected 52. In other words, for our hypothesis to hold there will have to be 2 missing sonnets or, at least, 2 places where the sonnet total is increased without addition of actual sonnets. Now Sonnet lxxvii with its mention of 'blanks' seems to hint at a similar possibility: 'Look

[1] See Frank Kermode, 'On Shakespeare's Learning', *Wesleyan University Centre for Advanced Studies Monday Evening Papers* II (1965) 7–10. L. C. Knights's *Explorations* (New York 1947) 77 finds Shakespeare's interest in 'the passage of time and the allied themes of death and mutability' 'sufficiently obvious'. And indeed a few minutes' work with a Shakespeare concordance (scores of entries under *Time*, dozens under *Day*, 18 under *Hour*, 7 under *Year*, etc.) shows that temporal conceptions and images figure prominently in the *Sonnets*.

[2] The 360th line of the sequence appropriately brings a reference to geniture: 'Till whatsoever star that guides my moving / Points on me graciously with fair aspect' (xxvi). It is *perhaps* coincidence that 'The Lover's Complaint' consists of 47 seven-line stanzas or $23\frac{1}{2}$ sonnets (the number of degrees of maximum declination of the sun; and that the line-total of the whole array is 14×152 (14-line sonnets) + 15 (xcix) + 12 (cxxvi) + 7×47 ('The Lover's Complaint') = 2484, Censorinus' estimate of the natural years in the *annus magnus platonicus*.

what thy memory cannot contain, / Commit to these waste blanks
...'[1] Editors usually give a biographical explanation of these lines,
perhaps speculating that Shakespeare wrote lxxvii as an occasional
sonnet to accompany the gift of a book with blank pages.[2] Some such
interpretation is no doubt right. But may we not also take 'blanks' in
a secondary sense as referring to blanks within the sequence itself?
May not the blanks, in short, be blank sonnets, numerological make-
weights like the blank chapters in *Tristram Shandy*?

This remains empty speculation, however, unless we can locate the
2 blank sonnets. But fortunately this is easy: in fact, the 1609 print
indicates them typographically (Pl. 4). Scholars have assumed that
the 2 sets of parentheses between cxxvi and cxxvii indicate the 2 lines
by which the former stanza falls short of the fourteen-line sonnet
norm; and perhaps incidentally they do serve this unusual purpose.
But, if so, they perpetrate a numerological and typographical pun.
For, as a little reflection will show, their primary function is much
more likely to be the important one of marking the 'waste blanks'
referred to in lxxvii and more recently in cxxv. On the second occasion the blanks are by implication identified as stanzas; since they are
put in the same category with the adjacent Stanza cxxvi. It is 'more
short than waste': in other words, metrically short and irregular (and
therefore an indicator of the pyramid pattern) rather than waste like
the blanks after it (indicators of the seasonal pattern). The question
may be asked, Why only 2 blank sonnets? Would it not have been
more economical of effort to combine the 153 and $3 \times 52 = 156$ totals
by having 3 blanks? Perhaps; but we should then have missed the
beautiful effect whereby the poet reduces himself formally as well
as verbally to nothing, in cxxxvi—'For nothing hold me'.[3]

We can now approach the fuller meaning of certain phrases that

[1] Accepting, as is usual, Theobald's and Malone's emendation of 1609 *blacks*.
[2] E.g. Dover Wilson 181: 'Perhaps he is presenting a table-book...a mirror and
a pocket-dial...to another and older friend than the rest of the sonnets were
addressed to.' Of course it is quite possible that the *Sonnets* originally accompanied the gift of, say, an hour-glass (such a gift was common: see e.g. Nichols,
Progresses of Queen Elizabeth i 117, or Panofsky, *Studies in Iconology* 82 n.);
and the 'blanks' could refer to blank pages, maybe in a presentation copy of the
Sonnets. My point is that from a literary-critical point of view this need not be
the whole explanation.
[3] Perhaps he would also have lost an ambiguity in *blanks*—2 blank sonnets, 2
'blanks' or pupils of eyes ('You live in this, and dwell in lovers' eyes', lv).

may refer to the structure. Sonnet lii, for example, mentions the 'long year'. A year might of course be described as long in a subjective sense; still, if this phrase had a structural reference, an exact meaning could be attached to it. For the 3 year-parts into which the 156-stanza sequence falls are not quite equal in length, though all contain 52 stanza-weeks. The first comprises 52 regular sonnets; but the second includes a fifteen-line stanza and the third a short twelve-line stanza, to say nothing of 2 blanks. Thus the year-parts are normal, long and short, just as the irregular stanzas are of normal length (cxlv), long (xcix) and short (cxxvi) in terms of line totals.

If the internally referring ambiguities are to be treated rigorously, Sonnet civ presents a difficulty:

> Three winters cold,
> Have from the forests shook three summers' pride,
> Three beauteous springs to yellow autumns turned,
> In process of the seasons have I seen,
> Three April perfumes in three hot Junes burned,
> Since first I saw you fresh which yet are green.
> Ah yet doth beauty like a dial hand,
> Steal from his figure, and no pace perceived...

The introduction of the beloved as 'the world's *fresh*[1] ornament' in the First Sonnet encourages us to take civ as structurally referrent. Yet it speaks of 3 years, whereas from a structural point of view only 2 years of 52 stanza-weeks have elapsed by civ. This problem of a numerological year concealed prior to civ can only be solved by considering the whole 1609 array, to which we now turn.

The array consists of 154 sonnet-stanzas, 2 blanks and 47 stanzas of 'The Lover's Complaint': 203 in all. Of this 203-stanza array, the centre is clearly Sonnet cii. Considering the sonnets alone, however, it is only approximately true to say that the centre lies between lxxvii and lxxviii, with the new half signalized, as in *Astrophil and Stella*, by new invocations of the Muse (lxxviii, lxxix). On analysing the symmetry more closely, we find that lxxvii contains the line centre not only of the pyramidal 153-sonnet sequence omitting cxxxvi, but also —allowing for the net shortfall of one line in xcix and cxxvi—of the 154-sonnet sequence. Now the 26-sonnet section defined by the two

---

[1] My italics. *Fresh* is not a common word in the *Sonnets*, and one of the few other occurrences is xvii 6: 'And in fresh numbers number all your graces'.

centre sonnets lxxvii and cii (and symmetrical in relation to the pairs of contiguous invocation sonnets)[1] has a notable property: its line total is 365. Since 14 is not a factor of 365, this annual measure for the centre section has to be contrived by adding an extra line ($26 \times 14 + 1 = 365$); hence the fifteen-line Stanza xcix. It appears that we have located the missing third structural year referred to in civ, where the lines 'Ah yet doth beauty like a dial hand, / Steal from his figure, and no pace perceived' can now be seen to refer back to a promise in lxxvii, the first sonnet of the 365-line centre section: 'Thou by thy dial's shady stealth mayst know, / Time's thievish progress to eternity.'

Flanking the centre section of 365 lines are two equal sections each of 24 sonnets. The more obvious is the section following, ciii–cxxvi, which begins and ends with the image of a glass ('Look in your glass …more, much more than in my verse can sit, / Your own glass shows you, when you look in it', ciii; 'Time's fickle glass', cxxvi) and which contains many suggestive references to hours ('Love alters not with his brief hours', cxvi; 'short numbered hours', cxxiv; 'Time's fickle glass, his sickle, hour', cxxvi). The 'glass' of lxxvii on one side of the ambiguity refers to a mirror; but this mirror turns, through the process of aging, into an hour-glass, bringing us to recollect that the mirror is an attribute of Time.[2] This clearly marked group terminates in the so-called 'coda' Sonnet, the irregular Stanza cxxvi. To match it, before the first centre sonnet, is an equivalent twenty-four-sonnet group, liii–lxxvi, which also contains many references to hours.[3] (It is noteworthy that, on the contrary, hours receive no mention anywhere in the centre section lxxvii–cii, where the dial hand steals unperceived.) The two hour-groups frame this central annual section, as indeed Sonnet v may perhaps be taken to hint:

[1] I.e. the 365-line year runs lxxvii (centre), lxxviii (invocation), lxxix (invocation), …, c (invocation), ci (invocation), cii (centre). Considered as a group, the sonnets mentioning Muses (xxi, xxxii, xxxviii, lxxviii, lxxix, lxxxii, lxxxv, c, ci, ciii) disclose many patterns. They number 10, thus forming yet another pyramid. And their total corresponds to the sum of the traditional 9 pagan Muses plus the tenth Christian Muse, the beloved: 'Be thou the tenth Muse, ten times more in worth / Than those old nine' (xxxviii; cf. also, however, *Anth. Graec.* v 95). The contiguous pair of Muse sonnets lxxviii and lxxix is perhaps noticed in a self-referring ambiguity in the latter sonnet: 'my sick Muse doth give another place.'

[2] Panofsky, *Studies in Iconology* 82 n.

[3] In lvii (*bis*), lviii, lxi, lxiii and lxviii.

Those hours that with gentle work did frame,
The lovely gaze where every eye doth dwell
Will play the tyrants to the very same. . .

The language here is very rich; besides meaning 'fabricate' and 'enclose with a circumscribing border such as that of a picture or mirror (glass)', *frame* has also a technical sense: 'the outwork of a clock or watch, consisting of the plates and pillars'.[1]

The initial section of 52 sonnet-weeks discussed above precedes the first twenty-four-sonnet section. After the second section of 24 sonnets follows the twenty-eight-sonnet section cxxvii–cliv that concludes the sequence. This represents yet another temporal measure, the month (both the twenty-eight-day lunar month and, counting the 2 blanks before cxxvii, the thirty-day solar month). Alternatively, the last 2 sections of the sequence may be regarded as forming a single run of 52 sonnets, so that the phrase 'brief hours and weeks' (cxvi), coming as it does in a sonnet that belongs both to an hour-group and a week-group, makes a double structural reference. We thus arrive at the ambiguous mannerist array shown in the table below.

		SONNETS				'THE LOVER'S COMPLAINT'
i–lii	liii–lxxvi	lxxvii–cii centre section	ciii–cxxvi	(2 blanks)	cxxvii–cliv	i–xlvii
52	24	26 (365 lines)	24		28	47
				52		

A division of 'The Lover's Complaint' after 24 stanzas—ending 'it is thy last' and containing references to 'the swiftest hours' (l. 60) and 'many a blasting hour' (l. 72)—would lead to more sustained symmetries, of the form

52	24	(365)	24	52	23
a	*b*	**C**	*b*	*a*	*d*

or

[1] *OED* iii 11 b, citing J. Harris, *Lexicon technicum* (1704). It is possibly relevant that pillars often were identified or confused with pyramids in Shakespeare's time, and that the part of the 153-sonnet pyramid after the first framing hour-section liii–lxxvii is a 78-sonnet pyramid.

52	24	(365)	24	28	24	23
a	*b*	***C***	*b*	*d*	*b*	*e*

But our innumerate modern imaginations are probably best content with a general impression of the broad lines of the design by which Shakespeare carries out his self-injunction: 'he that calls on thee, let him bring forth / Eternal numbers to outlive long date' (xxxviii).

Epilogue: Numerology and the literary artifact

It has not been my primary intention to apply numerological analysis in complete acts of criticism. Instead I have tried to determine the iconic function and stylistic varieties of some common types of external structural patterns. Beyond relating these to other constituent elements and indicating thematic relevance, there has been little attempt to rise above the level of simple interpretation to synthesis of artistic unity, let alone value judgement. I postponed questions of value, from a conviction that to dwell on them at this stage would be premature. Of course no part of reading or of criticism remains uninformed in some sense by values: critical amorality is impossible. However, as with any system of poetic organization, elementary competence in the conventions is a prerequisite of useful value judgements. Rhetoric presupposes grammar; and we would hardly value a critic's evaluations of Augustan couplets if he knew nothing of caesura.

All the same, the preceding pages have often implied that numerological analysis has a vital contribution to make to criticism. Yet those inimical to the approach have denied it any relevance to literature at all. I may be therefore forgiven a few tentative remarks about the function of numerology in the literary model and its bearing on evaluation.

To take the second point first, it should be clear that no necessary connection obtains between numerological organization and literary value. We have noticed some fine Elizabethan poems with highly patterned external structures; but even in that period there may be as many with trivial patterns or none at all. Conversely, poetry with complex, ingenious, even subtle numerology may have little poetic merit. Readers of Chapter 7 will recall Chapman's 'Amorous Zodiac': other extreme examples are Henry More's philosophical epics and Benlowes' *Theophila* (1652), whose formal symbolisms have warranted extensive analyses by Professor Røstvig and Dr Qvarnström. Thus it is reckless to claim, as John T. Shawcross does in *Hartford Studies in Literature* i (1969), in relation to Dryden's numerology, that 'this kind of witcraft offers a phenomenalistic criterion for aesthetic evaluation'. Numerology can no more offer a criterion for evaluation than prosody can, or rhetoric. Good poets have been known to neglect either of these elements successfully, just as novelists have dispensed with plot and dramatists with external action.

Like any other system of formal organization, numerology may have varying degrees of relevance to the point and value of a work. At one extreme, it may be a constructional aid private to the author, of interest subsequently to the genetic critic alone. Modern instances often lie at this extreme. Numerology devised at a time when number patterns were in vogue may expect more attention from the reader (like rhetorical schemes in the sixteenth century, or Augustan diction, or modern narrative devices). At such a time, all numerology is potentially relevant, and indeed in a general way actually so. That is, no critic can afford to ignore it, any more than he would ignore the blank verse of a Shakespearean play, even though the metrical constituent may not be immediately accessible to his intuition or eventually affect his assessment. At the other extreme, numerology— again like any other formal element—may be a significant factor in determining the whole effect of a work. Our appreciation of Homer's catalogue of ships, of Petrarch's *Trionfi*, of Spenser's *Amoretti and Epithalamion*, of Milton's *Paradise Lost*, in each case alters as it takes in the numerological structures I have hypothesized. Some of Cowley's frivolous bagatelles would be pointless frivolous bagatelles but for their plays on the triumphal pattern. And estimation of the stance and tone of Marvell's *Horatian Ode* is crucially affected by numerological analysis.

The relation of numerology to meaning, which is of theoretical interest, remains obscure. Some critics regard numerology as the key to all literary knowledge; others dismiss it as an extraneous cryptic curiosity. Consideration will show that neither extreme position is tenable.

With respect to the latter, the partial analogy with small-scale metrical organization is instructive. Prosodically considered, verse presents a surface structure, determining scansion, and a deep structure, in which the functional interplay of rhythm, metre, grammatical accent and juncture has expressive value. The deep prosodic structure may provide an immediate accompaniment to the chain of discourse (as in Pope's famous mimesis of woodcutting); or it may operate in a more implicit way, independently of semantics, according to a separate communicative system. This is the system whereby, at the crudest level, triple metre generally suits a light mood and, at the finest, the alternation of long and short lines in *Lycidas* produces one of the most elusive effects in our literature. Even though the substratum of metrical organization is largely synchronous with the phonemic substratum of syntax, significant prosodic features may not be perceptible without interrupting the reading process for study. So with numerology. Here the surface structure consists of external divisions such as stanzas. The organic patterning of the external divisions and of distribution of matter between them is nowadays unconscious—or else conducted according to private rules. Only formerly was it governed in part by shared conventions, and even then these need not always have been consciously formulated. Here we must be careful to avoid confusion between the numerological structure and the imaginative structure, of which the former is arguably part. Thus, a metrically central image is not necessarily central in the figurative sense of being thematically important—though it will very likely have more interest than previous criticism has allowed. Sometimes numerology accompanies the chain of discourse (as, for example, in self-referring passages), but often it is purely iconic and to that extent independent of the semantic sequence. Hence the feeling of Professor Bush and others that numerological interpretations are imposed 'from outside' and extraneous to the literary work as such. This thinking is circular: numerological patterns are necessarily extraneous to a literary model defined to exclude them. Of course it is true that the numerological structure only becomes apparent when we interrupt the normal modern process of reading to make a relatively close inspection. But the same is true of many other non-semantic elements, both formal and substantive. What reader is aware of the metrical patterns, sound patterns, rhetorical schemes, thematic parallels, allusions and mythic analogues of *Paradise Lost* while he is actually reading? Nor is it wholly clear that a normal reading might not formerly have taken in many numerical features that escape our own attention. Earlier readers would naturally look for what they had been trained to find significant, just as we ignore what experimental science has taught us to find non-significant.

The contrary error, attaching excessive importance to numerology, is attributable to a variety of motives, the most intellectually respectable of which relates to its special status as a significant but extra-semantic constituent. It appears to hold out the seductive hope of an independent check on the interpretation of difficult works—number symbolisms often being exactly determinate. Numerological criticism even seems to avoid the pitfalls of the intentionalist fallacy, in that numerical patterns, though undeniably successful, in the sense of being actually achieved, must also have been intended, since they can scarcely occur without deliberate effort. However, this prospect of simplifying the critical process often proves in the event to be a mirage. The number symbolisms may turn out to be very abstract, or the numbers may have several possible symbolisms, so that a content arrived at through the ordinary semantic process must be invoked to clarify them. Alternatively, it may prove hard to show that the pattern is not a random one, without recourse to the argument that it reflects the content. Instances of numerology making a clear and rich statement independently of the semantic element are rare.

Nevertheless, numerological analysis will usually help the interpretative critic to clarify the articulation of parts and to decide where to lay emphases. External structure generally reflects content, so that structural emphases are moral emphases. Moreover, consideration of the numerology may sharpen issues about the relation between form and value. This relation, about which we know very little, is especially problematic in the case of structures that are formal yet meaningful, meaningful yet intrinsic at the reader's option. Evaluating the patterns themselves presents further problems. Is numerology more integral and 'better', for example, when it directly reinforces the narrative or internal imaginative structures? Given that the external centre has iconic significance, should we prefer structures in which these formal mid points coincide with subjective *foci*, with 'central' passages in the ordinary figurative sense of the term? This was my own initial assumption. But then, what about the elaborate avoidance of this coincidence in many mannerist works? One can hardly reject a whole structural style out of hand. The independence of external structures points to the value of numerology during periods when form was almost cultivated in its own right, as a pattern of creation.

Questions about the value of numerology mainly arise in estimating how well a work is made. That is to say, numerology belongs primarily to literature considered as artifact. Like many other features of the literary artifact, it may remain unnoticed until concern with quality leads us to examine the workmanship. This examination may sometimes be optional; as it certainly is when the numerology was devised for the discipline and stimulation of the poet's own invention. But if a critic never made such optional examinations, his appreciation of style would remain very limited. In this case the limitation is partly historical: the view of numerology as extraneous is the result of conditioning by centuries of prose, which has taught readers to move relatively quickly along the semantic line. But centuries of verse conditioned renaissance readers to think of the literary model more as an artifact, in which meditation might frequently dwell, finding ever new aspects of a world image generated, like the universe itself, by mathematical patterns. If we are to appreciate works constructed according to such a poetic, it can only be by temporarily entering into the older attitude. This should present no theoretical difficulty to those who still accept the artifact model, or who agree with Northrop Frye that 'the primary literary aim' is 'producing a structure of words for its own sake'. However, numerology can also be accommodated in the model of literature as communication. In the naive application of communication theory, every sort of formal organization in literature is regarded as a 'redundancy', that is, a means of confirming the primary semantic signal. Numerology, as we have seen, may either fall into this category or constitute a secondary signal. The more correct application, however, treats the literary communication not as a work's semantic statement or theme but as its point or unity. From this position numerology, prosody, syntax, semantic elements, even themes, are all seen to be redundancies: any particular element, therefore, is to some degree at least notionally dispensable, in the case of an ideal reader. To the ideal critic, however, each is intrinsic to any well-unified work, essential to a rich response.

The hope for the future of numerological criticism is that it will become less controversial and defensive, taking its place among other approaches, particularly those that deal with neighbouring constituents (prosody, internal structural analysis). To do so, however, it must overcome three fundamental weaknesses.

First, ignorance about number symbolism. For familiarity with systems of philosophical number symbolism, with associational symbols and with their social and historical distribution is a *sine qua non* of effective numerological analysis. Professor Røstvig has done valuable work in this direction. But certain others seem content to attach to numbers whatever meanings they think convenient, without troubling about historical possibility. Early objectives, therefore, should include rigorous historical studies of the sources of number symbolism, to be followed, ideally, by a dictionary on historical principles. Such a dictionary might help us to decide whether a symbolism was common knowledge, or learned, or esoteric, or occult. It would certainly show both sceptics and lazy numerologists that numbers cannot mean anything one likes.

The second weakness of numerology has been a failure to devise sufficient safeguards against fanciful and affectively fallacious interpretations. Professor Bush's talk of 'learnedly uncritical freewheeling' is a not unfair criticism of many attempts at numerological analysis, including some of my own. Because the approach is new, enthusiasts understandably tend to neglect method and accumulate discoveries indiscriminately. They fail to relate numerology closely enough to other constituents; to consider with sufficient tact when a numerological approach is suitable; to meet the challenge of other critical approaches; and to set adequately stringent standards of objectivity for their own. The lack of constructive correction is a particularly damaging deficiency. Only through the dialectic of different opinions can we refine a numerological interpretation to the point at which affective fallacies are evaporated off and value inferences precipitated.

At present the problem of how to avoid inventing unintended patterns is perhaps the most troublesome of all. I have opened the discussion of this problem in *Spenser and the Numbers of Time*; but far deeper thinking about it is needed. Obviously the restrictions of ordinary scholarly method apply. These are not always adequate, however, with this unfamiliar material. Thus, establishing a number symbolism's availability will rule out some nonsense; but it will not exclude learned affective fallacies. And calculating the probability of random occurrence is another elementary precaution with its loopholes, as the case of small symbolic numbers illustrates. True, probability theory can show certain patterns to be almost inevitable. However, a pattern need not be improbable to have been intended; whereas even complex structural 'patterns' would still occur—very seldom, yet just as probably as any other permutation—if literature were produced by some random mechanical process. When patterns involve several numbers, a useful check on inventiveness is to avoid indiscriminate mingling of different categories of number symbolism. And it goes without saying that no manipulation of a number into parts should be attempted without adequate authority. (Though it must be said that authors did not always check their own inventiveness in these respects.) Finally, the critic ought to consider alternative structural interpretations honestly and give reasons, at least to himself, for discarding them. If doubt still remains it should not be suppressed except by suppressing the whole interpretation.

And yet, after all these precautions, some analyses remain plausible to the numerological critic but not to many of his readers. Further work may show us how to formulate criteria that exclude such interpretations. But we should also be prepared for the possibility that the risk of affective fallacies is inalienably bound up with the subjectivity of criticism.

For it should be emphasized that these problems are far from being peculiar to numerology. Many other constituents in theory present, to varying degrees, much the same difficulties—and would present them in practice, too, if familiarity had not made us oblivious, or if they involved ideas so obviously outmoded as number symbolisms. Thus, how do we know that any literary constituent is ever significant? How can we ever be sure that a theme is not of our own making? Or a subtlety of rhythm? In short, though numerological criticism gives no quick relief from problems of the relations between structure, meaning and value, making them if anything more acute, it has the salutary effect of exposing weaknesses in the general constitution of criticism. Accommodating numerology should eventually improve the literary model and tighten the standards by which we judge critical method.

The third weakness in the present state of numerological criticism is less serious, and can even be regarded positively as an opportunity. I refer to the narrow limits of our knowledge of the extent and variety of numerology. So far we have concentrated almost exclusively on symmetries and on Pythagorean or theological number symbolisms. But the range of structural types that could be considered is immense: it includes such diverse possibilities as circular forms (coronas, zodiacs and the like); architectural models; musical models; games; knots; acrostics; chronograms; and figure poems. Of course no special virtue attaches to gross coverage of types: for reasons already stated it is better to work and rework in depth on a few patterns in a few works. Nevertheless, our knowledge of the scope of numerological applications should be extended far beyond the present bounds. The prospects in this field are rich and exciting: it can hardly fail, for example, to yield valuable insights into Elizabethan literary structure.

In the longer term, we may expect numerological study to make several contributions to historical literary criticism. It should provide a great stimulus to macro-prosody (a subject long due for resuscitation): it should help to break many deadlocks in interpretation: and it should generally enhance appreciation of literature written in periods when much effort went into constructing formal patterns. Particularly with mannerist poetry, the continued practice of numerological analysis will not only bring individual works into sharper interpretative focus, but also cultivate some of the sense of structural style enjoyed by the poets themselves and their first readers.

Appendix 1

A SPECIAL AND PARTICULAR RESEMBLANCE OF
HER MAJESTY TO THE ROUNDEL

First her authority regal
Is the circle compassing all:
The dominion great and large
Which God hath given to her charge:
Within which most spatious bound
She environs her people round,
Retaining them by oath and liegance
Within the pale of true obeisance:
Holding imparked as it were,
Her people like to herds of deer.
Sitting among them in the mids
Where she allows and bans and bids
In what fashion she list and when,
The services of all her men.
Out of her breast as from an eye,
Issue the rays incessantly
Of her justice, bounty and might
Spreading abroad their beams so bright,
And reflect not, till they attain
The farthest part of her domain.
And makes each subject clearly see,
What he is bounden for to be
To God his prince and common wealth,
His neighbour, kindred and to himself.

The same centre and middle prick,
Whereto our deeds are dressed so thick,
From all the parts and outmost side
Of her monarchy large and wide,
Also fro whence reflect these rays,
Twenty hundred manner of ways
Where her will is them to convey
Within the circle of her survey.
So is the queen of Britain ground,
Beam, circle, centre of all my round.

George Puttenham, *The Art of English Poesy* (1589) sigs. N 3v–4v

Appendix 2

THE AMOROUS ZODIAC

i

I never see the sun, but suddenly
My soul is moved, with spite and jealousy
Of his high bliss in his sweet course discerned:
And am displeased to see so many signs
As the bright sky unworthily divines,
Enjoy an honour they have never earned.

[Introduction:
solar month begun:
lunar month begun

ii

To think heaven decks with such a beauteous show
A Harp, a Ship, a Serpent, and a Crow,
And such a crew of creatures of no prices,
But to excite in us th'unshamefast flames,
With which (long since) Jove wronged so many dames,
Reviving in his rule, their names and vices.

iii

Dear Mistress, whom the gods bred here below
T'express their wondrous power and let us know
That before thee they nought did perfect make,
Why may not I (as in those signs the sun)
Shine in thy beauties, and as roundly run,
To frame (like him) an endless zodiac.

208

iv

With thee I'll furnish both the year and sky,
Running in thee my course of destiny:
And thou shalt be the rest of all my moving,
But of thy numberless and perfect graces
(To give my moons their full in twelve months' spaces)
I choose but twelve in guerdon of my loving.

v

Keeping even way through every excellence,   [*Day begun*
I'll make in all, an equal residence
Of a new zodiac: a new Phoebus guising,
When (without altering the course of nature)
I'll make the seasons good, and every creature
Shall henceforth reckon day, from my first rising.

vi

To open then the spring-time's golden gate,   [*March, Aries:*
And flower my race with ardour temperate,   *spring begun*
I'll enter by thy head, and have for house
In my first month, this heaven-Ram-curled tress:
Of which, Love all his charm-chains doth address:
A sign fit for a spring so beauteous.

vii

Lodged in that fleece of hair, yellow, and curled,   [*Day begun*
I'll take high pleasure to enlight the world,
And fetter me in gold, thy crisps'[1] implies,[2]
Earth (as this spring spungy and langoursome
With envy of our joys in love become)
Shall swarm with flowers, and air with painted flies.

viii

Thy smooth embowed brow, where all grace I see,   [*April, Taurus*
My second month, and second house shall be:
Which brow, with her clear beauties shall delight
The earth (yet sad) and overture confer
To herbs, buds, flowers, and verdure gracing Ver,
Rend'ring her more than summer exquisite.   [*Spring completed*

[1] Close curls'; see *OED* s.v. *Crisp* sb. 4.
[2] Entwinings, tangles; latinizing coinage, not in *OED*; cf. *implexus*.

x

All this fresh April, this sweet month of Venus,
I will admire this brow so bounteous:
This brow, brave court for love, and virtue builded,
This brow where chastity holds garrison,
This brow that (blushless) none can look upon,
This brow with every grace and honour gilded.

x

Resigning that, to perfect this my year   [*May, Gemini*
I'll come to see thine eyes: that now I fear:
Thine eyes, that sparkling like two Twin-born fires,
(Whose looks benign, and shining sweets do grace
May's youthful month with a more pleasing face)
Justly the Twins' sign, hold in my desires.

xi

Scorched with the beams these sister-flames eject,   [*Summer begun*
The living sparks thereof earth shall effect
The shock of our joined-fires the summer starting:
The season by degrees shall change again
The days, their longest durance shall retain,
The stars their amplest light, and ardour darting.

xii

But now I fear, that throned in such a sign,
Playing with objects, pleasant and divine,
I should be moved to dwell there thirty days:
O no, I could not in so little space,
With joy admire enough their plenteous grace,
But ever live in sun-shine of their rays.

xiii

Yet this should be in vain, my forced will   [*June, Argo navis*
My course designed (begun) shall follow still;   (*Cancer*)
So forth I must, when forth this month is wore,
And of the neighbour signs be born anew,
Which sign perhaps may stay me with the view
More to conceive, and so desire the more.

xiv

It is thy nose (stern to thy bark of love)
Or which pine-like doth crown a flowery grove,
Which Nature strived to fashion with her best,

That she might never turn to show more skill:
And that the envious fool, (used to speak ill)
Might feel pretended fault choked in his breast.

xv

The violent season in a sign so bright,   [*July, Leo*
Still more and more, become more proud of light,
Should still incense me in the following sign:
A sign, whose sight desires a gracious kiss,
And the red confines of thy tongue it is,
Where, hotter than before, mine eyes would shine.

xvi

So glow those corals, nought but fire respiring
With smiles, or words, or sighs her thoughts attiring
Or, be it she a kiss divinely frameth;
Or that her tongue, shoots forward, and retires,
Doubling like fervent Sirius, summer's fires
In Leo's month, which all the world enflameth.   [*Summer completed*

xvii

And now to bid the boreal signs adieu   [*August, Virgo*
I come to give thy virgin-cheeks the view
To temper all my fire, and tame my heat,
Which soon will feel it self extinct and dead,
In those fair courts with modesty dispread
With holy, humble, and chaste thoughts replete.

xviii

The purple tinct, thy marble cheeks retain,
The marble tinct, thy purple cheeks doth stain
The lilies duly equalled with thine eyes,
The tinct that dyes the morn with deeper red,
Shall hold my course a month, if (as I dread)
My fires to issue want not faculties.

xix

To balance now thy more obscured graces   [*September, Libra*
'Gainst them the circle of thy head enchases
(Twice three months used, to run through twice three houses)
To render in this heaven my labour lasting,
I haste to see the rest, and with one hasting,
The dripping time shall fill the earth carouses.[1]

[1] Bumpers drunk as toasts; see *OED* s.v. *Carouse* sb. 1, 2.

xx

Then by the neck, my autumn I'll commence,   [*Autumn begun*
Thy neck, that merits place of excellence
Such as this is, where with a certain sphere
In balancing the darkness with the light,
It so might weigh, with scales of equal weight
Thy beauties seen with those do not appear.

xxi

Now past my month t'admire for built most pure   [*October, Scorpio*
This marble pillar and her lineature,
I come t'inhabit thy most gracious teats,
Teats that feed love upon the white Riphees,[1]
Teats where he hangs his glory and his trophies
When victor from the gods' war he retreats.

xxii

Hid in the vale twixt these two hills confined
This vale the nest of loves, and joys divined
Shall I enjoy mine ease; and fair be passed
Beneath these parching Alps; and this sweet cold
Is first, this month, heaven doth to us unfold,
But there shall I still grieve to be displaced.   [*Autumn completed*

xxiii

To sort[2] from this most brave and pompous sign   [*November, Corona*
(Leaving a little my ecliptic line   *australis*
Less superstitious than the other sun)   *(Sagittarius)*
The rest of my autumnal race I'll end[3]
To see thy hand, (whence I the crown attend,)
Since in thy past parts I have slightly run.

xxiv

Thy hand, a lily gend'red of a rose
That wakes the morning, hid in night's repose:
And from Apollo's bed the veil doth twine,
That each where doth, th'Idalian minion guide;
That bends his bow; that ties, and leaves untied
The silver ribands of his little ensign.

[1] The Riphaei: cold northern mountains.
[2] Sally out, make a sortie (*OED* v²); perhaps with the overtone 'apportion,
   assign' (*OED* v.¹ I I), referring to the stanzaic pattern.
[3] Punning between 'cause to cease' (*OED* I 4), referring to the seasonal pattern,
   and 'complete' (*OED* I I), referring to the pattern of months.

xxv

In fine, (still drawing to th'Antarctic Pole)   [*December, Capricorn*
The tropic sign, I'll run at for my goal,
Which I can scarce express with chastity,
I know in heaven 'tis called Capricorn
And with the sudden thought, my case¹ takes horn,
So (heaven-like), Capricorn the name shall be.

xxvi

This (wondrous fit) the wintry solstice seizeth,   [*Winter begun*
Where darkness greater grows and day decreaseth,
Where rather I would be in night than day,
But when I see my journeys² do increase
I'll straight dispatch me thence, and go in peace
To my next house, where I may safer stay.

xxvii

This house alongst thy naked thighs is found   [*January, Aquarius*
Naked of spot; made fleshy, firm, and round
To entertain Love's friends with feeling sport;
These, Cupid's secret mysteries enfold,
And pillars are that Venus' fane uphold,
Of her dear joys the glory, and support.

xxviii

Sliding on thy smooth thighs to this month's end;   *February, Pisces*
To thy well fashioned calves I will descend
That soon the last house I may apprehend,
Thy slender feet, fine slender feet that shame   [*Day completed:*
Thetis' sheen³ feet, which poets so much fame,   [*lunar month completed:*
And here my latest season I will end.   *winter completed*

L'ENVOI

xxix

Dear mistress, if poor wishes heaven would hear,
I would not choose the empire of the water;
The empire of the air, nor of the earth
But endlessly my course of life confining
In this fair zodiac for ever shining,
And with thy beauties make me endless mirth.

¹ Body.
² Days (*OED* I 1); daily courses through the heavens (*OED* II 2 d); days' labours
  (*OED* III 5).   ³ Beautiful, bright.

xxx

But gracious love, if jealous heaven deny
My life this truly-blessed variety,
Yet will I thee through all the world disperse,
If not in heaven, amongst those braving fires
Yet here thy beauties (which the world admires) *[Solar month completed:*
Bright as those flames shall glister in my verse. *day completed*

Bibliography
Check list of editions cited on more than one occasion

ADAM. *See under* PLATO.

APPELBAUM. *See under* MAXIMILIAN I.

BENJAMIN, ADRIAN. 'A Note on the Structure of *Astrophil and Stella*'. Forthcoming in *The Review of English Studies*.

BOAS. *See under* FLETCHER.

BONGO, PIETRO [PETRUS BUNGUS]. *Numerorum mysteria*. Bergamo 1591.

BROOKS, DOUGLAS *and* FOWLER, ALASTAIR. 'The Structure of Dryden's *Song for St Cecilia's Day, 1687*.' *Essays in Criticism* XVII (1967) 434–47.

BROWNE, SIR THOMAS. *The Works of Sir Thomas Browne*. Ed. Geoffrey Keynes. 4 vols. 1928.

BURCKHARDT, JACOB. *The Civilization of the Renaissance in Italy*. Vienna and London n.d.

CAREW, THOMAS. *The Poems of Thomas Carew and his Masque 'Coelum Britannicum'*. Ed. Rhodes Dunlap. Rev. edn, Oxford 1957.

CAREY *and* FOWLER. *See under* MILTON.

CARTARI, VICENZO. *Imagini delli dei de gl' antichi*. Venice 1647. Facs. ed. W. Koschatsky. Graz 1963.

CASE, ROBERT, H. (ed.). *English Epithalamies*. Chicago and London 1896.

CHAPMAN, GEORGE. *The Poems of George Chapman*. Ed. Phyllis B. Bartlett. 1941.

CHARTROU, JOSÈPHE. *Les entrées solennelles et triomphales à la rennaissance 1484–1551*. Paris 1928.

CHEYNEY, C. R. *Handbook of Dates for Students of English History*. 1961.

COLONNA, FRANCESCO. *Hypnerotomachia Poliphili*. Ed. Giovanni Pozzi and Lucia A. Ciapponi. 2 vols. Padua 1964.

COWLEY, ABRAHAM. *Poems*. Ed. A. R. Waller. *Cambridge* 1905.

CURTIUS, ERNST ROBERT. *European Literature and the Latin Middle Ages*. Tr. Willard R. Trask. 1953.

DEKKER, THOMAS. *The Dramatic Works of Thomas Dekker*. Ed. Fredson Bowers. 4 vols. Cambridge 1953–61.

DONNE, JOHN. *Donne's Poetical Works*. Ed. H. J. C. Grierson. 2 vols. Oxford 1912.

DRAYTON, MICHAEL. *The Works of Michael Drayton*. Ed. J. W. Hebel. 5 vols. Oxford 1961.

DRYDEN, JOHN. *The Poems of John Dryden*. Ed. James Kinsley. 4 vols. Oxford 1958.

DU BARTAS [GUILLAUME DE SAL LUSTE SIEUR DU BARTAS]. *Divine Weeks*. Tr. Joshua Sylvester. 1613.

DUNLAP. *See under* CAREW.

FELLOWES, E. H. (ed.). *English Madrigal Verse 1588–1632*. Revised and enlarged F. W. Sternfeld and D. Greer. Third edn, Oxford 1967.

FIERZ-DAVID, LINDA. *The Dream of Poliphilo: Related and Interpreted by Linda Fierz-David*. Tr. Mary Hottinger. Bollingen Series XXV. New York 1950.

FLETCHER, GILES *and* FLETCHER, PHINEAS. *Poetical Works*. Ed. F. S. Boas. 2 vols. Cambridge 1909.

FOWLER, ALASTAIR. *Spenser and the Numbers of Time*. 1964.
See also under BROOKS; LEWIS; MILTON; RØSTVIG; WILLS.

GIORGIO, FRANCESCO. *De harmonia mundi*. Paris 1545.

GORDON, D. J. '*Hymenaei:* Ben Jonson's Masque of Union'. *Journal of the Warburg Institute* VIII (1945) 107–45.

GRIERSON. *See under* DONNE.

HEBEL. *See under* DRAYTON.

HERFORD, SIMPSON *and* SIMPSON. *See under* JONSON.

HERRICK, ROBERT. *The Poetical Works of Robert Herrick*. Ed. L. C. Martin. Rev. edn, Oxford 1963.

HIEATT, A. KENT. *Short Time's Endless Monument: The Symbolism of the Numbers in Edmund Spenser's 'Epithalamion'*. New York 1960.

HOPPER, VINCENT FOSTER. *Medieval Number Symbolism*. New York 1938.

HOTSON, LESLIE. *Mr W. H*. 1964.

JONES. *See under* SURREY.

JONSON, BEN. *Ben Jonson*. Ed. C. H. Herford, Percy Simpson and Evelyn Simpson. 11 vols. Oxford 1925–52.

KANTOROWICZ, ERNST. *The King's Two Bodies*. Princeton, N.J. 1957.
'Oriens Augusti—Lever du Roi'. *Dumbarton Oaks Papers* XVII (1963) 119–77.
'Dante's "Two Suns"', in *Selected Studies*. New York 1965.

KERNODLE, GEORGER. *From Art to Theatre: Form and Convention in the Renaissance*. Chicago 1944.

KINSLEY. *See under* DRYDEN.

KIRKCONNELL, WATSON. *The Celestial Cycle*. Toronto 1952.

KRISTELLER, PAUL. *Andrea Mantegna*. 2 vols. 1901.

LEWIS, C. S. *Spenser's Images of Life*. Ed. Alastair Fowler. Cambridge 1967.

L'ORANGE, H. P. *Studies on the Iconography of Cosmic Kingship:* Instituttet for sammenlignende kulturforskning, Serie A: Forelesninger xxiii. Oslo 1953.

MARGOLIOUTH. *See under* MARVELL.

MARTIN. *See under* HERRICK.

MARVELL, ANDREW. *The Poems and Letters of Andrew Marvell.* Ed. H. M. Margoliouth. 2 vols. Oxford 1927.

MAXIMILIAN I. *The Triumph of Maximilian I.* Tr. and ed. Stanley Appelbaum. New York 1964.

MAZZEO, JOSEPH ANTHONY. 'Cromwell as Machiavellian Prince in Marvell's "An Horatian Ode"'. *Journal of the History of Ideas* XXI (1960) 1–17.

MILTON, JOHN. *The Poems of John Milton.* Ed. John Carey and Alastair Fowler. 1968.

NICHOLS, JOHN. *The Progresses and Public Processions of Queen Elizabeth.* 3 vols. 1823.

OGILBY, JOHN. *The Entertainment of. . .Charles II in his passage through the City of London to his Coronation.* 1662.

OTIS, BROOKS. *Virgil: A Study in Civilized Poetry.* Oxford 1963.

PALME, PER. '*Ut Architectura Poesis*' in *Idea and Form.* Ed. N. G. Sandblad. Acta Universitatis Upsaliensis, Figura Nova Series I. Uppsala 1959.

PANOFSKY, ERWIN. *Studies in Iconology.* New York and Evanston, Ill. 1962.

PEVSNER, NIKOLAUS. 'The Architecture of Mannerism' in *The Mint: A Miscellany of Literature, Art and Criticism.* Ed. Geoffrey Grigson. 1946.

PICO DELLA MIRANDOLA, GIOVANNI. *Opera omnia.* 2 vols. Basel 1573.

PLATO. *The Republic of Plato.* Ed. James Adam. 2 vols. Cambridge 1929.

POOLE, R. L. 'The Beginning of the Year in the Middle Ages' in *Proceedings of the British Academy* X. 1921.

POPE, ALEXANDER. *The Poems of Alexander Pope.* Gen. ed. John Butt. 11 vols. 1939–69.

PUTTENHAM, GEORGE. *The Art of English Poesy.* Ed. Gladys D. Willcock and Alice Walker. Cambridge 1936.

QVARNSTRÖM, GUNNAR. *Poetry and Numbers.* Scripta Minora Regiae Societatis Humaniorum Litterarum Lundensis, 1964–5, II. Lund 1966.
The Enchanted Palace. Stockholm 1967.

RICCIOLI, GIOVANNI-BATTISTA, S. J. *Almagesti novi. . .tomus primus.* 2 parts. Bologna 1651.

RINGLER. *See under* SIDNEY.

ROCHE, THOMAS P., JR. *The Kindly Flame: A Study of the Third and Fourth Books of Spenser's 'Faerie Queen'.* Princeton, N.J. 1964.

RØSTVIG, MAREN-SOFIE. 'The Hidden Sense' in *The Hidden Sense,* Norwegian Studies in English IX. 1963.
'Structure as Prophecy: The Influence of Biblical Exegesis upon Theories of Literary Structure' in *Silent Poetry: Essays in Numerological Analysis.* Ed. Alastair Fowler. 1970.

SCALIGER, JULIUS CAESAR. *Poetices libri septem.* Lyons 1561. Facs. ed. August Buck. Stuttgart 1964.

SEGAR, SIR WILLIAM. *Honour, Military and Civil.* 1602.

SHEARMAN, JOHN. *Mannerism.* 1967.

SIDNEY, SIR PHILIP. *The Poems of Sir Philip Sidney.* Ed. W. A. Ringler. Oxford 1962.

SINGLETON, CHARLES S. 'The Poet's Number at the Centre'. *Modern Language Notes* LXXX (1965) 1–10.

Spectator, The. Ed. D. F. Bond. 5 vols. Oxford 1965.

SPENSER, EDMUND. *The Works of Edmund Spenser: A Variorum Edition.* Ed. Edwin Greenlaw *et al.* 10 vols. Baltimore, Md 1932–57.

SURREY, HENRY HOWARD, EARL OF. *Poems.* Ed. Emrys Jones. Oxford 1964.

TUVE, ROSEMOND. *Allegorical Imagery.* Ed. Thomas P. Roche, Jr. Princeton, N.J. 1966.

VALERIANO, PIERIO. *Hieroglyphica...commentariorum libri lviii...Accesserunt loco auctarii, hieroglyphicorum collectanea, ex veteribus et recentioribus auctoribus descripta, et in sex libros digesta.* Frankfort 1613.

VENTURI, A. 'Les triomphes de Pétrarque dans l'art représentatif'. *Revue de l'art ancien et moderne* XX (1906).

WALLER. *See under* COWLEY.

WALLERSTEIN, RUTH. *Studies in Seventeenth-Century Poetic.* Madison and Milwaukee, Wis. 1965.

WEINBERG, BERNARD. *A History of Literary Criticism in the Italian Renaissance.* 2 vols. Chicago and Toronto 1961.

WEISBACH, WERNER. *Trionfi.* Berlin 1919.

WHITMAN, CEDRIC H. *Homer and the Heroic Tradition.* Cambridge, Mass. 1958.

WILLCOCK *and* WALKER. *See under* PUTTENHAM.

WILLS, RICHARD. *De re poetica.* Tr. and ed. Alastair Fowler. Luttrell Society Reprints XVII. Oxford 1958.

WILSON, J. DOVER (ed.). *The Sonnets.* Cambridge New Shakespeare. Cambridge 1966.

WIMSATT, W. K. *and* BROOKS, CLEANTH. *Literary Criticism: A Short History.* 1965.

WITHINGTON, ROBERT. *English Pageantry.* 2 vols. Cambridge, Mass. and London 1918–20.

WITTKOWER, RUDOLF. *Architectural Principles in the Age of Humanism.* Third edn rev. 1962.

YATES, FRANCES A. *The French Academies of the Sixteenth Century.* Warburg Studies XV (1947).

Index

Aaron 66
Abarbanel, Giuda (Leone Ebreo) 72n
Accorgimento 39n
Achilles 92
Addison 86; on epic action 129;
    on Milton's chronology 131
Adonis 46 53 103
Aemilius Paullus 27 28
Aeolus 95
Agamemnon 92
Age expressed numerologically 102
Ages, of history 135n; of man 135n,
    188n
Alberti, Leon Battista xi 32
Alchemic symbolism, in Colonna 44
    46; in Cowley 77; in Donne
    73f; in Dryden 85
Alexander, Peter 183
Alma 111 159n
Alphabetic numerology 7f 13
Altar 104f 173
Ambiguity 1 2 143n 146; in sym-
    metry of *Astrophil and Stella*
    176–80; of Donne's 'Ecstasy'
    107f; of Palazzo Branconio 109;
    of *Faerie Queen* 110–12; in
    triumphs 75–82 103. *See also*
    Self-referring passages
Ambrose, St 136
Ammonius 184 n
Amoret 47–58 *passim* 111
Amphion 83

Anacreontics 181f
anacyclesis 83
Anger 51n 52
Anna 120f
Aphrodite 149. *See also* Venus
Apocalypse 36
Apollo 24 48 119. *See also Sol*; Sun
Appian of Alexandria 28 31
Aquarius 141n 142 213
Arcade of honour 30 Pl. 6
Architecture 9f 133; analogies with
    118 (baroque) 18 (column) 180
    (garden) 108–11 (Palazzo
    Branconio) 122 (rococo); false
    analogies with 91; Perrault on
    122; symbolism drawn from 83f;
    triumphal arch in 32; *ut architec-*
    tura poesis xi 17 122 188. *See*
    also Baroque; Mannerism;
    Palace; Pevsner; Shearman
Argo navis 145 208 210 Pl. 1
Aries 141n 147 209
Ariosto, Lodovico 111
Aristotle 33 87 126
Arithmology 20. *See also* Numerology
Arrow 45f
Artegall 57n 58 111f
Artemis 149
Art history, extension of terms from
    89–91. *See* Baroque; Mannerism;
    Rococo
Arthur, King 29

Hawes, Stephen 38
Henry VI 29
Henry, Prince 3f
Hera Teleia 149
Herbert, George 145n
Herbert, Mary, Countess of Pembroke 175
Hercules 45
Hermes Trismegistus 116 119 158n
Herodotus 13
Herrick, Robert: 'Another New-Year's Gift' 146; *Epithalamy to Sir T. Southwell* 151; Harleian MS Epithalamium 153; 'New-Year's Gift' 146
Hersilia 40
Hexaemeric poetry 136–9
Heywood, Thomas 68 154 189n
Hieatt, A. Kent 13 15 106n 162–73 *passim*
Hippo 40
Hippolytus 40f
Homer, alphabetic numerology 13; *Iliad* 91–3 199; chronological structure 129; duration of action 128f; Pope's translation 39n 129; *Odyssey* 175
Honeywood, Michael 188n
Honour 39
Hope 51n 52
Hopkins, G. M. 22
Hopper, Vincent Foster 130
Horace 71n; centralized symmetry 63f; crowns himself 63f; *exegi monumentum* 188; inexact symmetry 95 122; *Odes* 188; *Satires* 63f 71n
Horae 60n 170f
Hotson, Leslie 187n 190f
Hours 6; Books of 134; equal and unequal, distinguished 60n 135n 165n; *Horae* 60n 170f; iconography 135; nocturnal 157; numerological representation 13–15 80 134 136 (Augustine, Virgil) 140 (Dryden) 143 (Chapman) 139 (Cowley) 137 (Traherne) 156–61 *passim* (epithalamia) 161–73 *passim* (*Epithalamion*) 195–7 (Shakespeare); **12** 59–61; **24** 13–15; **60** 80; unity of time defined in terms of 126f

Hour-glass 193n 195
Howard, Henry, *see* Surrey
Howard, Lady Frances 150
Hudibras 130n
Hyginus 145
Hyman, L. W. 79n
Hymen 149 156n; associated with **8** 152f; circle 7n; dignified numerologically in epithalamia 67f 104f 171f; invoked 68 104 157 163 171f
Hypnerotomachia 31 44–7 51 53 57

Iamblichus 171n
Imeria 45
Imitation, of nature 15–17; of previous numerology, by Boccaccio 63f; by Cowley 13–15; by Dryden 85 113; by Du Bartas 138; by Milton 132; by Pico 137
Imola, Rambaldi da 35
Incontinence 45
Infirmity 52 54
Ingegneri, Angelo 127
Ingpen, William 20
Intentionalism 22 201
Isis 51

James I 18n 153
Janus 134 147
Jealousy 51n
Jerome, St 7 34
Jerusalem 25 66
Johnson, Samuel 22n 125f
Jones, Emrys 22n 101
Jones, Inigo 32
Jonson, Ben 17f; Epithalamium for Weston 154 157; *Haddington Masque* 67f 135n; *Hymenaei* 150–3 154 188n; *King's Entertainment* 121n; *Love's Triumph* 32f; 'New-Year's Gift' 146f; 'To the Lord Treasurer' 188n; 'To the Memory of My Beloved' 70; on **5** 150f; on **8** 152
Joseph 40f
Josephus 37 43n 44
Joshua 66
Joy 45
Judith 40
Julius Caesar 27 43

Ronsard, Pierre de 128n
Ross, Alexander 66
Ross, Man of 87
Rossetti, D. G. 22 124
Rossi, Niccolò 127
Røstvig, Maren-Sofie 4n 199 203;
'The Hidden Sense' 3n 8n
11 17n 132n 155 158n 188n;
'Structure as Prophecy' 66 96
185n
Royal entry, *see* Triumphal entry
Ruricius 64 69

Sabbath, final 130
Sagittarius 141n 144f 212
St Barnaby's Day 15 140 162–70
passim 181n. *See also* Solstice
St Lucy's Day 15
St Paul's 119
Saluste, Guillaume de, *see* Du Bartas
Salviati, Lionardo 33
San Gallo, Antonio da 32 Pl. 10
Sansfoy *et al.* 110
Sardo, A. 66
Satan 85
Saturn 82
Saubert, Johann 3n
Sayers, Dorothy 35
Scaliger, J. C. xi 11n 16; on epi-
thalamium 149 151n 154
Scève, Maurice 174n
Scipio Africanus 28 36 38 40f
Scorpio 141n 145n 212
Scudamour 47–58 *passim* 111f
Seasons, iconography 15 134 135;
in Spenser 59–61; symbolized
numerologically by Carew 157f;
by Chapman 143–6; by Spenser
167–72; *Horae* 60n 170f
Segar, Sir William 30 133f
Selden, John 2
Self-referring passages xi 22 200;
disuse 113; in Chapman 5
140–6; in Dryden 113; in
Shakespeare 184 187 188n 192n
194f; in Sidney 178; in Spenser
164 168 171; triplet 113 140
Serpent 208
Severus 184n 189
Shadwell, Thomas 85
Shakespeare: *As You Like It* 153;
Love's Labour's Lost 26n
Sonnets 183–97; and *Psalms*

190f; blanks 192–4 Pl. 4;
irregular stanzas 183f 186 193–
5; Muse sonnets 194f; monu-
mental 188f; pyramidal struc-
ture 186–91 196n; symmetry
194–7; temporal numbers 192–
7; total **153** + **1** 184f; 'The
Lover's Complaint' 183f 192n
194 196
Venus and Adonis 46 102f
Shame 41 49 51f
Shamelessness 45
Shawcross, J. T. 114n 199
Shearman, John 21f 90 103f 106n
108n 109 116 180
Shirley, James 31
Sidney, Sir Philip 3; *Astrophil and
Stella* 175–80 194; distribution
of Songs 175–7; Penelope game
175f; symmetries 177–80; 'O
Sweet Woods' 107f
Sidonius 64f 68f
Signs 136 139 140–6 158n 190n. *See
also* Constellations; Zodiac
Simondius, tomb of 133
Singleton, Charles S. x 97
Sirius 143 211
Sixtus V 187
Smith, Hallett 104n
Sol invictus 26; *iustitiae* 27 35f 73
100f; *oriens* 26f 36 37n 73; non-
monarchic application 83. *See
also* Sun
Solar month 136 142 144 214
Solomon's Temple 25 66
Solstice 143; imitated numerologi-
cally by Cowley 14f; by Dryden
140; by Spenser 14f 162–70
passim 181n
Somme le roi 25
Sonnet 2f 174–97; as stanza 174;
calendrical arrays 181f; with
other forms 175–7 181f 183
Sorrow 52
Sovereign, key word indicating
central accent 71n
Space in renaissance thought 17 19 62
Spectator, The 13 131
Spence, Joseph 87
Spens, Janet 104
Spenser, Edmund 6 15 46 64n
Amoretti and Epithalamion 169
181f 199